I think that you are perhaps the only great publisher in America and will have to suffer for it.

—Gregory Corso, late March 1957

Lawrence Ferlinghetti (City Lights).
Bob Campbell/San Francisco Chronicle/Polaris.

Pity the nation—oh, pity the people who allow their rights to erode and their freedoms to be washed away. My country, tears of thee, sweet land of liberty

—Lawrence Ferlinghetti, October 3, 2007

The People v.
Ferlinghetti

To Gary & Rudy —

My dear friends who
are _SO_ supportive of
my professional &
personal life.

Enjoy the read!

David

The People v. Ferlinghetti

The Fight to Publish Allen Ginsberg's "Howl"

Ronald K. L. Collins
and
David M. Skover

ROWMAN & LITTLEFIELD
Lanham • Boulder • New York • London

Text Permissions/Acknowledgments

"Finishing the Hat," words and music by Stephen Sondheim
© 1984 RILTING MUSIC, INC.
All Rights Administered by WB MUSIC CORP.
All Rights Reserved Used by Permission
Reprinted by Permission of Hal Leonard LLC

Excerpts as submitted from "HOWL" FROM COLLECTED POEMS 1947–1980 by ALLEN GINSBERG. Copyright © 1955 by Allen Ginsberg. Reprinted by permission of HarperCollins Publishers.

HOWL by Allen Ginsberg. Copyright © 1986, 1956 by Allen Ginsberg, used by permission of The Wylie Agency LLC.

"Pity the Nation" by Lawrence Ferlinghetti, from BLASTS CRIES LAUGHTER (09), copyright © 1988, 1998, 2002, 2014 by Lawrence Ferlinghetti. Reprinted by permission of New Directions Publishing Corp.

"To the Oracle at Delphi" by Lawrence Ferlinghetti, from HOW TO PAINT SUNLIGHT, copyright © 2001 by Lawrence Ferlinghetti. Reprinted by permission of New Directions Publishing Corp.

"Autobiography" by Lawrence Ferlinghetti, from HOW TO PAINT SUNLIGHT, copyright © 2001 by Lawrence Ferlinghetti. Reprinted by permission of New Directions Publishing Corp.

"Poetry as Insurgent Art" by Lawrence Ferlinghetti, from POETRY AS INSURGENT ART, copyright © 2007 by Lawrence Ferlinghetti. Reprinted by permission of New Directions Publishing Corp.

"Populist Manifesto" by Lawrence Ferlinghetti, from ENDLESS LIFE, copyright © 1976 by Lawrence Ferlinghetti. Reprinted by permission of New Directions Publishing Corp.

Published by Rowman & Littlefield
An imprint of The Rowman & Littlefield Publishing Group, Inc.
4501 Forbes Boulevard, Suite 200, Lanham, Maryland 20706
www.rowman.com

6 Tinworth Street, London SE11 5AL, United Kingdom

Copyright © 2019 by The Rowman & Littlefield Publishing Group, Inc.

British Library Cataloguing in Publication Information Available

Library of Congress Cataloging-in-Publication Data

978-1-5381-2589-2 (cloth)
978-1-5381-2590-8 (electronic)

♾ ™ The paper used in this publication meets the minimum requirements of American National Standard for Information Sciences—Permanence of Paper for Printed Library Materials, ANSI/NISO Z39.48–1992.

Printed in the United States of America

To Susan Abby Cohen

Whose pragmatic and loving ways first tolerated,
and then encouraged, our poetic passions

Other Related Books by the Authors

- *Mania: The Story of the Outraged and Outrageous Lives That Launched a Cultural Revolution*
- *The Trials of Lenny Bruce: The Fall and Rise of An American Icon*

Contents

viii   *Contents*

Prologue

The "Self-Made Man"

I am a self-made man
And I have plans for the future

      —Lawrence Ferlinghetti, *A Coney Island of the Mind*

*A*merican Maverick.

Stop the frame there—behold the man!

Those two words portray much about the man who devoted decades to perfecting the art of freedom writ large. As a poet, painter, playwright, social activist, environmentalist, bookseller and book publisher, he charted his own life course with creative imagination and pragmatic conviction.

College man, Navy man, newspaper man, businessman, artistic man, and dissident man—it's all part of his DNA. His modus operandi: Quiet when many are shouting / outspoken when most are silent. His words: "Poetry is the shadow cast by our streetlight imaginations." More words: "Pity the nation whose people are sheep, and whose shepherds mislead them." Still other words: "I am waiting for the war to be fought which will make the world safe for anarchy." There is yet more—a life cast large on a canvas unwilling to yield to the limits of its borders.

The man, the American maverick of whom we speak: **Lawrence Monsanto Ferlinghetti**.[†]

At five score, there is still poetic breath left in his literary lungs. The streams of his consciousness pour out into his latest novel, *Little Boy*, published this year.[††] It is the story of one man's extraordinary life and the madness of the century in which that life was situated—"a story steeped in the rhythmic energy of the Beats, gleaming with Whitman's visionary spirit, channeling the incantatory power of Proust and Joyce," said his publisher. "This is Lawrence Ferlinghetti's last word." In *Little Boy*, Ferlinghetti ventures homeward to where he began his career as a writer, journalist, and short story author—one who took his first impressionistic cues from Thomas Wolfe and Henry David Thoreau, among others.

Quiet and detached, words were his window to the world. He traded in them in the marketplace as an unrepentant poet, alternative bookseller, and fearless book publisher. Print gave him his voice. In those ways, and so many others, Ferlinghetti stands proud on his island of liberty. Its shores beckon a world gone mad to heed the words of the poet Emma Lazarus: "Give me your tired, your poor, your huddled masses yearning to breathe free."

His fame as a poet is vast (millions of copies of his books have been sold); his talent as a painter is widely recognized (his works have been displayed in galleries and museums throughout the world); and his manifesto as an activist is manifest ("Poets, come out of your closets"). Many awards rest on his mantels, and popular culture has tapped into both his beat and bravado. He was a major figure in the cultural

---

[†]He grew up using the name Lawrence Ferling Monsanto, and then in 1937 changed it to Lawrence Monsanto Ferling. Thereafter, in January of 1955 he returned to his birth name, Lawrence Ferlinghetti.

[††]Ferlinghetti's literary agent for his 2019 novel was none other than Sterling Lord, the famous figure who represented Jack Kerouac. In January of 1958, Allen Ginsberg wrote to Ferlinghetti: "Sterling Lord here and took me . . . to supper and I asked him to try to peddle my [*Howl*] book to foreign countries [since] he's had a lot of success with Jack." Nothing came of it. Later, in July of 1970, Ferlinghetti wrote to Lord to persuade him to authorize City Lights to publish some of Kerouac's posthumous works, but Ferlinghetti recalled, "I never got the time of night from him." In the 1980s, however, Lord sold Ferlinghetti's novel *Love in the Days of Rage* to Dutton.

revolution known as the "Beat Generation," and gave a publishing presence to several of the great figures of that movement. And, of course, he was the man who in 1956 breathed publishing life into Allen Ginsberg's poetry. All of this and volumes more have been and will continue to be chronicled by historians. Important as that is, our charge is not to add to that bounty.

How, then, to paint his portrait? How to sketch his life? Color him what?

Turn here, turn there, turn where? To the law and the outlaw, to the poet and the publisher, to the crime and its consequences. Yes, start there: that story, our canvas.

Lawrence Ferlinghetti. Tag him an outsider. His name is absent from the pages of the law. It does not appear in any First Amendment treatise or free speech casebook. It is not a name law students learn about, or one that lawyers or judges tout. The Supreme Court has never cited his name as a precedent for press freedom. And yet, like Benjamin Franklin Bache (1769–1798), the rebel colonial printer and publisher, Ferlinghetti buttressed the tradition of dissident expression. He did so at a pinpoint in the modern era when many minds were closed, when candid literature was still taboo in many circles, when selling banned books was still a crime, and when even the publication of a poem could bring a criminal indictment.

Click the clock back 62 years and you'll find the story of *People v. Ferlinghetti*, a most unusual one. It is a story about a rebellious poet, a revolutionary poem (Allen Ginsberg's "Howl"), an intrepid book publisher, and a bookseller unintimindated by threats from federal and local officials—the purported keepers of our moral canons. There is much color in that story: the bizarre twists of the trial, the swagger of the lead lawyer, the savvy of the seasoned ACLU lawyer, the sway of the young ACLU lawyer, the absence of the poet-author Ginsberg, and the surprise verdict rendered by a Sunday school preacher who presided as judge. There is also the remarkable record of a book publisher who combined an erudite calm with an ardent conviction to protect principle. The precedent set by that publisher (and bookstore owner and poet) first changed his world and then reconfigured ours—it set in motion a new era in press and poetic freedom. Though that precedent never found its way onto the pages of the *Supreme Court Reports,* it did, nonetheless, weave its way into the quilt of the American culture. Since then, the precedent has stood, though Ferlinghetti's work remains unfinished—the rock of the law remains to be pushed.

The People v. Ferlinghetti is the true story of a maverick American who refused to play it safe and who in the process gave staying power to freedom of the press in America, first in 1957 and then again in 2007—his "howl" for liberty. It is a story of two friends: a poet (Allen Ginsberg) and a publisher (Ferlinghetti). It is a story easily lost to time—in the shadows of those whose company Ferlinghetti kept (great literary figures), or in the aftermath of the movement (the "Beat Generation") he helped launch. Beyond those borders, however, there lingers the story of a most unusual man who foresaw the great potential of a poem to change the culture and the law. Our aim is to retell that slice of his life story, not in tried-and-tedious lines but rather with the brio with which it was lived.

The greatest debts are often owed to those whose sacrifices are like the air we breathe—essential but unnoticed. This is the case of Lawrence Ferlinghetti—a name known in poetic circles but largely unheard of outside those quarters. Yet, for those who value the freedom of American mavericks—the liberty to rail against repression of the kind that robs men and women of their true worth—that name deserves a place in the American mind and in the annals of our free speech history.

Call him radical, rebellious, or revolutionary. Brand his City Lights bookstore a gathering place for lonesome outcasts, excitable poets, road-weary literati, Percy Shelly devotees, restless radicals, gender-benders, feisty feminists, and for the rest of the avant-garde crowd. Still, to stand there on Columbus Avenue in the shadow of the man and his San Francisco shop is to relive those moments when liberty first took refuge there and then spread across space and time to successive generations . . . including those yet to be born.

America's free-spirited book publisher / defender of the outsider / uninhibited bookstore owner / dissident poet / democratic socialist / mild-mannered anarchist-like firebrand / Walt Whitman visionary / American maverick: this is his story, the story of a quiet man who has long had more than a streak of Tom Paine in the fighting folds of his soul.

· 1 ·

"It's the Only Way to See"

Finishing the hat. How you have to finish the hat.
How you watch the rest of the world from a window while you
*   finish the hat. . . .*
Studying a face. Stepping back to look at a face
leaves a little space in the way like a window.
But to see, it's the only way to see.

—Stephen Sondheim, *Sunday in*
the Park with George (1983)

*D*ickensian. That is how Lawrence Ferlinghetti's life has been characterized. His biographer, Barry Silesky, described it as "a Dickens novel—both parents gone before he was two, abandoned at six, sent away by his caretakers as a teenager after leading his gang into petty crime." But just as for Pip of Dicken's *Great Expectations* or the namesake of his *David Copperfield*, benevolent Fate raised our young hero "out of the backwash" and enabled him "to become Lawrence Ferlinghetti, publisher, poet, novelist, painter, spokesman of his time."

There is much truth and insight in this analogy. In our eyes, however, it portrays Ferlinghetti's life circumstances without fully capturing the essence of his psyche, his being. For that, one needs to move from Charles Dickens to Stephen Sondheim. In his brilliant and groundbreaking musical, *Sunday in the Park with George*, the composer-lyricist depicts Georges Seurat, the French post-impressionist painter, in the process of creating his greatest pointillist work, *A Sunday Afternoon on the Island of La Grande Jatte*. Georges reveals the core of his mind and the crux of his soul in the heart-wrenching song, "Finishing the Hat."

1

He remains distanced from the outside world, detached from all others, essentially alone . . . physically, mentally, emotionally, and spiritually. Only that enables him to see. Only that makes him an artist.

Admittedly, any comparison of Ferlinghetti to Seurat might seem exaggerated. Nevertheless, when it comes to the spirit of the artist, Ferlinghetti and Sondheim's Seurat are soul mates. "Lawrence is just not interested in [particular] people," one of Ferlinghetti's lifelong friends reportedly declared. "It enables him to have the kind of vision he has, to see things without getting emotionally involved in the ordinary way." In other words, Sondheim's words, "But to see, it's the only way to see."

One can almost imagine Ferlinghetti sitting on his dark leather reclining chair in his San Francisco home as the late sunlight struggles to filter through the three elongated windows behind him. He might be reading a Christopher Hitchens book. As his eyes scan the pages, his attention is caught by this line: The mark of a contrarian is "the decision to live at a slight acute angle to society." Indeed, when he was well into his 90s, Ferlinghetti continued to live that experience: he protested that San Francisco, his bohemian haven on "the edge of the world," had become a city of "corporate monoculture." To understand him, one must have an appreciation for the ironic, for the absurd, for the Promethean need to rebel. For the dissident, the fight against dumbing acquiescence is unending. Percy Shelley was of such a disposition as was William Blake, both defiant poets. So, too, with San Francisco's Poet Laureate Lawrence Ferlinghetti, the man who devoted his life to trading in defiant words.

Writer & Publisher. There is something about being a writer and publisher, about communicating to the world through printed words that demarcates oneself from the rest of humankind. The printed word, unlike the spoken one, requires a distance from those receiving the message.[†] However personal the message, its medium is detached. If one thinks of Ferlinghetti as a writer—first as a journalist and thereafter as a poet—then both the art and the publishing medium suit the man. He is, after all, a private person, a reserved man, a calm individual, and

---

[†]Tellingly, when it came to proposing marriage to Selden Kirby-Smith or to congratulating Allen Ginsberg on his historic 6 Gallery reading of "Howl," Ferlinghetti opted to send telegrams rather than communicating in person.

someone removed from most of the conventions and conversations of daily life. Predictably, "he was often quiet, and given to disappearing into some distraction in the middle of a conversation." Blend his writer-publisher character traits with these: radical, rebellious, uninhibited, and daring. Stir that mix well and you have Lawrence Ferlinghetti, the dissident writer born on March 24, 1919 in Yonkers, New York, the last of five sons.

* * *

Ferlinghetti had a markedly unusual youth. His father (Charles Ferlinghetti) was an Italian immigrant who died of a heart attack before Lawrence was born; later, illness separated him from his French mother (Clemence Mendes-Monsanto) when he was not yet two. Thereafter, it was tug-and-turn: an uncle and aunt adopted him, and then his uncle alienated both; his aunt took him to Strasbourg where he learned French and lived for a few years; then it was back to New York to reside for a short time with his reunited uncle and aunt; when his aunt separated permanently from her husband, Lawrence was placed in an orphanage when he was six; then when his aunt took work as a govern-ess for a well-to-do family (the Bislands), the boy came back into his aunt's fold only to have her run off without any notice; the Bislands adopted him and sent him off to an elite private school (Riverdale Country School) until the 1929 stock market crash made that option too costly; then at 10 he was transferred to Bronxville public school and boarded with a family who rejected him after he was busted for shoplift-ing; at that point, the Bislands packed him off to a highly disciplined religious school (Mount Hermon) in Greenfield, Massachusetts.

In sum, "most of his formative years had been disconnected and isolated." A pattern of such abandonment, a course of such instability, and an early ping-pong existence could not but foster a deep-set need to protect himself in the future. What better way, then, but to shield himself from getting too close, too familiar, too reliant? It is not diffi-cult to perceive Ferlinghetti's beginnings as the crucible in which his mettle was tested and strengthened. By distancing himself from others, he acquired the perspective that empowered his artistry. Thus he came to see his world.

· 2 ·

The Biography of a Bookstore

*C*ity Lights Pocket Books. The name evokes "the head, heart, and undersoul" of the political, artistic, and literary communities of San Francisco in the 1950s. America's first all-paperback bookstore, named after Charlie Chaplin's famous 1931 movie, *City Lights*, opened in June of 1953 in the Classical Revivalist-styled building at 261 Columbus Avenue. The pie-shaped one-room storefront featured classic and modern literary works, art and pop culture books, leftist and progressive political tracts, and uncommon newspapers and magazines. From late morning until midnight during the week and 2:00 a.m. on weekends, the store was a beacon for bohemians who dropped in to browse the stacks or hang in the basement where they read quietly or rapped coolly. The atmosphere was, in short, alternative.

To know City Lights Books is to know Lawrence Ferlinghetti. Like the Chaplin movie, here is a man who aligned his being with the "perennial outsider," those "disposed, alienated, victimized by the immense mechanization of the modern world. . . . Though he didn't see himself as a victim like Charlie, he clearly felt himself one of the 'common men' threatened by the mass forces of the bureaucratic, materialist, conformist world." It was in that world that Lawrence was the odd man out, the Camus-like stranger, and the Chaplin character. Although City Lights bookstore was in the foreground of Ferlinghetti's life story, there was much in his background that illuminated it.

* * *

In ways typical of junior journalists, blue-collar workers, and wartime servicemen, Ferlinghetti was very much the common man. In the play of events, he was once an Eagle Scout, a newspaper boy, a junior

4

high school journalism enthusiast, a lobster fisherman, a mailroom clerk at *Time Magazine*, the circulation manager of his college newspaper, and a Navy ensign patrolling for submarines off the East Coast. He also had leadership qualities: during World War II, he commanded a submarine chaser (USS *SC1308*) that screened the beaches of Normandy, and after VE Day he navigated a troop ship (USS *Selinur*) in the Pacific Theater. His patriotism, however, bowed to pacifism once he witnessed the horrors of the atomic aftermath of Nagasaki.

By contrast, in ways both cultural and literary, Ferlinghetti is an American with learned flair and a French tongue. He is a man with an intellectual side: a journalism degree from the University of North Carolina, an M.A. from Columbia University (his thesis was on John Ruskin and the British painter J. M. W. Turner), and a Ph.D. in literary studies from the Sorbonne in Paris (his dissertation, written in French, was titled "The City Symbol in Modern Poetry: In Search of a Metropolitan Tradition"). In all of this, he studied under several revered literary figures, including Columbia Professors Mark Van Doren, Jacques Barzun, and Lionel Trilling. Once he ventured to San Francisco, he taught French in adult education programs for a brief time, and translated irreverent and satirical poems by the French surrealist Jacques Prévert, which were published in popular culture and radical literary magazines. From early on, he kept the close company of avant-garde literary minds such as Kenneth Rexroth (famed poet, translator, and essayist) and Kenneth Patchen (experimental poet and novelist).

He had his artistic side, which appeared as early as 1948 when he was in Paris working on his dissertation. As he recalled it, "a guy I was rooming with left his painting equipment behind, so I picked it up and gave it a try." Soon enough he was obsessed and took to training himself to draw in the free studio of the Parisian Académie Julien. The more he painted, the more he liked it. His mind's eye led him to creating images that were both hopeful and haunting. True to his art, he composed poems that "painted pictures,"† which were collected and pub-

---

†In August of 2016, Ferlinghetti admitted: "I never wanted to be a poet; it chose me, I didn't choose it; one becomes a poet almost against one's will, certainly against one's better judgement. I wanted to be a painter, but from the age of 10 these damn poems kept coming. Perhaps one of these days they will leave me alone and I can get back to painting."

lished in 1955 as *Pictures of the Gone World*. On canvas and in word, and "like the Symbolist poets," he knew "that ellipses—those gaps that viewers and readers must fill in with their own imagination—are essential to retain the mystery of both poetry and art." And Ferlinghetti had his political side: He was committed to a "left-leaning, libertarian, and anarchistic political philosophy." He first entered the political realm and the First Amendment free speech arena when he railed against artistic censorship in the context of San Francisco's Rincon Annex Post Office mural controversy. The walls of the art-deco building displayed vibrant murals painted by Russian-born Anton Refregier and funded by the Work Projects Administration. The artist completed his paintings in 1948 with *War & Peace*, which pointedly juxtaposed Nazi book-burning scenes with FDR's promises of the "four freedoms" for speech and worship and from want and fear. The San Francisco American Legion and Veterans of Foreign Wars, among others, viewed the murals as subversive and Communist propaganda. Ferlinghetti had a different view. In a 1953 *Art Digest* article, he defended the murals. As he saw it, they portrayed "a democratic array of Indians, conquistadores, padres, nuns, miners, railroad and ship workers, businessmen . . . soldiers, patriots . . . bridge builders, and builders of the United Nations," among others. Ultimately, the California State House resolution to remove the murals did not pass and the political squabble subsided.

* * *

No matter the parameters of his persona, drama is a word that would never suit the man. Although he openly associated with the Beat Generation's most celebrated literary figures, he shared none of their madcap ways. He was no woman-chaser/car-crazed Neal Cassady, no booze-broken Jack Kerouac, no gun-packin' Bill Burroughs, no fast-fix Herbert Huncke, and no madness-prone Allen Ginsberg. He was not a jumper, junker, or jester. Though he witnessed and tolerated their detrimental or dangerous life experiments, he never became personally or psychically involved in the mania that pointed down those paths. "I was the last of the Bohemian generation when I arrived from Paris," Lawrence explained. "I arrived in San Francisco four years before Allen Ginsberg and the Beats did. I was still wearing my French beret."

Older than most of the key Beat figures, the tall, slim, then clean-shaven man with radiant light-blue eyes, strong jaw, and receding hair presented more the image of a respectable small businessman than a beatnik, even though he seldom wore a tie and jacket. Moreover, neither his personality nor his poetry shared the feverish chaos of Beat lifestyles or the frenetic energy of their writing styles. Ferlinghetti knew talent when he saw it, however, and was willing to make the literary and monetary most of it. In time, he would discover that talent. Before then, he had to build a business. Thus, Ferlinghetti poured his passion into his work: selling and printing books.

If Ferlinghetti was progressive in matters bearing on artistic freedom, he was equally savvy when it came to matters involving business. In June of 1953, he co-founded City Lights Pocket Books with Peter Martin; it was America's first all-paperback bookstore. Eighteen months later, he became the sole proprietor of City Lights after buying his partner out when Martin returned to the East Coast. Shortly afterwards, Lawrence launched City Lights Publishing and started the Pocket Poets Series, inexpensive editions of poetry in volumes small enough to be put into one's pocket. Inspired by the bookstore-publisher combo prevalent in Paris, he replicated the business strategy: "It seemed like a logical thing to do. I never understood why bookstores here didn't do it. The bookstore's a natural source of publicity for the press, and a place to sell the books." By the mid-1990s, City Lights was publishing a dozen or so books per year while the bookstore produced its own profits. The monetary result: "the shop and the enterprise grossed about $2 million annually."

As a matter of political principle and economic prudence, Ferlinghetti never felt the need to prevail on government subsidization of the *City Lights* foundation. "For *City Lights* and myself," he explained, "we've never applied for a grant from the National Endowment for the Arts." This was so "because from the Leftist point of view, it's rather hypocritical to attack the government's policies, and on the other hand, take money from it in the form of grants."

* * *

In 1954, someone walked into City Lights Books. He was brazen and insecure, a young man who was looking for a publisher to jumpstart his literary career. He was not without baggage; he had criminal, psychological, and financial problems. Indeed, his luck seemed to be running out. But his unorthodox genius sparked something in Lawrence Ferlinghetti. That something provided Lawrence with a rare opportunity to combine his financial prowess with his poetic artistry in the service of a cultural cause. That man, a nascent poet, was Allen Ginsberg.

Young Allen Ginsberg (at City Lights).
Joe Rosenthal/San Francisco Chronicle/Polaris.

· 3 ·

"Howl"

The Poem Struggling to Be Born

*There was something wonderfully subversive about
"Howl", something the poet had hidden in the body
of the poem because it was too dangerous to say
openly, something we had to uncover and decode.*

—Jonah Raskin

*I thought I [would] just write what I wanted to without
fear, let my imagination go, open secrecy, and scribble
magic lines from my real mind.*

—Allen Ginsberg

*L*awrence saw what others did not. He sensed what others could not. He understood the mind of an angry poet in ways that others had not. Most significantly, he dared to publish what others would not. The publisher and the poet—Lawrence Ferlinghetti and Allen Ginsberg—were made for one another, different as they were. Allen needed a beacon, someone to shed a bright light on his poem. Lawrence needed a revolutionary work to publish as part of his City Lights Book's "Pocket Poet" series. Before Allen's words were set to print, they first had to be reduced to type, which meant tapping into the deep and dark well of his subconscious.

* * *

9

Madness was on his mind. There had been so much of it in his past and present. Would it ever end? Would his life dreams simply disintegrate into nothingness? At age 29, Allen Ginsberg sat on the precipice of dark despair. "I am no closer to the end of the line except death than I was ten years ago and more removed from the innocence that then gave promise of sweetness thru experience," he wrote shortly after his birthday in 1955.

He had money problems: with a meager $30 a week in unemployment checks, Allen denied himself and Peter Orlovsky, his lover, anything but the essentials. "Money problems of reality are not ghostly at all, they're solid as a rock I keep hitting my head on," he moaned. He had boyfriend problems: much as he adored him, Peter's see-saw mood swings—forlornly weeping at one moment and blithely chattering at the next—exhausted and depressed him. He had sleeping problems: he dreamed of Joan Vollmer, the woman his friend Bill Burroughs accidently killed, now forgotten in a foreign grave. And even more disturbing, he had writer's block: though he had studied his novelist friend Jack Kerouac's "Rules for Spontaneous Writing" and tacked them onto his wall, he couldn't get the right focus, muster enough energy, or tap the inspiration to follow them. It all weighed heavily on his mind, leaving him helpless to do much more than "trouble deaf heaven with . . . bootless cries."

Mottled sunshine filtered through the window facing Montgomery Street in the San Francisco room that Allen used as his study and bedroom. Narrow dappled rays fell across a simple wooden table on which his typewriter rested amid journals and papers. A slat of soft afternoon sun illuminated the plywood shelves hinged along the wall, where his books and records were haphazardly stacked. The early August light brought the lines of the roomy and plush armchair into sharp contrast. What radiant sound there was came from a 3-speed Webcor monaural phonograph, on which Bach's intense but jubilant Mass in B Minor often played.

Ginsberg was alone in his room, sitting at his typing table. Since Peter had hitchhiked to New York in late July to bring his brother Lafcadio back to San Francisco, Allen now had uninterrupted time to confront his desolation and to jump-start his writing. But how could he do that? The answer was in front of him, right there on the wall. Like chlorophyll that transforms light to life energy, Kerouac's "rules" for spontaneous writing finally worked to free his inhibitions. When Allen turned his inner madness outward, he released decades of demons that had haunted him.

> *I saw the best minds of my generation*
> *generation destroyed by madness*
> *starving, mystical, naked,*
> *who dragged themselves thru the angry streets at*
> *dawn looking for a negro fix.*

With those words, Allen aligned his life with his poetry. True to what Kerouac had advised—*"come from within, out"*—Ginsberg allowed his "subconscious to admit" its "own uninhibited" message. Typing away as if he were in a trance, he was *blowing* it out of his system like a crazy jazzman hopped up on pure, uncut spontaneity.

> *who poverty and tatters and fantastic minds*
> *sat up all night in lofts*
> *contemplating jazz,*

Allen was on to something new. With rebel flair, he broke away from the short, pretty, rhyming lines typical of mainstream poetry. Echoing Walt Whitman, he hollered out long lines that spoke to the ear—but his were harsh and angry lines. He latched onto the word "who" as the base to begin each furious strophe, often dividing his thought into the triadic structure that he had learned from the poet William Carlos Williams.

> *who bared their brains to heaven under the El*
> *and saw Mohammedan angels staggering*
> *on tenement roofs illuminated,*

Here was a reference to Bill Cannastra, one of the best of those minds. His flesh became words, agonizing words, in a line that harkened back to Bill's tragic subway death when, in a playful antic, he stuck his head outside the window of a speeding subway car. Now Allen built momentum with each repetitive and rhythmic "who." His subconscious spit out another anguished memory—this one of Carl Solomon, prisoner of an asylum who, like others, screamed when his brain made contact with burning electrodes.

who sat in rooms naked and unshaven
listening to the Terror through the wall,

Poor Naomi, Allen's troubled mother, was never freed from her own madness. In his mind's eye, Allen saw the unbearable lunacy that he had witnessed only weeks earlier at Pilgrim State Hospital, where his mother was a patient.

who demanded sanity trials accusing the radio of hypnotism,
& were left with their insanity
and their hands and a hung jury,

Nothing, however, quite rivaled the craziness that sucked the life out of David Kammerer the night that Lucien (pronounced Looshun) Carr, Allen's bizarre Columbia University colleague, stabbed the man who adored him again and again. The specter of that horrifying 1944 killing struck Allen's psyche as he typed away.

who cut out each others hearts on the banks of the Hudson
life's a drama on a great lost stage
under the crimson streetlamp of the moon,

And then there was the memory of Herbert Huncke, the drug and sex addict who first taught Allen what it truly meant to be "beat." Herbert revealed to him unforgettable physical and mental suffering when he showed up on his doorstep in the bitter winter of 1948.

who wandered all night with their shoes full of blood
on the snow banks of East River looking for the door
to open on a roomful of steam heat and opium,
picking his scabs and saying who is my friend?

There were more "whos"—78 of them in total in the first draft of the poem. They ran the gamut from his friends' 1945 pranks and capers in Joan Vollmer's upper West Side apartments; to the 1949 car chase with the police in hot pursuit of Allen and two of his felonious friends;

to the notorious sexploits of Neal Cassady, the hero of Kerouac's *On the Road*.

Allen used sex slang ("ultimate cunt and come") to sharpen his images of promiscuity. And unconcerned about the popularity of his message or the vulgarity of his words, he defied cultural conventions and legal taboos by flying the banner of homosexual freedom, a freedom born out of his experiences and fantasies.

who let themselves be fucked in the ass
by saintly motorcyclists, and screamed with joy,
who were blown by those human angels, the sailors,
caresses of Atlantic and Caribbean love,

With nocturnal energy, Allen typed as light sunk into darkness. His acute concentration blocked out whatever discomfort he felt from the hardness of his high-backed wooden chair. The pulse of his "bardic breath" rhythms propelled him; the flow of his foot-long free-verse lines sustained him; and the power of his compassion for human affliction emboldened him. He interjected literary devices—repeating words to suggest sounds ("who lit cigarettes in boxcars boxcars boxcars racketing through snow") and juxtaposing inapposite images to give new impressions ("who listened to the crack of doom on the hydrogen jukebox")—and was energized by the special effects they created.

Allen *typed typed typed typed typed*. He filled seven pages of single-spaced strophes, rejecting inapt words or inferior phrases with "xxxx" strike-outs. Winding down to the end, he knew that he had done it. He had breached the dam that obstructed his poetic imagination. And with the fury of a Hebraic prophet, he had railed on behalf of the madmen and madwomen in his life. The poem was a "gesture of wild solidarity, a message into the asylum, a sort of heart's trumpet call," he later recalled.

Low on adrenaline, Allen put a final sheet of paper into his manual typewriter. He needed to declare explicitly his sympathetic identification with Carl Solomon, his friend in the asylum, the man he treated as the poetic symbol of mad victimization in a cruel and loveless world. Eking out his last bit of energy, he typed a few lines more, addressing the friend who had recently been committed in Pilgrim State Hospital:

Carl Solomon!
I am with you in Rockland

where you're madder than I am
I am with you in Rockland
where you stay for the rest of your life

Finally, exhilaration gave way to exhaustion. Rising slowly from his writing table, Allen collapsed into the sofa bed across the room, and drifted into a peaceful sleep.

* * *

"Your HOWL FOR CARL SOLOMON is very powerful," Jack Kerouac wrote to Allen from Mexico City. Ginsberg had sent the original draft of the poem to him shortly after he had composed it. Jack's words meant a lot to Allen, coming as they did from the man who had tutored him in spontaneous writing. In a reply letter, Allen acknowledged the debt to his friend: "I realize how right you are, that was the first time I sat down to blow, it came out in your method, sounding like you, an imitation practically. How far advanced you are on this."

The manuscript contained, however, numerous strike-outs and initial revisions marked in pink pencil. Immediately, they caught the critical eye of the master of spontaneous prose. "I don't want," Kerouac added, the poem to be "arbitrarily negated by secondary emendations. . . . I want your lingual SPONTANEITY or nothing . . . the first spout is the only spout." Such spontaneity was the fuel that was igniting Kerouac's own burst of poetic energy. Allen Ginsberg's *Howl for Carl Solomon* was a sign that Jack Kerouac was right.

This avant-garde writing style much appealed to the avant-garde Lawrence Ferlinghetti. He knew Ginsberg from his frequent visits to City Lights. Ferlinghetti "saw him as another of those far-out poets and wandering intellectuals who had started hanging out" in the three-year-old North Beach bookstore. They occasionally strolled together, taking Lawrence's dog, Homer, for a walk and ending up at Mike's, a pool hall, for beers and burgers. Ferlinghetti also knew Allen's work, having recently rejected *Empty Mirror*. But *Howl for Carl Solomon* was different. It was, in Lawrence's estimation, "the most significant single long poem" written "since World War II." So he offered to publish the work, when completed, as the fourth volume of "Pocket Poets." Allen was ecstatic. Finally, he would join the publishing ranks of his fellow Beats—Jack Kerouac, John Holmes, and William Burroughs. "City Lights Bookstore here . . . will put out 'Howl' (under that title) next year," he boasted to Jack.

With the return of Peter and his teenage brother, some of the madness of "Howl" hit home. Lafcadio spent up to six hours a day in the bathroom, and squawked tirelessly about making millions of dollars on schemes like inventing a rocket ship to go to the moon. It drove Allen nuts, and at a time when he needed all his concentration to complete his poem. Since Peter worked at the post office and Allen took part-time odd jobs, there was enough money for him to rent a hideaway. He did just that on September 1, 1955, when he moved to 1624 Milvia Street in Berkeley. Allen adored his respite from the madness on Montgomery Street; he described it as a "35 per mo. ivy-covered one room (plus kitchen & bath) cottage on side-street, garden and apricot tree around, private and Shakespearean." Its backyard was "filled with vegetables and flowers." It was a place where he could "write a lot."

Recent Ferlinghetti in front of bookstore.
Stacey Lewis.

· 4 ·

The Publisher

"When Do I Get the Manuscript?"

𝒜llen's home was a heaven on earth to him. There, in an almost mystic state, Jack Kerouac was fixated on the death of Jesus Christ. His diaries and journals were filled with entries about and drawings of the crucifixion. In his Columbia University days, he sat in his dorm room and listened to the *St. Matthew Passion* by Johann Sebastian Bach; he considered it to be divinely inspired. That work about Good Friday, one of the greatest choral compositions ever created, was a favorite of Jack's.

Now, the magnificent first Chorus of the *Passion* played at full volume. Its slow, heavy, and rhythmic pulse beat on and on, as though capturing the sounds of Christ's footsteps as he dragged the cross on his whip-torn shoulder to Golgotha. The tension of the orchestral opening pulled on Jack's god-loving soul as he listened to it on the Webcore phonograph at Allen's Milvia Street cottage. Lost in his reveries, assorted images flitted through his mind: like those of the dusty roads on which he bummed rides out of El Paso after leaving Mexico / like those of the star-filled evening when he slept on a Santa Barbara beach a couple of days before / like those of the sexy blonde in a strapless bathing suit who gave him a lift in her Mercury convertible / like those of the tender night that he spent sleeping with Carolyn Cassady / and like those of the joyful reunion that he had just experienced with his old friend Ginsberg.

Allen was excited when he first told Jack about an upcoming

17

poetry event at a hip artsy hangout called 6 Gallery, with an illuminated number 6 floating above its windowed entry doors. He had talked about the place with Michael McClure, a 23-year-old poet whom he had met a year earlier at a San Francisco writing workshop. Michael had told Allen that Wally Hedrick, one of the owners of 6 Gallery, was willing to host a poetry bash. Since McClure himself lacked the time to do it, he suggested that Ginsberg organize it, although he promised to read a few poems. Thrilled to do so, Allen now asked Jack to join the event he was planning. Perhaps Jack could recite something from *Mexico City Blues*. Kerouac declined; he didn't like performing before strange crowds. He agreed to come, however, being especially eager to witness Allen's first public reading of his spontaneous "Howl."

Jack knew some of the people who were slated to participate in the upcoming 6 Gallery happening. In fact, he had been with three of them, only a week or so earlier, at one of Kenneth Rexroth's Friday evening literary soireés. Gary Snyder and Philip Whalen, former room-mates at Reed College who were both poets and serious students of Buddhism, were there. Gary and Philip planned to recite some of their recent works, and Rexroth accepted an invitation to give a few remarks to kick things off.

Kerouac thought well of Snyder. Gary was a "lumberjack" he-man, "wiry and fast and muscular," but with a sensitive spiritual soul. There was "something earnest and strong and human hopeful" that Jack appreciated in Gary. Whalen struck a slightly different chord in Jack. The "big fat bespectacled quiet" Philip came across to him as a goofy "booboo," though "goodhearted." Nonetheless, what tickled Kerouac about both of them was that they were familiar with his writings and liked them.

Rexroth, too, had complimented Kerouac's work in a recent KPFA FM-radio broadcast. Yet that was not enough to win Kerouac's friend-ship. He was uncomfortable around the "bow-tied wild-haired old anarchist fud" who held himself out as the eminence grise of the San Francisco literary scene. And he particularly disliked Rexroth's arro-gance, as when Kenneth put people down with "his snide funny voice." That Friday night at the soirée, Kerouac was the brunt of Rexroth's sarcasm. It happened when the evening's discussion turned to Bud-dhism. Jack was going on about the *Pure Land Sutra*, one of several spiritual works he had read. Gary and Philip, familiar with the meditation manual, joined in. Jack was jubilant: "Why, there are other people who have read these texts!" The haughty Rexroth, unwilling to yield the limelight to this dilettante, brought him down a notch: "Everybody in San Francisco is a Buddhist, Kerouac! Didn't you know that?"

The other poet slated to appear at 6 Gallery was Philip Lamantia. Jack had known Philip as a friend years earlier in New York, where they used to bop back and forth from Latin dance halls to black jazz clubs. And they shared similar outlooks on life, poetry, and spirituality. To Kerouac, Lamantia was an "out-of-this-world genteel-looking Renaissance Italian" type, with a priestly air.

Describing the 6 Gallery program, Allen told Jack about the advertising campaign that he had orchestrated. One hundred printed postcards were mailed, and handbills hung in numerous North Beach bars to publicize the event. The postcards were everywhere, including stacks of them at City Lights bookstore. They read:

6 POETS AT 6 GALLERY

Philip Lamantia reading ms. of late John Hoffman—Mike McClure, Allen Ginsberg, Gary Snyder & Phil Whalen—all sharp new straightforward writing—remarkable collection of angels on one stage reading their poetry. No charge, small collection for wine and postcards. Charming event.

Kenneth Rexroth, M.C.

8 PM Friday Night October 7, 1955

6 Gallery 3119 Fillmore St.
San Francisco

Jack looked forward to that special Friday night. Would listening to the poets be nearly as glorious as listening to Bach? Would experiencing "Howl for Carl Solomon" be like experiencing the *St. Matthew Passion*? He hoped so.

For Lawrence Ferlinghetti, it would not be a moment that tilted towards Kerouac's spiritual heavens. There was something more pragmatic and poetic at stake, namely, a perfect poem for his "Pocket Poem" series. He had seen an early draft of the poem and by then knew Allen well enough. All that remained was to wait, bide his time.

* * *

Kenneth Rexroth was eager to get things started. Kerouac and the boys rolled in a bit late, coming from Vesuvio's bar with Lawrence and Kirby Ferlinghetti in an old model Austin. Jack saw that Allen's postcards and promo had worked. The gallery, located at 3119 Fillmore, was jam-packed. Some 150 Bohemians, anarchists, musicians, poets, painters, professors, visionaries, and cynics had journeyed to the "Negro section" of the city to hear six poets at 6 Gallery. Clad in "various costumes, worn-at-the-sleeves corduroy jackets, scruffy shoes," and "books sticking out of their pockets," the non-conformists crammed into the old converted auto-repair shop[†]—two adjoining rooms with dirt floors and a bathroom door that would not lock. They stood under a big-beamed ceiling, and mingled alongside seven pillars that ran up and down the center of the space. Seizing the opportunity, the already lubed Kerouac and his Boston Irish friend worked the crowd for a booze collection.

Jack took in the first half of the event sitting at the edge of the platform, guzzling from his jug and noting the madcap drift of things. The poets sat in large chairs, arranged in a semi-circle, on a small low platform at the back end of the place. A surrealist sculpture—splintered pieces of orange crate floating in Plaster of Paris—hovered behind them. Rows of folding chairs were filled with countercultural types; the overflow squeezed into every inch of space left in the smoke-clouded environment.

Sporting a bowtie and a pinstripe cutaway, Rexroth stood before a makeshift podium. He began by joking, "This is a lectern for a midget who is going to recite the *Iliad* in haiku form"; he then commented seriously on San Francisco as a unique island of bohemian culture, like Barcelona of the Spanish Anarchists. Rexroth handed the program over to Lamantia, who read John Hoffman's surrealist poetry and turned to

[†]6 Gallery was originally a carriage house built in 1906. A station for stagecoaches, it was reworked in the 1950s into an automobile repair shop, which was thereafter converted into a cooperative art gallery founded by six artists (Wallace Hendick, Hayward King, Deborah Remington, John Allen Ryan, David Simpson, and Jack Spicer).

McClure, who recited his "Point Lobos Animism" poem before yield-ing the spotlight to Whalen, who delivered two poems—"Plus Ça Change" and "The Martyrdom of Two Pagans." With his eyes closed and his back to the poets, Kerouac nodded at the lines he liked, some-times shouting out "wow"s and "yes'es" of approval between swigs from his gallon of Thunderbird.

After the intermission, Rexroth took to the orange-crate podium once again to silence the audience. Jack and his buddy, Bob Donlin, stumbled back into the room, hauling more jugs of cheap California burgundy to pass around during the second half of the night's program. It was around 11:00 p.m.

"Hey Natalie," Jack yelled, as his eyes caught Natalie Jackson's red hair. Neal, dressed in his railroad brakeman's uniform with watch and vest, stood behind her, his arms encircling her waist. She took a "big slug" from the jug, and so did her man. Jack hoped to loosen things up. So many of these so-called "hip" types had just sat and stood there lifelessly during the first half.

As Kerouac moved in their midst, he eyed his former girlfriend, Jinny Baker, a 23-year-old Japanese woman. Jack was taken aback: she was "beautifuller than ever." "Jinny," he called out. Theirs was a love that had gone sour, and she apologized for her role in that: "I was wrong." It didn't matter now. He was there to hear Allen, so he appeased her with a convenient "I am madly in love with you," and walked on. When the houselights dimmed, Neal Cassady looked over to Peter Orlovsky, with whom he had spoken earlier. The two of them waited for their poet-hero to begin. Kerouac, Ferlinghetti, Snyder, and Whalen—all of whom already had read the first part of "Howl"[†]—were also eager to hear the bard vocalize his clarion call.

Slightly intoxicated, the curly black-haired young man nervously strode from the back of the gallery to take the stage. Clean-shaven and wearing a charcoal-gray suit, white shirt, and tie, he cut a formal figure—as if he were about to give a funeral oration. Uneasily shifting his feet, Allen Ginsberg found his center of balance and announced the title of his new poem:

[†]Ginsberg chose to read only Part I of "Howl" at the 6 Gallery, since it was the only section that he considered complete enough to be performed in public.

"Howl for Carl Solomon"

Glancing at his manuscript through black horn-rimmed glasses, he began in a calm, quiet, but pointed tone:

> *I saw the best minds of my generation destroyed by madness, starving, hysterical, naked, dragging themselves through the negro streets at dawn looking for an angry fix, angel headed hipsters exploring for the ancient shuddering connection between the wires and the wheels of the dynamo of night,*

Allen started slowly, pausing at each comma, punctuating adjectives with staccato force. His words bespoke the craving in the hungry soul for a bond to the heavenly force that governs the constellations. With every "who," he breathed deeply and propelled his voice forward to build rhythmic pulse. The base word "who" grounded him. He gained more confidence as he launched defiant images with each new strophe.

> *who burned cigarette holes in their arms protesting the narcotic tobacco haze of capitalism, / who passed out supercommunist leaflets in Union Square weeping and undressing, while the sirens of Los Alamos wailed them down, . . . / who screamed on all fours in the subway, and were dragged off the roof waving genitals and manuscripts,*

All this talk of genitals made Ruth Witt-Diamant very uncomfortable. It was not so much that the founder of the San Francisco Poetry Center and a sponsor of poetry readings at 6 Gallery was a blue-nosed prude. Hardly. But Allen's sexually explicit language—the "cocks," "cunts," getting "blown" and "fucked in the ass"—was a bit too scandalous for her tastes. Such "obscene" words at a general public performance, not to mention the open drinking, all in the presence of minors, could well bring down the law. Gesturing frantically at Rexroth, she signaled that Ginsberg must moderate his expletives. Kenneth, by contrast, appreciated the significance of the poetic breakthrough that he heard; he would not raise a finger to curtail it. There was nothing for Ruth to do, except tolerate Allen's uninhibited vernacular: *who copulated ecstatic and insatiate with a bottle of beer.*

Though exuberantly drunk, Jack Kerouac heard the human horn of Allen's voice blowing long and powerful phrases, exhaling his pent-up fury like a jazzman wailing on an atomic saxophone. It was spontaneous poetry in action. He heard it beat down to his soul; he felt it shake down to his bones. Jack wanted Allen to take it to the next exhilarating level. Caught up like a brother-in-arms, he shouted out his support: "Go! Go! Go!" And go Allen did . . . all the way back to a place in time and a place in Jack's mind.

> *who journeyed to Denver, who died in Denver, who came*
> *back and waited in Denver / watched and went away finally to find*
> *out the future, / who fell on their knees in hopeless cathedrals praying*
> *for each others' salvation . . .*

The words rang in Neal's ears. Denver . . . the slums of Denver, the bums of Denver, the altars of Denver, the joyrides of Denver, the jails of Denver, the whores of Denver. Pavlovian Denver. He responded, "Go! Go! Go!"

Allen now came to the strophes in his poem that were the most personal and poignant for him, those dedicated to his mother and to his friend Carl Solomon. His voice deepened with a tenderness born in empathy, as he pledged solidarity to the madman he met in an asylum.

> *ah, Carl, while you're not safe I am not safe, and*
> *now you're in the total soup of Time –*

Ferlinghetti sat back calmly and took in the spectacle of it all. The crowd could not contain itself. The audience joined in a thunderous cadence: "Go! Go! Go!" They stomped their feet; they snapped their fingers; they clapped their hands. "Go! Go! Go!" Feeding on their life force, Allen now increased his speed, raised his pitch, and amplified his volume, as he pushed his voice to its maximum power. Swaying with the rhythm of his lines, he chanted his ending with hypnotic rabbinical passion.

Relentless. Merciless. Wondrous. The unspoken had been spoken . . . for some 14 metaphoric minutes. Madness had been outed. It was a howling manifesto that transcended logic and embraced mysticism. Every woman, man, and minor there experienced it. Rexroth cried.

Neal rushed up to the stage. He grabbed Ginsberg's hand, shook it heartily, and said, "Allen, my boy, I'm proud of you." Allen was touched. As he looked around, he saw Jack. Did he appreciate the subterranean meaning and the inspired sound of the poem? Indeed, he did. Kerouac had heard the future, and he told Allen that "Howl" would make him famous in San Francisco. Not to be outdone, Rexroth demurred: "This poem will make you famous from bridge to bridge."

After Gary Snyder concluded the program with his reading of "A Berry Feast," the poets went out to celebrate. They ate at Sam Wo's Chinese restaurant, where Jack first learned to eat with chopsticks, and then resorted to a favorite hangout, The Place, for yet more drink . . . cocksure that a corner to the counterculture had been rounded. "We had gone beyond a point of no return," Michael McClure recalled, "and we were ready for it, for a point of no return." We knew "at the deepest level that a barrier had been broken."

Ferlinghetti was similarly confident, similarly impressed, though he did not join his friends at Sam Wo's. Rather, he and his wife returned to their top-floor apartment at 339 Chestnut Street. Though he had seen the manuscript before this evening, he had never *heard* Allen's poetic howl. Having done so convinced him more than ever that this poem was destined for Pocket Poem publication. And so, as the story goes, he proceeded straight to his study where he composed a telegram to Ginsberg.[†] In the historical shadow of Emerson's cele-

---

[†]Ginsberg's archivist and biographer, Bill Morgan, has written: "The following day Ferlinghetti supposedly sent him a telegram paraphrasing Emerson's letter to Whitman. . . . Later, in 1964, Allen couldn't remember if Ferlinghetti had really sent a telegram or not. In some ways it seems unlikely, since even short telegrams were expensive, but Lawrence distinctly remembers sending it via Western Union. A twenty-year search of Ginsberg's archive has failed to turn up the telegram, but in sentiment, it certainly happened, if not in fact." Morgan's reference to Ginsberg's recollection is based on a 1964 letter that Allen wrote to his Italian translator, Fernanda Pivano: "Ferl[inghetti] sent telegram only ironically, I don't remember if he really did that." In contrast, Michael Schumacher, another Ginsberg biographer, maintains that both Allen and Lawrence Ferlinghetti confirmed in interviews that such a telegram was sent and received, though no other evidence of it exists. Whatever the fact of the matter, the significance of such a telegram would have been readily understood by Ginsberg, an avid reader of Whitman. Almost exactly 100 years before the 6 Gallery reading, on 21 July 1855, Ralph Waldo Emerson wrote to Walt Whitman to thank him for the gift of a copy of *Leaves of Grass*. Emerson considered it "the most extraordinary piece of wit and wisdom that America has yet

brated response to Whitman's *Leaves of Grass*, the telegram read: "I greet you at the beginning of a great career. When do I get the manuscript?"

* * *

He could not purge the name from his mind . . .

Moloch. *Ba'al* Moloch. The Sacred Bull. The Canaanites, Ammonites, Moabites, and other Punic cultures in the ancient Near East feared Moloch's fury. To appease him, they offered up their first-born children to be burned or slaughtered. This pagan figure, however, was an enemy of the Hebrew God. "You shall not give any of your offspring to sacrifice them to Molech," *Leviticus* sternly instructed the Jews, "and so profane the name of your God: I am the LORD."

Allen Ginsberg came face to face with Moloch one evening in late August of 1955. It happened after he and Peter had taken peyote. Strolling the streets of San Francisco, he was overcome by a demonic presence. The piercing eyes of a monster startled him. As they approached Powell and Sutter Streets, the sinister face of a Death Head loomed ever larger. It stared down at them, as if eager to seize their souls. Allen had seen this mask of Moloch before, ten months earlier at Sheila Williams's apartment. Then, too, peyote had expanded his visionary perception. When he looked out her open window, he spied the image of Moloch through the wisps of night fog. It was the silhouette of the tall tower of the Sir Francis Drake Hotel, with three lit windows that he imagined to be the eyes and nose of this King of Evil. Writing to Jack Kerouac, Allen recounted his foreboding encounters with Moloch: "We wandered on Peyote all downtown," and saw "Moloch-smoking building in red glare downtown St. Francis Hotel, with robot upstairs eye & skull face, in smoke, again."

Now, weeks after the 6 Gallery triumph, Allen sat in a cafeteria at the base of the Drake Hotel. He muttered "Moloch," "Moloch," "Moloch" to himself. Sipping coffee, he penned that mantra into snippets for the second part of "Howl." Those same words had rung in his ears earlier when he rode the Powell Street cable car. With each *clang, clang, clang* of the trolley, his mind chanted in rhythm with the sound: *Moloch, Moloch, Moloch.*

---

contributed." And he continued: "I greet you at the beginning of a great career, which yet must have had a long foreground somewhere, for such a start."

Ginsberg then revised that text over and over at his Milvia Street cottage, much to Jack Kerouac's dismay. While he was staying with Allen in the fall of 1955, Jack acted as his writing coach, counseling him to stick to the principles of spontaneous composition. But "no 'spontaneous' poem was more thoroughly rewritten" than "Howl." For months after debuting Part I of "Howl," Allen typed one draft after another of Part II—some 17 typewritten drafts followed the handwritten original. As the manuscript evolved, "Moloch" took on more ominous tones.

> *What sphinx of cement and aluminum bashed open their skulls and ate up their brains and imagination?*
> *Moloch! Solitude! Filth! Ugliness! Ashcans and unobtainable dollars!*
> *Children screaming under the stairways! Boys sobbing in armies! Old men weeping in the parks!*

Hunched at his typewriter for hours on end, Allen elaborated on the characteristics of the pagan god. As he added, deleted, and modified again and again, he murmured aloud, "Moloch," "Moloch," "Moloch." Gary Snyder, who shared the tiny one-room cottage with him, was flabbergasted by Allen's trance-like trope. Sitting cross-legged, Japanese-style, on the floor rug, Gary struggled to concentrate through the background muttering, as he translated Han Shan from the Chinese. Finally, he called out in jest: "Moloch who reaches up at night thru the bottom of the toilet bowl and grabs my pecker every time I try to take a crap!" Laughing at Gary and himself, Allen was not deterred. He worked on, using "Moloch" as his poetic base, to rail against the demon who infiltrated men's minds, implanted his evils there, and condemned all who opposed him.

> *Moloch! Moloch! Nightmare of Moloch! Moloch the loveless! Mental Moloch! Moloch the heavy judger of men!*

Fine-tuning his lines, Allen read aloud to correct the rhythm and to build rhetorical power. His recitation at 6 Gallery convinced him that "Howl" must be crafted for the ear, so dramatic flourish became his tuning fork. With metaphorical momentum, Allen denounced the forces of military-industrial capitalism that, like Moloch, devoured children.

Moloch whose mind is pure machinery! Moloch whose blood is running money! Moloch whose fingers are ten armies! Moloch whose breast is a cannibal dynamo! Moloch whose ear is a smoking tomb!

More was soon to come—the section about Allen's mentally plagued mother Naomi—and when it did the result would be a poem unlike any other.

· 5 ·

The Bust

Law and Literature

$\mathcal{H}$e had the manuscript now and was busy putting all the parts of *Howl* together for publication. All was moving fairly well on that score. Still, Lawrence was concerned. Three or so months after he offered to publish "Howl for Carl Solomon," he faced the specter of censorship.[†] He suspected that he "would be busted, not only for four-letter words," but also for the poem's "frank sexual, especially homosexual content." How could he bring this great Whitmanesque work to life if the government might abort it at the outset? Unless he could solve that riddle, he stood to lose not only the poem but all that he had created to make his bookselling and publishing dreams a reality.

It wasn't merely a matter of winning a censorship case; it was also a matter of affording to stay in the game. "We were just a little, unknown bookstore. We didn't have any resources for hiring lawyers," Ferlinghetti realized. So he contacted Lawrence Speiser, who headed the Northern Chapter of the American Civil Liberties Union. Good news. The ACLU agreed to defend him if anything came up. The prospect also pleased Allen. "Civil Liberties Union here was consulted and said they'd defend it if it got into trouble, which I almost hope it does,"

[†]Legally speaking, there were also possible issues of defamation and invasion of privacy relating to statements published about Carl Solomon. Fortunately for Ginsberg and Ferlinghetti, Solomon never filed any such actions.

Allen told his father. "I am almost ready to tackle the U.S. Govt out of sheer self delight. There is really a great stupid conspiracy of unconscious negative inertia to keep people from 'expressing' themselves."

Before Allen could fight the good fight, however, he needed to finish revising "Howl" and selecting other poems for the book. Ginsberg made the final modifications to "Howl" by the end of April 1956; and Ferlinghetti and he went back and forth until they decided on nine additional poems, including "A Supermarket in California, Sunflower Sutra," and "America." There was also the matter of the title: Lawrence persuaded Allen to "call it simply 'Howl,' making 'for Carl Solomon' a dedication, and thus implying a more universal significance." The contents of "Howl" likewise changed: the original Part IV was taken out[†] and the work ended with "A Footnote to Howl."

Because the famed poet William Carlos Williams had responded so favorably to an earlier draft of "Howl," Allen urged that he be invited to write an introduction to the book. Ferlinghetti agreed and wrote to him. Williams accepted. He penned 500-plus words that spoke eloquently to the poem's compelling meaning and emotional force:

> He proves to us, in spite of the most debasing experiences that life can offer a man, the spirit of love survives to ennoble our lives if we have the wit and the courage and the faith—and the art! to persist. . . . Hold back the edges of your gowns, Ladies, we are going through hell.

Before the manuscript was ready to send to the printers, two other items needed attention. Allen inserted an epigraph quote by Walt Whitman for the book; the two unattributed lines that he chose from *Song of Myself* captured perfectly the essence of "Howl."

Unscrew the locks from the doors!
Unscrew the doors themselves from their jambs!

[†]In a 1998 interview, Ferlinghetti stated that he had persuaded Ginsberg to "leave out a whole section of 'Howl,' one whole, single-spaced page with a roman numeral at the top. I don't know what happened to that page," he noted. "There's no trace of that page anywhere."

Similar to his unpublished collection of poems, titled *Empty Mirrors*, Allen dedicated *Howl and Other Poems* to his Beat pals. The dedication was to Allen's closest three friends—Jack Kerouac, William Seward Burroughs, and Neal Cassady—and to their writings. The dedication referred, all in all, to 13 unpublished manuscripts, and concluded whimsically: "All of these books are published in Heaven." The fourth friend to be acknowledged was Lucien Carr; he was recognized for being "recently promoted to Night Bureau Manager of New York United Press." Although the first printing of *Howl and Other Poems* mentioned Lucien Carr in the dedication, subsequent printings did not. Lucien objected strongly to the use of his name. "I value a certain anonymity in life," he wrote Allen, "I hope that you bear that idiosyncrasy in mind in your next book—'Moan.'" That meant that Allen had to delete Lucien's name ASAP. In a January 15, 1957 letter to Ferlinghetti, Ginsberg wrote:

> My friend Lucien objects violently to using his name in the dedication. His reasons are varied and personal and real enough for him—I never asked his OK. . . . What can be done about omitting the line in the dedication in the second printing? Is it too late for immediate action?. . . . I am bound by honor to Do something about it no matter how much it fucks everything up.

Not pleased, of course, Larry took it in stride: "*Howl* will be delayed an extra two weeks due to the deletion of Lucien Carr. . . . The total cost comes to $25, which I could use as soon as possible, to pay the bill."[†]

* * *

One of the things Lawrence Ferlinghetti liked about young Allen Ginsberg was his ability to promote himself and others. Part of the success of 6 Gallery was due to the publicity campaign that Allen orchestrated before the event. Now he did much the same for the forthcoming publication of *Howl and Other Poems*. Kenneth Rexroth's wife, Marthe, cranked the ditto master at San Francisco State College to make the first copies of the manuscript, and Ginsberg sent out more than 100 aniline-purpled ditto copies to family, friends, and literary mentors such as professors Mark Van Doren and Lionel Trilling.

[†]As fate would have it, Carl Solomon also took exception to Ginsberg using his name; he even threatened to sue Allen, though nothing ever came of it.

But that was just prologue. The real thing, a print run, was still in the making. Before that could happen however, lawyers would have to lend their eyes and then their approval to what could be contraband—a legally obscene poem.

* * *

Lawrence Ferlinghetti had foresight. Much as he liked "Howl," and ready as he was to publish it, he was not unmindful of the risks associated with publishing a work with colorful and homoerotic words. Hence, he arranged with Villiers Publishers in London, a small poetry printer and vanity press, to print the first run (1,500 copies) of the fourth volume of his Pocket Poet Series. As he knew, Villiers was a reliable house that charged reasonable prices for its saddle-stitched letterpress work. The printer insisted, however, on the substitution of asterisks for "four-letter" words. Villiers was sensitive to this since *Miscellaneous Man*, one of its earlier projects, ran into censorial trouble in San Francisco because of "obscene" language. It did not want to repeat that scenario. Reluctantly, Ferlinghetti agreed, as did an equally unenthusiastic Ginsberg.

Bound for the Artic Circle on the *Pendleton*, Allen scanned the galleys of his book. They were a complete mess. His carefully divided long lines were haphazardly broken on the printed page. Because detailed instructions had not been given to the printer, the stylistic integrity of his poems was seriously compromised. "This being my first book I want it right if can," Ginsberg wrote to Ferlinghetti. The "poems are actually sloppy enough written, without sloppiness made worse by typographic arrangement. . . . It looks like the whole book will have to be reset practically. . . . I will pay that no matter how much up to $200, which I guess it may well cost." Allen could not fathom the thought that his poetic debut would be marred by such a jumble. "I mean you can't tell *what* I am doing," he continued, "it looks like just primitive random scribbling in pages. I had not intended the prosody to be *that* arbitrary." Ferlinghetti was not about to leave Ginsberg in his distraught state; he ordered a new printing, but this time with precise guidelines.

When Allen received the corrected galleys in August, he sighed in deep relief. His long lines had been restored properly, and for a fraction of what he had been willing to pay. "Everything worked out fine with the typography—it looks much better this way and it seems to have been real cheap to do—$20 is nuthin," Ginsberg told Ferlinghetti. In a moment of insecure humility, he admitted: "I shuddered when I read the poetry tho, it looks so jerry-built sloppy and egocentric most of it. . . . Reading it through I'm not sure it deserves all the care and work you've put into it and the encouragement you've given me." Still, Allen showed his gratitude for Lawrence's efforts to bring his "Howl" to light: "But what the hell, thank you anyway for all your courtesy and I hope few people will see it with such jaded eyes as I do. . . . I wonder if we will actually sell the thousand copies."

To ensure the sale of those copies, Ginsberg aimed to increase the buzz about *Howl and Other Poems* in literary circles. He provided Ferlinghetti with a list of some 100 luminaries to receive complimentary copies, including Kenneth Rexroth, Kenneth Patchen, W. H. Auden, T. S. Eliot, and Ezra Pound. Books were even mailed off to Charlie Chaplin and Marlon Brando.

Allen's apprehension over sales was relieved when Richard Eberhart's piece, "West Coast Rhythms," appeared in the *New York Times Book Review*. The essay was a godsend. "The West Coast is the liveliest spot in the country in poetry today," it began. The story mentioned the Poetry Center at San Francisco State College, Kenneth Rexroth, Kenneth Patchen, Gary Snyder, Philip Whalen, and Michael McClure, too. But the lion's share of its attention was devoted to a "remarkable Poem" that had created "a furor of praise or abuse whenever read or heard. It is a powerful work, cutting through to dynamic meaning." This compelling work—"profoundly Jewish in temper"—was portrayed as a "howl against everything in our mechanistic civilization which kills the spirit . . . It lays bare the nerves of suffering and spiritual struggle." And finally, in words that delighted the Buddhist poet, Eberhart added: "Its positive force and energy come from a redemptive quality of love, although it destructively catalogues evils of our time from physical deprivation to madness."

All this good ink came just as *Howl and Other Poems* worked its way through U.S. Customs without incident, ready for distribution to bookstores everywhere. Allen Ginsberg was ecstatic, Louis Ginsberg proud, Lionel Trilling surprised, Ezra Pound dumbfounded, and the radical French-educated Lawrence Ferlinghetti happy as a Jacobin on Bastille Day.

Eberhart's article propelled Ginsberg and *Howl* into the limelight. *Life* magazine and *Mademoiselle* planned to cover the budding poetry movement and its star. Literary journals that had spurned him before now did everything to entice him to publish with them. It was a bright new day. "Beginning to get long admiring letters from starry-eyed Parkinson & N.Y. types about Howl," Allen wrote. "Agh! I'm sick of the whole thing, that's all I think about, famous author hood, like a happy empty dream. . . . How beautiful tho. I guess I feel really good about it."

* * *

Gregory Corso—he was a friend, a fellow poet, and a "Beat." Thus, when he heard the news, it shocked him—CENSORSHIP. To think that something as ridiculous as this could happen to Allen Ginsberg's poetic stroke of genius! In San Francisco, no less—the Bohemian city, the West Coast home of the Beats, and the site of the path-shifting 6 Gallery reading, where he had witnessed Allen's howling. Reading Ginsberg's letter from Tangier, Corso first learned of the U.S. Custom's seizure of a British shipment of *Howl and Other Poems*. The olive-skinned ex-con shook his shaggy hair in amazement. Greg replied to Allen from Barcelona: "[H]ow absurd of that man to seize the books." What was this dumb-ass official thinking? Why would this fool get bent out of shape over "fucks," "cunts," and "cocksuckers"? Words, words, words—they were just words—so what was the big fuckin' deal? The whole thing irked him.

Back in the Bay Area, the *San Francisco Chronicle* columnist Abe Mellinkoff held a similar opinion, though he was far more erudite. The headline of his March 28, 1957, "Morning Report" read: "Iron Curtain on The Embarcadero." The 44-year-old city editor knew the Collector of Customs, Chester MacPhee, and considered him to be "a nice guy and a good public servant." But his kind words ended there. With a dollop of sarcasm, Melinkoff stated: "[H]e knows no more about modern poetry than I do. What I mean [is that] he is ignorant on the subject. That's why I think he has a lot of nerve in confiscating 520 copies of a book" by Allen Ginsberg.

Melinkoff's column explained that *Howl and Other Poems* "was printed in England and picked up on the local docks as being too dirty for Americans to read." And for what compelling purpose? " 'The words and the sense of the writing is obscene. You wouldn't want your children to come across it,' " declared MacPhee. This justification addled the astute newspaperman. While he granted that Customs agents play an important role in searching for opium smugglers, "the collector has no duty to protect my children. . . . If he is going to pick up everything that is a menace to them, he is going to be confiscating night and day."

What caught the attention of the Customs men in connection with the *Howl* shipment was the name "Villiers." Not long before, they had seized copies of *Miscellaneous Man* for alleged obscenity; that magazine, published by William Margolis in Berkeley, was also printed by Villiers. The moral enforcers of the Tariff Act of 1930 were wise to the vulgar fare of the London-based printer. They went on a censorial hunt for anything that displayed the stamp "Villiers." It was up to the well-dressed MacPhee, who resembled the actor David Niven, to convince the public that *Howl* was such a threat to children that it must be quarantined. Lawrence Ferlinghetti, whose bundles of books were sequestered, was unconvinced: "I think MacPhee just saw the four-letter words in there, and wasn't capable of making any critical judgment on the literary or poetic value of the text."[†]

As already noted, the City Lights Books publisher anticipated MacPhee's move when he had earlier contacted the American Civil Liberties Union to defend against any Customs actions. Happily, Ferlinghetti didn't need the ACLU's assistance for the first shipment of *Howl*, which passed through without incident. Now, however, he summoned them to lift the quarantine on the second shipment of his books; on April 3, the ACLU informed MacPhee that it would challenge the legality of the seizure. Even so, Lawrence did not limit himself to legal recourse. He saw to it that a stock of 2,500 photo-offset copies were printed *in the U.S.*, thus depriving Customs officials of jurisdiction. And those books were quickly distributed for any and all to read. His shrewd move made a mockery of MacPhee's paternalistic logic— protecting American children from lurid lines of poetry.

The "obscene" author, of course, was in no place to assist his "obscene" publisher. Working in Tangier, Morocco, on Bill Burroughs's early draft of his ribald novel *Naked Lunch*, Ginsberg was both sympa-

---

[†]It is interesting that the customs officials seized *Howl and Other Poems* after Villiers had printed only asterisks alluding to such "four-letter words." Assuming that all of the mailed copies contained asterisks, it would then seem that Chester McPhee found obscenity by implication. Such asterisks, however, did not appear in later American printings.

thetic and opportunistic. On the one hand, he wrote to Ferlinghetti, "I guess this puts you up shits creek financially. I didn't think it would really happen. . . . Sorry I'm not there." On the other hand, he figured, "I suppose the publicity will be good." He urged Lawrence to "prepare some sort of outraged and idiotic but dignified statement, quoting the Customs man," Eberhart's *New York Times* article, and William Carlos Williams's introduction to *Howl.* "Mimeograph it up," he urged, "and send it out as a sort of manifesto publishable by magazines and/or news release."

Lawrence first lent an ear to Allen's publicity advice, and then wielded his pen. Because William Hogan, the *San Francisco Chronicle's* book review editor, turned over his Sunday column, "Between the Lines," to the bookseller, Ferlinghetti could respond publicly to the government's actions. In his printed statement, he made three basic points:

1. The publicity argument: "The San Francisco Collector of Customs deserves a word of thanks for seizing *Howl and Other Poems* and thereby rendering it famous. Perhaps we could have a medal made. It would have taken years for critics to accomplish what the good collector did in a day, merely by calling the book obscene."

2. The literary merits argument: "I consider *Howl* to be the most significant single long poem to be published in this country since World War II, perhaps since Elliot's *Four Quartets.*"

3. The dissent argument: If "Howl" is "a condemnation of our official culture, if it is an unseemly voice of dissent, perhaps this is really why officials object to it. In condemning it, however, they are condemning their own American world. For it is not the poet but what he observes which is revealed as obscene. . . . Considering the state of the world (not to mention the state of modern poetry) it was high time to howl."

With two slams from the *Chronicle*, Customs Collector MacPhee was put on the rhetorical run. But what really pulled the rug out from beneath him was notification that the U.S. Attorney's Office in San Francisco would take no legal action against *Howl.* With that, Customs had no alternative but to release the books, which it did on May 29.

Ferlinghetti's two-pronged strategy, hitting hard on both the publicity and legal fronts, had worked beautifully. It was a victory for free speech: Allen's dissident bardic voice could now be heard. It was a victory for the free market: Lawrence's pocket poet books could now be sold.

Until, that is, William A. Hanrahan's "sting" operation. Unlike the critics who carped at MacPhee's warnings, the Captain of the Juvenile Department of the San Francisco Police took them to heart. If the Customs officials were unable to "protect" San Francisco's children from Ginsberg's coarse verses, then he and his officers would come to their rescue. On May 21, 1957, Hanrahan sent two undercover agents to City Lights to buy a book of poems and a magazine. After paying Shigeyoshi ("Shig") Murao, the heavy-set store manager who "looked like a Japanese sage but had the culture of a hip American," they left immediately with their contraband, *Howl and Other Poems* and *Miscellaneous Man*.

Within two weeks, the plainclothes officers came back to the scene of the crime, and purchased yet another copy of *Howl*. Later on that same day—Monday, June 3, 1957—they returned to City Lights with two arrest warrants. Ferlinghetti and Murao were to be charged with the "willful and lewd" sale of "obscene and indecent" materials, and Lawrence with the publication as well, in violation of §311.3 of the Penal Code of California.

The task of making the poem-busts fell to officers Russell Woods and Thomas Pagee. They pulled up to the storefront, the one with the striped canopy that prominently advertised "BOOKS." Somewhat embarrassed, the two entered the small pie-shaped room, looking for their criminal suspects. They found only Shig and Kirby, Ferlinghetti's wife. When Kirby confronted them about the absurdity of it all, the response was routine: "it is all in the line of duty, ma'am." Though they looked like well-groomed college students and "were terribly nice," they were there on official business. A "John Doe" warrant was then handed to Shig. He took it in stride, and even kidded that "Shigeyoshi Murao, a Japanese-American, was being arrested as a 'John Doe' white man." The officers smiled, but didn't laugh. Without being handcuffed, Murao was escorted out of the store and into the squad car. It was only three blocks to the Hall of Justice.

Shigeyoshi Murao, Jake Ehrlich, and Ferlinghetti.
San Francisco Chronicle/Polaris.

On arrival, the suspect was taken down to the basement, where he was fingerprinted. The Kafkaesque reality of being busted for selling poems hit home when the cops took his mug shots, front and side. Then, the stench of urine overwhelmed Murao as he approached his dim cell. When the door locked behind him, his eyes immediately fixed on the "piss-stained mattress on the floor." He was in the drunk tank. Someone had seen the need to post a penal code section on the cell wall; above it, scrawled as graffiti, was an obscene word—"cocksuckers."

Murao suffered the stench as Ferlinghetti breathed in full lungs of fresh air in his Big Sur cabin,[†] the one near a canyon where gigantic "elbows of rock" rose up thousands of feet and then fell into the

---

[†]It was at that cabin in August of 1960 that Kerouac wrote most of what became his novel *Big Sur*, published in 1962.

breaking waters of the Pacific. While there, he received word of the bust; he even got newspaper clippings, and mailed one along with a letter to Allen in Tangier. On June 6, three days after Shig had been sprung by the ACLU on $500 bail, Lawrence left the enchanted redwood forest and turned himself in at the San Francisco Hall of Justice; "a picturesque return to the early Middle Ages," is how he described it.

The next day, Jack Kerouac, who was staying in Berkeley, wrote to Allen: Some "local dumb Irish cops rushed up on their own initiative and bought HOWL in the store and arrested the nice Jap cat who was instantly bailed out by the Civil Liberties Union, but I went there & there were no more HOWLS on the shelf." Worse still, Kerouac feared that American intellectuals were "so gutless they might knuckle under the dumb fat Irish cops in time and it'll be like Germany, a police state. I'm really worried."

Allen was also anxious: "I guess this is more serious than the customs seizure since you can lose real money on this deal if they find you guilty," he wrote to Lawrence. And he had his suspicions, too: "Who or what is behind all this attention? It appears like Customs were burned up when they had to let go and someone must have called juvenile police from customs, and asked them to take up and carry the ball from there." One more thing: "Are local newspapers being sympathetic?"

Indeed, they were. Beyond the news stories, the *Chronicle* ran an editorial with a damning headline that read: "Making a Clown of San Francisco." It published a column with the ominous headline: "Orwell's 'Big Brother' Is Watching over Us." And it featured a cartoon that portrayed a bulldog-faced policeman pounding a notice on a bookstore door. The caption: "Hanrahan's Law—All books must be fit for children to read—SFPD." And there was more of the same in other papers.

The editorial writers, columnists, and cartoonists lampooned what Captain Hanrahan had told reporters: "We have purchased" *Howl* and *Miscellaneous Man*. "They are not fit for children to read." To which came the editorial response: "Here is a new and startling doctrine and one which, if followed to the letter, would clear many of the world's classics from local bookstores, not excepting the Bible wherein is many a chapter and verse not recommended for perusal by tiny tots."

Gregory Corso was equally critical of the "Hanrahan's Law" mindset, but for different reasons: "How many children will read HOWL?"

"Hanrahan's Law." San Francisco Chronicle (June 6, 1957).
San Francisco Chronicle/Polaris

Some people are "afraid of what it might do to children—but children read nothing! Children know nothing—children are nothing!" Later, writing to Ferlinghetti from Paris, Corso was less flip. In a serious vein, he lamented the fate of those who print books by the Beats: "I think that you are perhaps the only great publisher in America and will have to suffer for it."

Justice William Brennan.
Benjamin Forte/CNP/Polaris.

· 6 ·

The High Court

Justice Brennan's Constitutional Handiwork

I'm afraid of what will happen in court—trial set
for August 6—maybe City Lights [will] lose, be
out of dough, & screw up the whole publishing deal.

—Allen Ginsberg

*A*llen and his lover Peter Orlovsky frolicked in far-off Naples, Venice, Paris, and Amsterdam, strolling in museums and sitting in cafés while savoring the charms of European culture. Back in the U.S.A., Larry and Shig met with their ACLU lawyers and prepared for trial. Concerned as Allen was about the prosecution of *Howl and Other Poems*, he was not the one within the punitive reach of the law.

Ferlinghetti, ever the radical poet, did not worry about his clash with Officialdom. He welcomed it. Even though he could be fined and jailed, he saw the golden lining in the storm clouds. Recall his sentiment: "It would have taken years for critics to accomplish what the good collector did in a day, merely by calling the book obscene." Notoriety had its benefits: a spike in sales and the prospect of long-term profits.

Indeed, before the trial was over, there would be several runs of *Howl* with more than 10,000 copies in print, and an LP-record deal in the works. And *Life* magazine and others were profiling it all. Even if Ferlinghetti were convicted, the San Francisco poet and publisher seemed unflappable: "I thought, well, I could use some time in the clink to do some heavy reading."

Shigeyoshi Murao viewed the world through a different lens: "In jail I had no noble thoughts for fighting for freedom of the press. . . . I had planned to live a quiet life of reading, listening to music and playing chess the rest of my life. Yet here I was involved in a case for selling obscenity."

That charge weighed heavily on his mind and his cultural sense of self. As Ferlinghetti described Murao, he was a "Nisei whose family had been interned with thousands of other Japanese-Americans during the war," and "to be arrested for anything, even if innocent, was in the Japanese community of that time a family disgrace."

There was, however, far more at stake than the fate of two young men. For a conviction in this case surely would entice Captain Hanrahan and his officers to return to City Lights or other bookstores to scan the shelves for copies of other "obscene" types of avant-garde literature. The Juvenile Bureau chief suggested as much when he alluded to a literary cache that had caught his attention: "We will await the outcome of this case before we go ahead with other books." And a conviction in the *Howl* case would set a precedent for other jurisdictions to follow. If *Howl* could be banned in California, then it could be outlawed in Illinois, New York, Georgia, Massachusetts, or anywhere else in the nation.

Allen knew that while the Beats had clashed with the law before, the *Howl* trial was the first time that their rebellious ideas and ideals were tested and tried by the State. It wasn't just *Howl*'s colorful words, such as "cock," "fucked," and "balled." It was also the poem's aggressive and activist message, those tirades against McCarthy-era politics and Norman Rockwell-era morality. That message was far more threatening to the conventions of the day than any barroom vernacular. The prosecution had much it could tap on to make its case in the minds of most judges or jurors of the day:

> *Exhibit A—Pro-Communism*: "who distributed Supercommunist pamphlets in Union Square weeping and undressing while the sirens of Los Alamos wailed them down"
>
> *Exhibit B—Pro-Homosexuality*: "who blew and were blown by those

human seraphim, the sailors, caresses of Atlantic and Caribbean
love"

Exhibit C—Pro-Promiscuity: "who sweetened the snatches of a million girls trembling in the sunset, and were red eyed in the
morning but prepared to sweeten the snatch of the sun rise,
flashing buttocks under barns and naked in the lake"

Exhibit D—Anti-Capitalism: "Moloch whose mind is pure machinery! Moloch whose blood is running money! Moloch whose
fingers are ten armies!"

Exhibit E—Anti-America: "Go fuck yourself with your atom
bomb," delivered in "America," one of the poems in the *Howl*
collection. "I'm sick of your insane demands," Allen insisted in
yet another declaration of anger and alienation in that poem.

Ginsberg railed against what America had become. This son of a
Communist mother and a socialist poet father loathed modern America's ethos, its logos, its "homophobos," and its mechanized mindset that
produced uniformity at the expense of individuality. By that measure,
Allen and his poems were un-American.

When the cultural lens widened, it became clear that the poem
was political. Thus the battle the Beats now waged was not merely over
some "dirty" words in literature, but over competing visions of the
nation: the perspective of an Eisenhower-like America that many held
dear versus that of a Whitman-like America that the Beats cherished.
What was at stake was the right to *dissent*, the right to attack that
"Moloch" America so determined to strangle the spirit of freethinking
youths.

Defending *Howl*, then, meant defending alienated cultural outlaws
who condemned modern America, the same outlaws who pointed to a
new vision of America yearning to be born. With Allen on the sidelines
and Larry and Shig on the frontlines, the battle for America's soul was
about to begin.

* * *

To look at him you'd never know that Lawrence Speiser was an
American Civil Liberties Union lawyer. He didn't fit the stereotype.
He had middle-America etched in the contours of his cheeks and fixed
on his forehead.

At the time of the *Howl* trial, Speiser was 34, and had the face

Jake Ehrlich with Ferlinghetti and Lawrence Speiser (right).
San Francisco Chronicle/Polaris.

and frame of a football jock—clean-cut, clean-shaven, tall, and broad chested. His all-American manner made him seem "square," the kind of guy the Beats lampooned. Few could guess that this World War II veteran would defend countercultural and radical types, even anarchists and communists. But defend them he did. Larry Speiser was part of a remarkable trio of pro bono lawyers who would represent the defendants (an anarchist publisher and his shop clerk) in *People v. Ferlinghetti* and *People v. Murao.*

As he prepared for the start of the trial in the Municipal Court of San Francisco, Speiser had his mind on another First Amendment case. This one did not involve poetry. It was a loyalty-oath case, in which he himself was the civil plaintiff-appellant, and which he had recently lost in the California Supreme Court. Thus, at the very time Speiser was working on *Murao/Ferlinghetti*, he was also petitioning the U.S.

Supreme Court to review the state's denial of a tax exemption because he refused to sign a loyalty oath.

Speiser had an impressive record as a civil liberties lawyer, especially for someone his age. True to that record, in the year following the *Howl* trial, he would win his own case in the Supreme Court. It was a 7–1 victory, with Justice William J. Brennan, Jr. writing for the majority.[†]

As it turned out, that same Justice Brennan would play a pivotal, though indirect, role in the *Howl* case, too. That was due to his opinion in still other First Amendment cases, *Roth v. United States* and *Alberts v. California*, decided in June of 1957, a few months before the *Murao/Ferlinghetti* trial began.

* * *

It was a mere 32 days after he was confirmed by the Senate, with Joe McCarthy railing against him, when William Brennan took his seat on the Supreme Court to hear oral arguments in cases nos. 582 and 61, *Roth v. United States* and *Alberts v. California*. He was the junior player sitting alongside constitutional giants William O. Douglas, Hugo Black, John Harlan, Earl Warren, and Brennan's former Harvard Law School professor, Felix Frankfurter.

The Court chamber where the *Roth-Alberts* oral arguments took place was a monumental paean to the law's grandeur. The constitutional dialogue began under the majestic 44-foot ceiling supported by 24 columns of Italian marble.

Prior to oral arguments, the Justice Department had shipped those materials under seal to the Court to demonstrate the kind of filth that would be legitimized if the Justices reversed the convictions of Sam Roth and David Alberts for advertising and selling obscene books and magazines. Now, Justices Tom Clark and William O. Douglas quietly distributed pornographic materials to their colleagues on the bench, out of the sight of those in the Court gallery, of course. In the very elevated quarters where decorum and propriety were the rule, some of the Justices eyed "stroke" mags as they listened to the nuances of American procedural and constitutional law. If only Allen Ginsberg had known, it would have made for a saucy and satirical poem.

[†]According to Thomas Emerson, a noted First Amendment scholar, the Supreme Court's "*Speiser* decision broke new paths in its recognition of the importance of taking into account the dynamics of a system of freedom of expression."

Justice Frankfurter was a pretentious jurist who wore his Harvard credentials on his lapel. He dominated the dialogue. The constitutionally conservative Justice peppered the parties with procedural, evidentiary, and jurisdictional questions. With professorial fervor, he tried repeatedly to pin Roth's counsel down to exactly what his position was on the legal status of obscene materials. The more he asked, the worse it got. Exasperated, the Justice said: "You can't just swim in the midst of the Pacific Ocean in these matters. You've got to get some footing on some . . . *terra firma.*"

Throughout the oral arguments, the timid Brennan spoke only once, and not for very long. He asked the Deputy District Attorney from California how to identify an offending photograph or movie frame, namely, that point at which an erotic magazine or film crossed the line from the constitutionally protected to the legally obscene. The response was non-responsive, no defining point, just common knowledge: "Every man in the street knows what obscenity is."

When all was said and done, the highly technical oral arguments made it easy for the audience to drift off and stare at the sculpted marble panels surrounding the chamber. Moreover, no one reasonably could have predicted either the outcome of the case or the landmark status it would later attain.

It was Monday, June 24, 1957, when the Court handed down its rulings. Sam Roth's obscenity conviction was upheld by a 7–2 margin, as was that of David Alberts, though by a 6–3 vote. While the judgment of the Court and some of the language in Justice Brennan's majority opinion surely must have troubled the civil-rights attorney Lawrence Speiser, there were aspects of the opinion that promised a new measure of First Amendment freedom for his clients.

Indeed, Brennan's opinion read like a tribute to the Roman god Janus, the great gatekeeper with two faces gazing in opposite directions. It was an opinion that pleased conservatives and liberals alike, even as it troubled them.

There was the conservative face. This face of the opinion frightened libertarians and pleased those who would censor sexual expression. After all, Brennan declared: "[T]his Court has always assumed that obscenity is not protected by the freedoms of speech and press." And then this: "[I]mplicit in the history of the First Amendment is the rejection of obscenity as utterly without socially redeeming importance." Worse still, there was a big blow to those who used blue vernacular: "There are certain well-defined and narrowly limited classes of speech, the prevention and punishment of which have never been thought to raise any Constitutional problem. These include the lewd and obscene. . . . It has been well observed that such utterances are no essential part of the exposition of ideas, and are of such slight social value as a step to truth that any benefit that may be derived from them is clearly outweighed by the social interest in order and morality."

Obscenity was, by definition, worthless—no analysis or balancing necessary. For prosecutors, that meant that if they succeeded in branding a book, movie, play, or poem "obscene," that was typically the end of the matter: off to the local holding-tank with the moral offenders. Such a destiny might, then, await Ferlinghetti and Murao. Would their judge or jury conclude that *Howl and Other Poems* was "no essential part" of the exposition of important ideas?

Then there was the liberal face of the *Roth* opinion. On that side of the opinion, there was hope for those who defended sexual expression in literature and the arts. Brennan provided language that inspired that assessment: "[S]ex and obscenity are not synonymous." Obscene material, he continued, is "material having a tendency to excite lustful thoughts." And then Brennan delivered a big blow to those who sought to outlaw blue vernacular: "All ideas having even the slightest importance—unorthodox ideas, controversial ideas, even ideas hateful to the prevailing climate of opinion—have the full protection of the guaranties, unless excludable because they encroach upon the limited area of more important interests."

The upshot? Messages about sex were no longer categorically obscene. There was also a strong suggestion in the opinion that a finding of obscenity hinged on evidence that a work pushed libidinal buttons. Finally, when messages about sex commingled with social commentary, they ranked higher on the First Amendment scale.

Legally, the most important portion of the *Roth* opinion, the words that would find their way into numerous state and federal obscenity laws, was Justice Brennan's famous formula for determining obscenity:

- "[W]hether to the average person,
- applying contemporary community standards,

- the dominant theme of the material taken as a whole
- appeals to prurient interest."

Each of these four prongs had its peculiar relevance to the *Howl* case. For Ferlinghetti and Murao, the *Roth* test could prove promising in the hands of a judge sensitive to the nuances of the law and the literary value of *Howl*'s unorthodox and controversial lines. *Murao/Ferlinghetti* would be the first obscenity case in the nation to apply the new *Roth* test. How would the earliest progeny of *Roth* be fashioned? Would the *Howl* judge take his cue from William Brennan's application of the obscenity test? It was, recall, the young Justice who had upheld the *Roth-Alberts* obscenity convictions. Or would the *Howl* judge turn instead to the more liberal side of the opinion for constitutional guidance?

Lawrence Speiser, the appellate law expert who resembled a defensive lineman, had to craft a constitutional argument that would spare Ferlinghetti and Murao the fate of Roth and Alberts. It was quite a formidable challenge, even for such a remarkable lawyer.

Municipal Judge Clayton Horn.
Art Frisch/San Francisco Chronicle/Polaris.

· 7 ·

The Judge

The Story of the Sunday School Bible Teacher

$\mathcal{T}$he trial was set for August 8, 1957. It was to be conducted at the Municipal Court for the City and County of San Francisco, located at 750 Kearny Street.[†]

Judge Byron Arnold, a newly appointed Republican judge, was to preside. But things didn't play out that way. The case was delayed for eight days, and the matter reassigned to the Honorable Clayton W. Horn, with the case calendared for August 16.

Judge Horn was a Sunday school Bible teacher. He was a man who cared about the moral character of his world and those in it. God was in the letter of the law. Morals mattered. And when woven together, they did not bode well for the defense.

In the weeks before he presided over the *Howl* obscenity trial, Judge Horn had imposed his moral vision in an unusual manner, which placed him in the national limelight. He had sat in judgment on a case involving five women charged with shoplifting; finding they were guilty as charged, Judge Horn sentenced them to serve time at a movie theater.

The five convicted women were confined for 219 minutes in a local theater for a court-ordered movie viewing of the *Ten Commandments*. The cinematic sentence did not end with the ladies watching Cecil B. DeMille's epic film starring Charlton Heston (Moses), Yul Brynner (Pharaoh Rameses), and Anne Baxter (Nefertiti). They had to

---

[†]The courthouse was leveled long ago; a Hilton hotel is located there today.

51

put pen to paper and discuss, in essay form, the moral lessons to be drawn from the movie.

The judge's sentence drew harsh criticism from the editorial page of the *San Francisco Chronicle*: "Municipal Judge Clayton Horn's freewheeling excursion into movie-reviewing and *belles lettres* in weighing penalties for five petty shoplifters fills us with wonder and no little trepidation."

Worse still, that lesson in morality, the editors emphasized, required the five misdemeanants to sit through a film filled with "violence, lust, sex, and orgies." Alongside the editorial was a derisive cartoon of Horn clad as Moses in robe and sandals, holding a graven tablet that declared: "THOU SHALT NOT MISS 'THE TEN COMMANDMENTS'—Judge Clayton Horn."

The Bay-area jurist resembled the actor Gene Lockhart, who in 1947 played a judge in the movie *Miracle on 34th Street*. Judge Horn, however, was no actor. Black robed, he would now sit in judgment over the much-publicized obscenity trial of Lawrence Ferlinghetti and Shigeyoshi Murao.

What were the chances that a judge who honored a vengeful God would rule in favor of the defendants? Would he castigate these purveyors of poetic protest because the works they published and sold were laced with lewd terms?

Or would he, newly chastened by the media's charges of moral self-righteousness, approach the case with a non-judgmental sensitivity to its significance for the American free-speech culture? Maybe, but again, what were the chances?

Whatever those chances were, the defense had to develop both a compelling trial strategy to convince Judge Horn† of the legality of *Howl* and a compelling constitutional record in the event of an appeal. For those tasks, Ferlinghetti and Murao had a dream team of lawyers.

* * *

Lawrence Speiser, who had headed the Northern California chapter of the ACLU, would take charge and select and prepare the wit-

†A few years after the *Howl* trial, Judge Horn would preside over an obscenity case involving the controversial comedian Lenny Bruce. Al Bendich (see photo), one of the defense lawyers in the *Howl* case, successfully defended Bruce.

nesses for trial. If the defendants were to win this case, those witnesses were crucial to substantiate that *Howl* had serious literary value and did not primarily appeal to "prurient" interests.

Albert M. Bendich became the next member of the legal team. He

Al Bendich, ACLU lawyer for Ferlinghetti and Murao (2013, with Ron Collins).
R. Collins.

was a bright but quiet 28-year-old lawyer, a recent graduate of the University of California's Boalt Hall Law School. Although a labor law practitioner, Bendich had desired for some time to work for the ACLU. Having applied in the spring of 1957, he was hired by the civil-rights organization, late in the summer and shortly before the *Howl* trial began, to succeed Speiser as staff counsel. At the time that he came on board, Bendich met with Speiser over his impending workload. Speiser assigned Bendich immediately to *Howl*, his very first free-speech civil liberties case.

The formidable charge of researching the main statutory and con-stitutional arguments and writing the legal memoranda submitted to the court fell to this novice. In effect, Bendich was the one who had to reconcile the contrary strands of the *Roth* opinion with the facts of *Murao/Ferlinghetti*. And he had to do this against the backdrop of a body of pre-*Roth* law that was largely hostile to the use of vulgarity in literature.

Jacob Wilburn Ehrlich was the final member of the team. He took the lead both at the trial and in the limelight. Ehrlich—"Never Plead Guilty" or "the Master" as he was popularly known—was a San Fran-cisco lawyer with a big ego and a bigger national reputation. In July of 1948, for example, he defended condemned murderer Caryl Chessman, forestalling his execution in an appeal from death row, a case that drew international attention.[†]

Practicing since 1922 in San Francisco, "the Master" had won hundreds of murder cases. In one of them, he secured a jury acquittal in a mere four minutes. In another, it took the jury only 13 minutes to find his client not guilty of murdering her boyfriend who died of three bullets to the back. He was also renowned as a divorce lawyer; he repre-sented celebrities such as Errol Flynn, Billie Holiday, and Howard Hughes.

Ehrlich was a show horse, a man of both substance and flash. In his day, he published several widely used tracts on the law, including *Ehrlich's Blackstone*. And in the courtroom he was *the* man to be heard and seen.

Never modest in his style, he was an impressive oral advocate and

---

[†]The defendant had been condemned to death for non-capital offenses: robbery, kidnapping, and rape.

an impeccable dresser. His trademark attire: expensive custom-tailored suits draped over well-polished cowboy boots. And then there were his legendary cuff links, some valued at more than $25,000. One of his favorite sayings spoke volumes on his sartorial tastes: "A man can always be underdressed, but never overdressed."

Little wonder, then, that he could command $1,000 per minute for a 15-minute court appearance for one of his well-heeled clients. Even the less fortunate among them were not spared his astounding bills: "When I defend a man in a capital case," he often quipped, "my fee is EVERYTHING he owns. The way I have got it figured, if I win him his freedom it is worth it, and if I don't, he won't need it anyway." Ehrlich's sharp and showy career was perfect material for Hollywood: he eventually was fictionalized in *Sam Benedict*, a popular TV series, with Edmond O'Brien playing his character.

For all his experience in representing accused murderers and lovelorn spouses, Jake Ehrlich had never argued a First Amendment case. He did it—and this time, with no payment—for the glory and glitz that such a victory might promise.

Deputy District Attorney Ralph McIntosh was the prosecutor in the *Howl* trial. Once a linotype operator at a newspaper by day and a law student by night, he was now a man with years of prosecuting behind him. While nowhere as knowledgeable in constitutional law as Speiser and Bendich, and while hardly a courtroom match for the suave and seasoned Ehrlich, McIntosh had earned a local reputation for being tough on smut.

He had long set his prosecutorial sights on porn movie houses and bookstores, charging them for their dirty flicks and girly magazines. He even went after Howard Hughes's 1941 film, *The Outlaw*, the one in which Hughes, as an eccentric producer and Hollywood movie mogul, emphasized Jane Russell's voluptuous cleavage throughout the rough-and-tumble western. The film and its pulp-fiction-like poster, a racy pic of a reclining Jane, revealing her scantily-clad breasts while packing a pistol just above her hiked-up skirt, proved too much for the San Francisco prosecutor. He would not tolerate such filth in his fine city.

But going after "smutty" poetry was something new for the old prosecutor of porn. McIntosh had no sense of the poem; it was all gibberish to him. What he did understand, however, were all the dirty words, those disgusting references to "cock" and "cocksucker" and "asshole" and "fucked in the ass." Now that was obscene. That was something the California criminal law need not tolerate and the First Amendment should not protect.

Surely, the Supreme Court's new *Roth* standard for obscenity would not license such rubbish to be peddled in bookstores and elsewhere. And so, in the tradition of the notorious 19th-century moral crusader Anthony Comstock, Ralph McIntosh aimed to prosecute that which he really did not comprehend. He would do so simply because there were foul and corrupting words lurking between the black-and-white covers of *Howl and Other Poems*.

While McIntosh would confront formidable opponents in the team of Ehrlich, Spieser, and Bendich, he did have, to all appearances, a morally sympathetic judge and a new Supreme Court decision with some helpful language in it. More generally, the prosecutor could rely on a strong tradition hostile to the nonconformist ways of those who engaged in "sustained shrieks of frantic defiance," as M. L. Rosenthal of the *New York Times* tagged Ginsberg's poetry several months earlier.

To put it all another way, Ralph McIntosh had one big thing in his favor. He had the STATE (the mighty "Moloch" as Ginsberg tagged the demonic figure in "Howl") on his side.

Worse still, from what everyone knew about Judge Horn, he was more likely to side with the likes of moral crusaders such as Comstock and McIntosh than with crass and crazed poets and those who defended them.

August 1956, San Francisco: Ferlinghetti and Shigeyoshi Murao sitting in court during HOWL trial, with Ehrlich at podium.

San Francisco Chronicle/Polaris.

· 8 ·

The Courtroom

Poetry on Trial

"BATTLE OF THE BOOKS IS ON"

"Howl' Trial Starts—a Sellout Crowd"

It was a declaration of war reported on the front page of the *San Francisco Chronicle*. What was at stake was a generational struggle of ideologies and attitudes—the old vs. the young; the established vs. the rebellious; the traditional vs. the unconventional; and the righteously proper vs. the irreverently vulgar.

The Beat Generation's "nakedness of mind," as John Clellon Holmes put it in 1952, was being exposed for all to see in a San Francisco courtroom. In that venue, the Beats would proclaim through "Howl" their *"will* to believe," a will that manifested itself "even in the face of an inability to do so in conventional terms." The contest of wills and words had begun.

This battle, of course, had singular importance for Ferlinghetti and Murao. But from the broader perspective of Western history, it fell into a long line of conflicts over the government's power to control morals and manners, a tradition that stretched back at least to the elected censors of ancient Rome. In this sense, *Murao/Ferlinghetti* was the latest episode in a relentless campaign to purify what entered people's minds. In America, that crusade had attacked such noted works as Nathaniel Hawthorne's *The Scarlet Letter*, Walt Whitman's *Leaves of Grass*, D. H.

Lawrence's *Women in Love*, Radclyffe Hall's *The Well of Loneliness*, and James Joyce's *Ulysses*. The larger implications of the *Howl* prosecution were certainly well understood by the San Francisco literary community. One day before the *Murao/Ferlinghetti* trial opened, Mayor George Christopher received a petition signed by 21 of the city's leading booksellers, urging him to "use all the power of your office" to stop police seizure of books. Decrying the "deplorable" arrests of Ferlinghetti and Murao, the petition declared: "This sort of censorship has no place in a democratic society," and "is harmful to San Francisco's reputation as a center of culture and enlightenment."

Although neither the first nor the last obscenity prosecution on American shores, the *Howl* trial nevertheless had a full measure of significance. Legal vindication of Ginsberg's poetry might confirm the cultural value of unorthodox literature more generally, and might cast a wider protective net of liberty for the likes of Jack Kerouac, Bill Burroughs, John Clellon Holmes, and Ferlinghetti himself.

Accompanying the *San Francisco Chronicle*'s headlines was a black-and-white courtroom picture of a new generation of young Americans sitting and standing there to witness history. It was all captured for posterity by press flashbulb cameras allowed in the chamber.

The photographs reveal a high-ceilinged courtroom divided into two large sections of benches abutted by carved railing. Some 150 people sat there. Huge windows permitted the summer sunlight to pour in. Seated on a swivel chair to the left of the judge's bench, Lawrence Ferlinghetti wore an olive-green corduroy coat and tie. A pensive Shigeyoshi Murao, his right hand under his chin, sported a light blue summer suit, a white-buttoned shirt, and a black knit tie. Jake Ehrlich was dressed with his typical sartorial splendor in a finely cut three-piece suit replete with a gold watch chain and a protruding multi-pointed handkerchief. When the trial† finally got under way on Friday, August 16, the courtroom was jammed—Standing Room Only. Henry Miller, the renowned author of *The Tropic of Cancer*, attended the trial in order

---

†A largely complete transcript of the *People v. Ferlinghetti* trial is offered in *Howl of the Censor* (1961), edited by Jake W. Ehrlich. Unfortunately, the Ehrlich transcript omits, among other things, the closing arguments of Lawrence Speiser and Albert Bendich.

to show his support for Ferlinghetti and the First Amendment. Unknown admirers did the same, as they openly displayed copies of *Howl* that they had brought with them. By stark contrast, the prosecutor refused to contribute to the spectacle: he carried copies of *Howl* and *Miscellaneous Man* in a brown bag, as if to suggest that even the display of their all-too-innocent covers might be seen as injurious to the decorum of the court. Employing a different strategy, Jake Ehrlich kept his copy of *Howl* in plain view, and even waved it boldly during the course of the hearings. As for Lawrence Ferlinghetti, he openly sold and publicly displayed numerous copies of *Howl* in his storefront window throughout the trial.

"Gentlemen, you may proceed." With those words from Judge Horn, the trial started.

The prosecution called its first witness, Russell Woods, the plainclothes officer who visited City Lights Bookshop on May 21 to pick up copies of *Howl* and *Miscellaneous Man* magazine. Ralph McIntosh's direct examination of the officer was surprisingly short and simple. Woods established that he had purchased and read *Howl*, and obtained an arrest warrant for the defendants. That was it. At this point, McIntosh offered a copy of Ginsberg's book into evidence, and turned the witness over to the defense for cross-examination.

Jake Ehrlich did not reveal the defense's hand that day. "It will be of no value to commence cross-examination today or to put in a defense," Ehrlich explained, "unless and until your Honor has read the book. Then we can call your attention to various parts." McIntosh offered no objection to a continuance. "You have the book before you," the prosecutor said to Judge Horn. "Naturally, you will have to read it to determine whether or not it is obscene or indecent." In complete accord, the judge postponed the trial for a week so that he could sample the forbidden fruit.

Since the defendants had waived a jury trial, the outcome lay with Clayton Horn. The trio of legal talents had made a calculated bet that their client's fortune was better entrusted to a Bible-believing judge than to a potentially prim-and-proper San Francisco jury. That calculation, of course, was a risky one, and the defense now hoped that the judge would fully prepare himself to appreciate the grave meaning and great import of Ginsberg's poems.

* * *

When the trial resumed on Thursday, August 22, the 2:00 pm hearing got off to a quirky start. The straight-laced prosecutor drew Judge Horn's attention to the bottom of *Howl*'s dedication page, which read: "All these books are published in Heaven."

"I don't quite understand that," Ralph McIntosh stated in all seriousness, "but let the record show anyway, your Honor, it's published by the City Lights Pocketbook Shop."

Had this evidence been offered with tongue-in-cheek, it might have suggested a playful understanding of Ginsberg's mindset. As it was, McIntosh's admission proved prophetic. It was the first of many examples of the linear mind clashing with the literary mind. Soon, it would become patently apparent that the elderly prosecutor was baffled by a great deal in *Howl*. Only time would tell whether his bewilderment would cripple the prosecution's obscenity case.

Rising from his chair, the confident and commanding Jake Ehrlich was now prepared to expose the legal strategy developed by the trio of attorneys for the defense. As was expected, he began by moving for a judgment that *Howl and Other Poems* was not obscene and that the defendants were not guilty of violating California Penal Code §311 for publishing and selling obscenity.

"I assume your Honor has now read the book," Ehrlich asked. "The question then arises whether as a result of your reading you have been able to form a judgment as to whether this book is or is not obscene. . . . If your Honor determines that the book is not obscene under the law, then, of course, that's the end of the issue."

Arguing for his motion, Ehrlich was careful to establish two key points of law critical to the defense. First, a prosecution for obscenity could not prevail on indecent words alone, taken out of context of the entire work. "I believe your Honor will agree with me that individual words in and of themselves do not make obscene books," he urged. "Some people think that certain four-letter words in and of themselves destroy mankind from a moral standpoint. This, of course, is not the law." Ehrlich drove this point home by alluding to the notorious example of censorial overreaching against Whitman's celebrated work: "I presume that I could take the classic, *Leaves of Grass*, and by cutting it to pieces find a word here or there or an idea that some people may not like."

Second, the defense emphasized that California's obscenity law penalized only intentional acts—in other words, that the defendants' purpose in publishing and selling *Howl* must be to provide the public an obscene work. In this regard, Ehrlich claimed, the prosecution failed utterly to prove its case. "There is not one word in the record going to the intent of the defendant in the sale of this book," he argued. "Nor is there any evidence before this court that any representation was made concerning the contents of the book, nor is there any evidence before the Court that . . . the purpose of the sale was the selling of a salacious, lewd or indecent book."

"The Master" had put the prosecutor on the ropes. Try as he might to disentangle himself, Ralph McIntosh's every effort seemed to enmesh him even more tightly. As he offered one counterargument after another, the frustrated prosecutor was rebuffed by the Court at almost every turn:

- *Prosecutor's Argument*: California's obscenity law prohibits obscene or indecent literature. Thus, a violation can be established by proof either of obscenity or indecency alone.
  Court's Response: No—the words are essentially synonymous. "You are flying in the face of the First Amendment," Judge Horn asserted. "I can stop you right there as far as 'indecent' is concerned. This Court . . . will follow the *Roth* decision as the basis of what may or may not be the subject of an . . . exception to the First Amendment, and these books are either obscene or not obscene." In Horn's mind, indecency was not a separate exception to the First Amendment. Thus, he concluded: "I am not going to quibble about the word 'indecent' or even consider that it is something lesser than obscene."
- *Prosecutor's Argument*: When it comes to the defendant's purpose in selling obscenity, lewd intent may be proved by the character of the literature itself.
  Court's Response: No—evidence that a book was sold, particularly where there is no suggestion of obscene character on its cover, is not sufficient alone to demonstrate lewd intent.
- *Prosecutor's Argument*: An inference of lewd intent can be drawn from the fact that a publisher or seller must have knowledge of what he is doing.
  Court's Response: No—at least as to Murao, the bookstore clerk.

"Going back to the salesman," the Judge posited, "there is nothing in the record showing that he has read these books or knew their contents or that there was any lewd intent on his part in selling them."

When the exchanges ended, even a cautious seer would have found the signs to be favorable for the defense. After all, Judge Horn had invoked the First Amendment as a shield against any prosecution under California criminal law for merely "indecent" words. Either *Howl*, taken as a whole, was obscene literature as defined by the *Roth* test, or it was protected expression.

Furthermore, Horn had managed to separate the prosecution's charges involving *Miscellaneous Man* from those involving *Howl*. Having done that, the case against the defendants for selling *Miscellaneous Man* could not stand. For one thing, the magazine had not been published by City Lights; for another, its innocuous cover gave no indication of its allegedly obscene character. Hence, McIntosh's failure to prove that the defendants had actual knowledge of its contents was fatal to the *Miscellaneous Man* charges.

Additionally, Judge Horn became increasingly cool toward the prosecution's entire case against Shigeyoshi Murao for criminal sale of an allegedly obscene work. Accordingly, he suggested that the charges against Ferlinghetti's clerk would soon be summarily dismissed. What remained to be seen was how the jurist would view the State's case against Ferlinghetti for the publication of *Howl*.

At this point, Judge Horn dealt a bad card to the defense. He denied its motion to dismiss the *Howl* case for insufficient evidence. So, the trial was on. Now it fell to Ehrlich, Speiser, and Bendich either to submit the case to the Court without a defense or to present testimony supporting the legality of *Howl*.

Judge Horn intended to keep tight reins on the trial proceedings. For example, he was quite precise as to the type of evidence that he would and would not entertain. He would accept opinion evidence from literary scholars, critics, or reviewers on the merits of *Howl*. In contrast, he would not hear testimony from psychiatrists or sociologists on the psychically damaging or socially corruptive potential of the work. On that score, Horn declared: "It is obvious that you are never going to get unanimous consent. . . . That's the reason why the freedom of the press should be so stringently protected, so that no one segment of the country can censor to the injury of the rest, what they can read, see and hear." This was yet another blow to the prosecution. The judge was sounding more and more like an ACLU devotee.

The prosecutor objected strenuously that the hearing "could get out of hand" as both sides offered expert witnesses "telling your Honor how you should decide." Judge Horn made it plain, however, who would be The Decider in his courtroom. He would not tolerate a panel of experts opining on *Howl*'s obscenity. For it was Judge Horn, and only Judge Horn, who would reach that conclusion as a matter of law. "I would not permit the direct question to be asked of such a witness, 'Do you consider this book obscene?' because that is something that the Court has to determine," Horn confirmed.

After a brief conference with the attorneys in his chambers, the judge brought the hearing to a close. He set the date of Thursday, September 5, for presentation of expert testimony concerning *Howl*'s inherent value as a poetic creation.

> *The trial, in its way, illustrated what "Howl" was howling about.*
>
> —Al Bendich

The *Murao/Ferlinghetti* trial was a cause célèbre for the San Francisco literati. Grand literary poobahs appeared in Judge Horn's courtroom on Thursday, September 5, to testify in defense of *Howl*'s poetic merits.

Lawrence Speiser had lined up a formidable team of impressive witnesses. There were six college professors from different disciplines: among them, Herbert Blau, professor of humanities and language arts at the San Francisco State College and director of the Actors' Workshop of the San Francisco Drama Guild; Leo Löwenthal, sociology and literature professor at the University of California at Berkeley, who had been a leading authority in the Frankfurt Institute before Hitler's rise; Mark Linenthal, professor of language arts and director of the Poetry Workshop at San Francisco State College; and Mark Schorer, chair of English graduate studies at the University of California at Berkeley, and a recognized novelist, short story writer, and essayist.

In addition, a recognized newspaper book review editor, Luther

Nichols of the *San Francisco Examiner*, would be called for the defense. And to add the weight of international literary success, two celebrated authors were to testify for the defense: Walter Van Tilburg Clark, recognized primarily for his novel, *The Ox-Bow Incident*; and Kenneth Rexroth, the prolific poet, translator of poetry, and essayist who was simpatico with the Beat Generation.

Notwithstanding the imposing credentials of the defense's nine witnesses, notable was the absence of three witnesses: Allen Ginsberg, the man who wrote *Howl*; Lawrence Ferlinghetti, the man who published *Howl*; and Shigeyoshi Murao, the man who sold *Howl*. None of those voices was ever heard in the course of the trial that lasted for weeks. Judge Horn never heard Allen describe the relationship between life as he lived it and the poem as he wrote it. The jurist never heard Ferlinghetti explain why he decided to have the book printed abroad. Moreover, it was never clear whether Murao even read the poems, and if he did what he made of them. Of course, one is left to wonder whether, if any or all of the three had taken the stand, the testimony would have helped or hindered the defense.

The defense's phalanx of outstanding literary authorities was assembled to serve one and the same important purpose. They were all to offer their expert opinions that *Howl*, in both its substance and its style, had serious literary merit, insofar as it dealt with significant social issues, or offered an impassioned critique of contemporary American life, or indicted the elements in modern society that corrupted, perverted or destroyed "the best minds" of Ginsberg's generation. Of course, if *Howl* had such literary merit, then the defense attorneys could argue that the poetry was "a step to truth," was not "utterly without redeeming social importance." In short, it could not be obscene.

Each of the nine witnesses, in his own way, contributed to building the defense's case. For example, Mark Schorer was key to establishing that "*Howl*, like any work of literature, attempts and intends to make a significant comment on or interpretation of human experience as the author knows it."

Ever the pedagogue, Schorer clarified in his steady and serene drawl the aesthetic structure of the poem, as if he were instructing his English students. A Fulbright and Guggenheim award-winning scholar, Schorer explained that Ginsberg created, in the first part of the poem, "the impression of a kind of nightmare world in which people representing 'the best minds of my generation' . . . are wandering like damned souls in hell." Part II turned to an "indictment" of "material-ism, conformity and mechanization leading to war," all "destructive of the best qualities in human nature." Finally, Part III addressed a friend "who is mad and in a madhouse," and "is the specific representative of what the author regards as the general condition." Stylistically, the poem used "the language of ordinary speech, the language of vulgarity," terms "absolutely essential to the aesthetic purpose of the work."

Without ever giving a direct opinion on the obscenity of *Howl*, something that Judge Horn would not have permitted, Schorer's testi-mony was a masterpiece of indirection on that very issue. How could *Howl* be obscene when it had such literary merit in its very theme, organization, and vulgarity?

The other defense witnesses testified much to the same effect. Book critic Luther Nichols, the future West Coast editor for Double-day, deftly characterized Ginsberg's life as a "vagabond one" that was "colored by exposure to jazz, . . . to a liberal and Bohemian education, . . . to a certain amount of what we call bumming around." All that experience led to this "howl of pain." Similarly, Van Tilburg Clark, whose cowboy-frontier novels explored deep philosophical issues, found in "all of the poems" in *Howl* a "thoroughly honest poet, who is also a highly competent technician."

Clearly, the most laudatory judgment on *Howl* came from the poet Kenneth Rexroth. "Its merit is extraordinarily high," Rexroth stressed. "It is probably the most remarkable single poem published by a young man" since the Second World War.

When Al Bendich, who conducted the direct examination of Rex-roth, asked him to describe the nature and theme of *Howl*, the poet of humanistic passion depicted Ginsberg's work as "the denunciation of evil . . . and a call to repent." It fit into a great Biblical tradition: "This is prophetic literature: 'Woe! Woe! Woe! The City of Jerusalem! . . . [Y]ou must repent and do thus and so.'"

With these words, Rexroth's testimony moved Ginsberg from the status of a crude poet to that of a chastising prophet. Without doubt, this characterization must have caught the ear of the Bible-revering judge. And as for Ralph McIntosh, it must have been inconceivable for him to imagine Biblical prophesies worded in the coarse vernacular of *Howl*.

As the defense witnesses aimed to demonstrate *Howl*'s serious literary merits, the prosecutor's cross-examination of them aimed to dethrone their lofty praise. In so doing, McIntosh hoped to convince Judge Horn that, indeed, Ginsberg's poetry was little more than its filth, its vulgarity, and its disgusting language—in short, obscene. McIntosh used two basic strategies to accomplish that.

First, there was the *What can this possibly mean?* strategy: Demonstrate that the average person on the streets of San Francisco would likely have no idea of what *Howl* was all about. Then, in the words of Justice Brennan in *Roth*, Ginsberg's poetry might be viewed, under "contemporary community standards," as having little "social value as a step to truth." That was the point of McIntosh's cross-examination of Mark Schorer:

> *McIntosh*: You understand what "angel-headed hipsters burning for the ancient heavenly connection to the starry dynamo in the machinery of night" means?
>
> *Schorer*: Sir, you can't translate poetry into prose; that's why it's poetry. . . .
>
> *McIntosh*: In other words, you don't have to understand the words to—
>
> *Schorer*: You don't understand the individual words taken out of their context. . . . You can no more translate that back into logical prose English than you can say what a surrealistic painting means in words, because it's not prose. . . .
>
> *McIntosh*: Each word by itself certainly means something, doesn't it?
>
> *Schorer*: No. . . . I can't possibly translate, nor I am sure, can anyone in this room translate the opening part of this poem into rational prose.
>
> *McIntosh*: That's just what I wanted to find out.

The prosecution employed a second strategy: *Were these words really relevant?* That is, demonstrate that Ginsberg's choice of "dirty" words was not really relevant to any socially valuable ideas. Then, applying the standards of *Roth*, Ginsberg's poetry (already shown to be incomprehensible "to the average person") might be viewed as little more than its lewd and sex-obsessed language, appealing primarily to the "prurient interests" of its readers. McIntosh's cross-examination of Luther Nichols emphasized this strategy:

McIntosh (reading "Footnote to *Howl*"): "The world is holy! The
soul is holy! The skin is holy! The nose is holy! The tongue and
cock and hand and asshole holy!" Now, are those last words
there, are they relevant to the literary value of Mr. Ginsberg's
work?

Nichols: . . . He's showing that everything is holy within a sense, the
sense that he is trying to convey here. . . .

McIntosh (reading "America"): "America when will we end the
human war? Go fuck yourself with your atom bomb." Now, the
word in there, that four-letter word, is that relevant to the literary merit of Mr. Ginsberg's work?

Nichols: . . . He doesn't want to temper it by saying it any less softly.
He's angry, and when you are angry sometimes you do use words
of this sort. I would say yes, it's relevant; it's in keeping with the
wrath he feels, with the language that he has used throughout
most of these poems.

Interestingly, in deploying his cross-examination strategies, the
prosecutor repeated again and again—indeed, no fewer than 24 times—
the very four-letter, and five, six, seven- and eight-letter words that he
deemed "obscene" terms violating the California penal law. And all of
this, of course, was done in open court.

Jake Ehrlich was prepared to bring the defense case to a close.
Before resting, however, he offered into evidence copies of admiring
reviews of *Howl*. Among them, a *New York Times Book Review* article
by Richard Eberhart, published only three days earlier, described Ginsberg's poems as "profoundly Jewish in temper." Much like Rexroth,
Eberhart depicted *Howl* as "Biblical" in its catalogue of "evils of our
time from physical deprivation to madness."

There were other reviews, some positive and some mixed, published in magazines such as *The Nation* and literary journals.

Predictably, Ralph McIntosh objected to the admissibility of all
the book reviews as being irrelevant. "The only possible reason that
[Mr. Ehrlich] could offer those would be if there was some testimony
by Mr. Ferlinghetti; if he were to take the stand and say that he relied
upon those book reviews in selling this book." Then, the prosecutor
explained, the reviews would be material to the publisher's intent in
issuing *Howl*.

With some impatience, Judge Horn overruled this objection. Judicial consideration of literary reviews in obscenity cases had become an established practice in New York, Horn observed, and "California has so far adopted a more liberal attitude than the State of New York." The book reviews were admitted, and the distinguished literary voices of Richard Eberhart, M. L. Rosenthal, and others now chimed in with those of the nine defense witnesses.

From the very start, Ralph McIntosh had not relished the prospect of expert witness testimony in this obscenity prosecution. He had argued vehemently at the end of the August 22 hearing that the opinions of poets, professors, and pundits as to the literary merits of *Howl* were entirely irrelevant. Hence, the prosecutor did not intend to prolong what he viewed as a charade of poetic puffery. He brought only two rebuttal witnesses to the trial for the sole purpose of demonstrating that even the experts would disagree as to the redeeming social value of Ginsberg's outlandish and tasteless creations.

The prosecution's witnesses paled, both as to credentials and credibility, in comparison to the illuminati called by the defense. David Kirk, an assistant professor of English at the University of San Francisco, testified that *Howl* had "negligible" literary value because it was "just a weak imitation of a form that was used 80 to 90 years ago by Walt Whitman." On cross-examination, however, Kirk proved no match for quick-witted Jake Ehrlich, as he twisted the young Ph.D. candidate into knots of self-contradiction and self-impeachment.

The comic relief of the *Howl* trial arrived with Gail Potter. Before taking the stand for the prosecution, the middle-aged woman had circulated small printed brochures to the courtroom spectators advertising her availability for private elocution lessons. On the stand, the San Francisco speech teacher and freelance writer declared with grandiose flair: "I have rewritten 'Faust'—took three years to do that, but I did it; I rewrote 'Everyman.'"

When laughter exploded, Judge Horn interrupted: "Ladies and gentlemen, we are not playing games; this is a trial that involves serious issues. . . . Try to maintain decorum in the courtroom; otherwise, I will have to clear it."

Once order was restored, the prosecutor asked Ms. Potter for her opinion of *Howl and Other Poems*. "I think it has no literary merit," she put it decisively. "You feel like you are going through the gutter when you have to read that stuff." Shuddering with dramatic disgust, she concluded: "I didn't linger on it too long, I assure you." Defense attorney Ehrlich responded by declining any cross-examination.

"The People rest, your Honor," McIntosh stated. It was now time for the prosecution to make its closing statement.

The Deputy District Attorney began by portraying the ordinary and unenlightened citizen of San Francisco as going to hell in a handbasket if exposed to such smut as *Howl.* "I made the comment in open court here that I read it; I don't understand it very well," he conceded. "In fact, looking it over, I think it is a lot of sensitive bullshit, using the language of Mr. Ginsberg. So then, if the sale of a book is not being limited to just . . . experts on modern poetry, but falls into the hands of the general public, that is, the average reader, this court should take that into consideration in determining whether or not *Howl* is obscene."

Here was a contemporary Cassandra, crying out the fall of the beloved city. "I would like you to ask yourself, your Honor," McIntosh bellowed, "would you like to see this sort of poetry printed in your local newspaper . . . to be read by your family, . . . or would you like to have this poetry read to you over the air on the radio as a diet?" With emotional charge, the prosecutor concluded: "In other words, your Honor, how far are we going to license the use of filthy, vulgar, obscene, and disgusting language? How far can we go?"

Jake Ehrlich's summation deflated the prosecution's dire warnings. Invoking James Joyce's *Ulysses* and Christopher Marlowe's *Ignoto*, he elevated lowbrow slang to highbrow status. "Fuck" was but a "plain, common Anglo-Saxon word . . . used in some beautiful poetry."

Reciting the whole of Marlowe's poem, he boldly proclaimed the final stanza:

I cannot buss thy fill, play with thy hair
Swearing by Jove, "Thou art most debonair!"
Not I, by cock! But I shall tell thee roundly,
Hark in thine ear, zounds I can fuck thee soundly.

Throwing down the gauntlet, he asked: "Would we, if he were alive today, arrest Christopher Marlowe for writing his poem?"

The defense lawyer then turned the tables on the prosecution: "You do not think common, lewd or lascivious thoughts just because you have read something in a book, unless it is your mental purpose to do so." Directing himself to *Howl*, Ehrlich adroitly summed up the merits of the poems' substantive concepts and stylistic choices. When the poet howled "Go fuck yourself with your atom bomb," he asked, "what prurient interest is Ginsberg generating with that cry of pain? The man is at the end of the road. He is crying out in the wilderness. Nobody is listening." Moreover, the language of the poems harbored no lewd intent or salacious appeal: "It isn't for us to choose the words. When Ginsberg tells his story, he tells it as he sees it, uses the words as he knows them, and portrays in his language that which he sees."

Building momentum in pace and pitch, Ehrlich proclaimed: "The problem of what is legally permissible in the description of sexual acts and feelings in art and literature is of the greatest importance in a free society. . . . The battle of censorship will not be finally settled by your Honor's decision, but you will either add to liberal educated thinking or by your decision add fuel to the fire of ignorance."

And then Ehrlich's climax: "Let there be light. Let there be honesty. Let there be no running from non-existent destroyers of morals. Let there be honest understanding. In the end the four-letter words will not appear draped in glaring headlights, but will be submerged in the decentralization of small thinking in small minds."

Somber silence in the courtroom. No one spoke. No one moved. Moments passed. Finally, Judge Horn inquired: "Gentlemen, is the matter submitted? . . . October 3rd at 2 pm for decision."

The three-week trial had come to a close. Now the work of McIntosh, Ehrlich, Speiser, and Bendich was over, but the real work for Judge Clayton Horn had just begun. During the one-month recess before issuing his decision, he poured through James Joyce's *Ulysses* and the obscenity cases concerning it, and carefully studied *Howl and Other Poems*.

* * *

Unlike Jack Kerouac and the Beat crowd, Clayton Horn was not getting smashed and carrying on in a frenzied manner. His life was far more staid, more cerebral, or at least it had become that way with the advent of the *Howl* trial.

What the judge was doing was of far greater importance than the mundane day-to-day routine of the fender-bender fare he had in his courtroom. Now he was faced with momentous law—*constitutional law*. Now he had to study that law, especially the new obscenity standards mandated by the Supreme Court. And now he had to comprehend that law, apply it to the facts of the case and author a legal opinion, something rare for a municipal court judge.

As he read in his chambers or reclined on his sofa at home, Judge Horn studied both literature and law. When he was not perusing *Ulysses* or *Howl,* he paged through the official appellate reports of the federal and state courts and strove to make sense of complicated statutes. Fortunately, the studious jurist had a most helpful work to assist him, this one less literary, more legal; less poetic, more practical. It was a "Memorandum of Points and Authorities" composed by defense counsel Albert Bendich and submitted to the court for its consideration.

In clear and crisp prose, the document methodically laid out the constitutional and statutory arguments that formed the backbone of the defense's trial strategies. Not only did it outline the logical sequence of legal analysis, but it provided case authority supporting every key point. Moreover, excerpts from the testimony of expert witnesses illustrated that, indeed, the defendant's case had been proven at trial.

The memorandum was divided into three parts. Part I addressed the order in which the legal issues were to be considered by Judge Horn, as the First Amendment required it. Part II interpreted the standards for constitutionally unprotected obscenity that Justice Brennan provided in *Roth.* And finally, Part III examined the higher standards to be met under California law before a defendant could be convicted for obscenity.

Each link in this chain of reasoning was carefully conceived and crafted. And at every point, the relevant law, whether the First Amendment or the California Penal Code, was given a reading that was both reasonable and strongly rights-protective. Of course, if the judge were convinced by that formidable chain, he would be led inescapably to a decision of "not guilty."

As Bendich understood the fundamental freedoms of speech and press, they prohibited the suppression of any literature by application of the obscenity test unless the trial court first determined that the work was utterly without socially redeeming value. Justice Brennan's majority opinion in *Roth,* Bendich explained, distinguished between "social speech" (that with redeeming value) and "non-social speech" (that without redeeming value), and it was only the latter that was to be tested under the "prurient interest" obscenity standard. "The *Roth* decision charges the trial court with the responsibility in every obscenity case," Bendich explained, "to see to it that this preference for freedom is not transmuted into a preference for prejudice."

This argument meant that Judge Horn needed to decide, first and foremost, whether *Howl and Other Poems* had any, even very slight, social value as a literary work. If it did, then a decision to acquit Ferlinghetti and Murao was to be made then and there, without any further consideration of the work's sexually stimulating potential.

Bendich marshaled piece after piece of powerful testimony from the defense's expert witnesses to persuade Horn that *Howl* must be viewed as having at least some literary merit. And the young ACLU attorney did not forget the jurist's penchant for Bible reading. Invoking the example of the Jewish prophet Hosea, he concluded: "Perhaps Ginsberg is a modern Hosea—only history will show whether, like Hosea, he will be considered a great social poet and critic. But it is obvious today that Ginsberg is saying much the same thing about our society as Hosea was saying about Israel."

And what was Ginsberg's connection to the prophet who chastised Israel for its infidelities? "Ginsberg, too, says that . . . we can save ourselves from destruction by our nightmare world . . . by focusing our attention upon the supreme values of love and reverence for everything human." That understood, the prosecution's case against *Howl* was a flimsy one—indeed, one not permitted by the First Amendment: "The prosecution has done no more than to question the meaning of the poem, admitting its ignorance in that regard, and has done no more than to cite out of context isolated words and phrases as questionable usage. The prosecution has not shown that this is a work which may be fairly described as hard core pornography or dirt for dirt's sake."

If the trial court were to determine, however, that *Howl*'s contents had essentially no redeeming value, then it would be required to move onto the *Roth* obscenity test. At that point, Bendich stressed, it was important to appreciate what the test was not about: "It does not consider whether material is shocking, degrading, vulgar, scatological or perverse where its tendency is to *disgust* the reader." In short, *Roth* had sliced off vulgarity from obscenity. What the test was about was "erotic allurement, sexual stimulation, aphrodisiac action." He put it plainly: "This comes very close to a requirement that the material be actually designed to 'sell sex' and, as such, to deal with no questions of social importance."

With this qualification, the obscenity test was designed to surgically remove from the community's discourse only that pornography that traded in acts rather than ideas. "A gesture calculated to excite lust, just as a picture or a story calculated to do the same, has no relevance to a question of how life should be lived by the community since it does not suggest social change or moral criticism," the memorandum stated. "[A] work which has as its probable effect no more than erotic arousal, or . . . stimulation to masturbation, does not argue social purpose."

Bendich contended that, under this constrained reading of *Roth*, *Howl* ought to survive the "prurient interest" test. "It is difficult in the extreme, if not impossible, to say logically that a work which has as its dominant theme the criticism of moral standards has also as its dominant theme the arousal of lustful desire. Here, at least, it would seem that the prosecution cannot have it both ways." He concluded: "The record is clear that all of the experts for the defense identified the main theme of *Howl* as social criticism. And the prosecution concedes that it does not understand the work, much less what its dominant theme is."

Much the same compelling logic guided Bendich's handling of the California obscenity statute and how it should be interpreted favorably to the defense. That is, the penal code required that both the obscenity of the work and the specific intent of the defendant be proved beyond a reasonable doubt and to a moral certainty.

But the facts could not establish that, Bendich argued. "No circumstantial evidence has been adduced by the prosecution . . . except that the defendant Ferlinghetti owns the City Lights Bookstore which is named as the publisher on the flyleaf of *Howl*." The memorandum continued: "There is no evidence . . . that Ferlinghetti sells erotica, that his bookstore caters to a prurient crowd. Indeed, so-called 'girlie' magazines will not be found there." Moreover, the bookstore was widely recognized for specializing in "literature for the intelligentsia."

Importantly, the civil-liberties lawyer observed, not even the feds had found Ginsberg's poetry to be criminal: "Although the Collector of Customs seized *Howl* on the charge that it was obscene, and referred the matter to the United States Attorney for institution of condemnation proceedings, the United State Attorney, after conferring with the United States Attorney General on the matter, notified the American

Civil Liberties Union, which had provided counsel for the defendants throughout, that condemnation proceedings would not be instituted."

At this point, it was only left for Bendich to conclude: "It is thus apparent that defendants at all times acted on the conviction that the material in question was not obscene; there has never been anything furtive or clandestine about the way defendants handled the material in question."

Only 14 pages long, the memorandum was a concise and convincing exercise of legal reasoning. Had Ginsberg and Ferlinghetti read the document, they likely would have found much of the subject matter ponderous, the writing technical, and the experience boring. But no other document, including *Howl* itself, might weigh as heavily on Judge Horn's mind as Bendich's memorandum of law. Perhaps even more than the trial testimony, that memorandum might best preserve their right to write as Beats.

Still, in all of this, there was a wild card. To what extent would the God-fearing jurist be persuaded by the defense?

'Howl' Not Obscene, Court Rules

WEATHER FORECAST
Bay Area: Partly cloudy today and tonight. High Friday, 62 to 67; low, 48 to 54. Westerly winds 12 to 25 miles an hour.
Full Report, Page 13

San Francisco Chronicle
THE VOICE OF THE WEST

FINAL

934 YEAR No. 277   CCCCAAA   FRIDAY, OCTOBER 4, 1957   10 CENTS   GArfield 1-1112

Racing Shutdown

State Money Crisis Threatened By Track Strike

Special to The Chronicle

SACRAMENTO, Oct. 3—The strike which has closed Tanforan and which may halt horse racing at California's remaining tracks could result in a State deficit this year, State Finance Director John M. Peirce said today.

The cancellation of Tanforan's fall meeting cut off tax receipts from parimutuel wagering. Now, with other racing sessions at other tracks threatened, Peirce said construction programs at California fairgrounds and colleges may have to be postponed.

"This situation threatens the delicate balance in the

San Francisco's

jack dooms
114 Kearny

We agree with the general viewpoint but don't care for biscuits

We endeavor in advertising to convey some stirring thoughts about Jack Davis clothes, figuring you can examine the merchandise closeup at leisure.

Commenting on this procedure, a customer said recently:

People buy an idea for the same reason they buy a biscuit—because it has savor and pleasure and excitement and impact as well as nourishment!

Ordinarily we think a customer is exactly right. But biscuits, even the tastiest, hardly represent impact and excitement to us. Don't even stack

'Howl' Not Obscene, Judge Rules

By David Perlman

"Howl and Other Poems," the booklet whose violent verse aroused the Police Department and the city's literary Bohemia for varying reasons, was cleared of obscenity charges in Municipal Court yesterday.

Judge Clayton W. Horn ruled that the volume was not lewd or pornographic and could not be censored.

He freed Lawrence Ferlinghetti, bookseller, publisher and a poet himself, from a misdemeanor accusation that could have meant a $500 fine and six months in jail.

He also found Shigeyoshi Murao, clerk at Ferlinghetti's City Lights Pocket Bookshop, not guilty.

In a 39-page decision studded with erudite quotations from many another obscenity case, Judge Horn laid down a set of rules which, he made clear, should guide the Police Department in the future when its officers go prowling after smut in the city's bookshops.

KNIGHT ORDER

With no settlement in sight Governor Goodwin J. Knight instructed his staff today to study the problem—to see whether a subsidies could be found and to determine what financial problems the State will face if the horses do not start running again.

In Los Angeles, President Nicholas Dedaurio of the striking Pari-Mutuel Employees Guild said "There's nothing to report—we offered to arbitrate, but up to now there's no official word from the employers on our offer."

In Santa Barbara, Chairman Dwight Murphy of the California Racing Board, who had sought vainly to mediate the dispute, predicted a long strike. Golden Gate Fields may have to cancel its fall meeting, scheduled to start October 28, he said.

He also said Santa Anita's big 55-day meeting, scheduled

See Page 2, Col. 3

Some Wind Damage Around City

Wind gusts swept intermittently through San Francisco yesterday—lopping off half a dozen eucalyptus tree branches in Golden Gate Park, loosening a giant cardboard tomato from a sign at Eighth and Market streets

The most pointed comment was in French.

"Howl not rightly bawdy," Judge Horn intoned. So the police and public might know, he translated: "Evil to him who evil thinks."

The Judge's decision was hailed with applause and cheers from a packed audience that offered the most fantastic collection of beards, turtle-necked shirts and Italian haircuts ever to grace the grimy precincts of the Hall of Justice.

It was hailed by J. W. Ehrlich, who led the defense crew with attorneys Lawrence Speiser and Albert Bendich of the American Civil Liberties Union. Ehrlich crowed:

"Every book that was ever worthwhile was condemned somewhere by someone."

The decision was greeted glumly by Assistant District Attorney Ralph McIntosh, who had read into the trial record with gusto all the four-letter words and allegedly dirty phrases that "Howl" contains (told McIntosh:

"It's just another case as far as the District Attorney's office is concerned.")

But the most ancient comment came from Ferlinghetti himself, who, when he had done dusting congratulatory hands with

10,000 COPIES

the book's admirers, said calmly:

"Come on, you chickens," the youngsters shouted at students who stayed inside.

Violence by Proxy

While his pals grinned, a Little Rock student punched at an effigy of a Negro

Women Tell Of Exposing Cancer Fraud

By Milton Silverman
Science Editor

Two San Joaquin Valley housewives got credit here yesterday for the exposure and conviction of a pair of the most notorious cancer quacks in California.

One woman, who agreed to serve as an undercover agent for state authorities, suffered serious internal burns.

The other, who insisted on helping to expose the quack, is scarred for life.

For an ugly moment it appeared a new riot might break out on the street before the school where blood was shed in adult riots and demonstrations last-week.

A Negro was hung in effigy and the straw-filled dummy set afire. The demonstrators shrieked and shouted in angry hysteria.

Sixty National Guardsmen quickly formed solid ranks. With rifles aslant across their

See Page 4, Col. 1

Central High 'Riot' Fails

Guard Breaks Up Student Walkout

LITTLE ROCK, Ark., Oct. 3 (AP)—Federalized National Guardsmen, rifles across their chests, today broke up a menacing throng of 75 white students who walked out of integrated Central High School.

The demonstrators had hoped to pull out with them most of the school's 2000 white students in a forceful protest against Negroes in their classrooms. But ringleaders admitted the demonstration was a flop.

EFFIGY BURNED

Braves Win 4-2 to Even World Series

NEW YORK, Oct. 3—The Milwaukee Braves squelched the New Burdette's fine pitching and Wes Covington's fine fielding to defeat the New York Yankees today, 4 to 2, and even the World Series at a game apiece.

There is no game tomorrow. The teams move to Milwaukee, where they'll meet Saturday, with the Braves' Bob Buhl scheduled to pitch against the Yankees' Bob Turley.

See Page 7, Col. 1

Hat in the Ring

Knowland Makes Formal Entry in Governor Race

By Earl C. Behrens, Political Editor

SACRAMENTO, Oct. 3—U. S. Senator William F. Knowland formally announced his candidacy for Governor today.

"I shall be a candidate for Governor in 1958," Knowland said in a statement read at a press conference in the Hotel Senator here. It was his official declaration that he would contend with Governor Goodwin J. Knight at the June primary. Knight already has announced he will run for re-election.

"I have made my decision to run for this high office," Knowland declared, "with no purpose other than, if successful and elected, to devote myself faithfully to the administration of the duties of the office for the term or terms to which I might be elected."

Four and a half hours after Knowland had made his announcement, Governor Knight issued a lengthy statement saying the Knowland "decision to run for Governor of California is properly viewed by the reasonable people as a hydra-headed bid for the Presidency of the United States."

The Governor said Knowland must declare "unequivocally that, if elected to the governorship, he will serve out his full four-year term—with his total attention on California, not on Washington." Otherwise, Knight said, the "voters will view his purported interest in their welfare with serious reservations."

PRESIDENCY

At his press conference the Senator left the door ajar to a possible future presidential candidacy when he stated:

"No one has a crystal ball," Knowland, told reporters in answer to a question. "I expect to serve out my term. I hope I shall be permitted to do so." He said his declaration that he intended to serve out his term was "not a Sherman-like statement, but is in keeping with my whole record in public life."

He noted that he had served out the "full term" of a prior office to which he had been elected, except that of Republican National Committee member. He left that job to enter military service in World War II.

The Sherman-like state-
See Page 7, Col. 1

Hoffa To Put Brewster Out of Jobs

By Jack Howard

The Western empire that Dave Beck created and made a cornerstone of the world's biggest union faces a major shakeup as the Teamsters meet in Miami Beach today to elect their leaders for the next five years.

Frank Brewster, Beck's comrade of 30 years, is all set to lose both his National vice presidency and the presidency of the 375,000-member Western Conference of Teamsters.

From the looks of a slate hand-picked by Jimmy Hoffa, Brewster's vice presidency will go to George Mock, an organizer operating out of Sacramento.

Brewster's $25,000-a-year Conference presidency is expected to go to Einar Mohn, now Beck's executive vice president but formerly a popular and respected Teamster organizer in California.

And to cap the internal upset

See Page 6, Col. 8

Canadian Hotel Burns, Four Dead

CHATHAM, Ont., Oct. 3 (AP)—At least four men died early today when fire destroyed the C.P.R. hotel, a 70-year-old landmark on the main street of this southwestern Ontario city.

·9·

The Verdict

Vindicated!

*What they all have in common is the conviction
that any form of rebellion against American
culture . . . is admirable, and they seem to regard
homosexuality, jazz, dope–addiction, and vagrancy
as outstanding examples of such rebellion.*

—Norman Podhoretz

That was the judgment of the Beat Generation printed on the pages
of the "liberal" *New Republic* for September 16, 1957. By a Columbia
classmate of Allen's, no less. That critical take on *Howl* and other Beat
works was echoed by other mainstream critics:

- James Dickey, *Sewanee Review*: *Howl* is an "exhibitionist welter of
  unrelated associations, wish-fulfillment fantasies, and self-righteous
  maudlinness."
- John Ciardi, *Saturday Review*: the poem has "a kind of tireless
  arrogance at least as refreshing as it is shallow."
- John Hollander, *Partisan Review*: *Howl* is a "dreadful little volume
  . . . very short and very tiresome."[†]

[†]A few years later, Ginsberg responded to his critics: "Poetry has been attacked by
an ignorant and frightened bunch of bores who don't understand how it's made, &
the trouble with these creeps is they wouldn't know poetry if it came up and bug-
gered them in broad daylight."

While Allen took it on the chin in some highbrow literary venues, other poetry experts praised his work in Judge Horn's courtroom. It was that laudatory image of Ginsberg and the Beats that was magnified countless times in the popular culture, including a two-page spread of *Life* magazine.

The boldface title: "BIG DAY FOR BARDS AT BAY: SAN FRANCISCO MUSE THRIVES IN FACE OF TRIAL OVER POEMS." The September 9, 1957, story gave a favorable assessment of the Beats: "As some of these photographs show, the poets are shouting their poems in nightclubs, at dance recitals, in art galleries, on radio and TV. Their work has gained respectful hearing from local and even national critics."

Four huge photographs depicted various Beat moments:

- Kenneth Rexroth, with head thrown back as if howling, recites poetry to the accompaniment of a jazz ensemble.
- Clad in a black dress and hat, a young amateur poet, Phyllis Diller, spoofs Dame Edith Sitwell, the English experimental poet.
- A "bohemian bard" performs his poetry, as a shirtless, muscular dancer in tights gives dramatic expression to his work.
- A hip Lawrence Ferlinghetti reads his *London*, while a sassy black woman ("Mrs. Florence Allen") does a mock striptease with her brassiere in plain view.

The other two photographs were taken of the *Howl* trial:

- An impassioned Jake Ehrlich, leaning forward against a banister, addresses the court while brandishing an open copy of *Howl*.
- A brooding Ferlinghetti and contemplative Murao observe their fates on trial.

The photographic message of those juxtaposed images was clear: a rebellious movement was emerging in the culture and battling in the courtroom. It was cool, James Dean cool. Lawrence Ferlinghetti was right. Censorship was *Howl*'s best publicity agent—*Howl* was enjoying modest success as some 10,000 copies were in print.

* * *

Kerouac's *On the Road* had finally taken off. After a wildly favorable *New York Times* review,[†] his phone never stopped ringing, and speaking requests were unending. "Everything's been happening here," Jack informed Allen. "Unbelievable number of events almost impossible to remember." In his letter of October 1, 1957, Kerouac wrote of his current life as "a big blurred Dostoevskyan party with socialites where I was the Idiot." And then this bit of capitalized advice to his friend: "NOW LISTEN VIKING WANTS TO PUBLISH HOWL AND YOUR OTHERS AND ALSO GROVE. THEY'RE RACING TO REACH YOU FIRST. TAKE YOUR CHOICE. I THINK HOWL NEEDS DISTRIBUTION. IT HAS NOT EVEN BEGUN TO BE READ."

Faithful to the publisher who had risked jail time and economic loss for him, Allen would not consider leaving the City Lights imprint. As he would later assure his friend Ferlinghetti, "I hear from Jack that both Viking and Grove interested in hardcover *Howl*, however that would be wrong etc. so don't worry as I said I won't go whoring in N.Y." That loyalty probably cost Ginsberg.

Worthy of Ginsberg's loyalty, Ferlinghetti wrote to his friend on Constitution Day (September 17, 1957): "Trial is not over yet—we're in court again this Thursday. . . . Question of Fucked in the Ass not yet settled . . . . Got to go. Later dad, Larry."

* * *

Approximately one month after *People v. Ferlinghetti*[††] had been submitted for consideration, Judge Clayton Horn rendered his decision. At 2:00 p.m. on Thursday, October 3, 1957, the judge announced his judgment to a crowded audience that, according to the *San Francisco Chronicle*, "offered the most fantastic collection of beards, turtle-necked shirts and Italian hair-dos ever to grace the grimy precincts of the Hall of Justice."

Remarkably, Horn issued his opinion in written form, a rare phenomenon for municipal judges. The typed opinion left little doubt where this jurist stood on questions of free speech: "The authors of

[†]Gilbert Millstein's September 7, 1957, review of *On the Road* singlehandedly catapulted Kerouac to fame.
[††]When the opinion in the case was issued, the name changed to *People v. Ferlinghetti* since the case against Murao had been dismissed.

the First Amendment knew that novel and unconventional ideas might disturb the complacent, but they chose to encourage a freedom which they believed essential if a vigorous enlightenment was ever to triumph over slothful ignorance. . . . The best method of censorship is by the people as self-guardians of public opinion and not by government."

Horn's opinion was pure John Stuart Mill, pure Louis Brandeis, pure Hugo Black, pure protection for dissident expression: "[L]ife is not encased in one formula whereby everyone acts the same or conforms to a particular pattern. No two persons think alike; we are all made from the same mold but in different patterns. Would there be any freedom of the press or speech if one must reduce his vocabulary to vapid and innocuous euphemism? An author should be real in treating his subject and be allowed to express his thoughts and ideas in his own words."

The Judge buttressed his rhetoric with legal analysis, carefully applying the rule of *Roth*. Obviously, the San Francisco jurist was impressed with Albert Bendich's Memorandum of Points and Authorities, as the structure and logic of his opinion closely tracked the defense attorney's rationales. Horn stressed: "the majority opinion in *Roth* requires a trial court to . . . decide in the first instance whether a work is utterly without social importance, *before* it permits the test of obscenity to be applied. . . ."

That crucial point was the first of twelve points Judge Horn listed for applying the law of *Roth* to the facts of *People v. Ferlinghetti*. "If the material has the slightest redeeming social importance it is not obscene," Horn wrote. Of course, this ruling alone could readily have ended the prosecution's case. Yet, the judge went on to elaborate eleven other criteria that needed to be considered before a work could be deemed obscene and a fit subject for censorship.

Among other things, the words contested must excite lascivious thoughts or arouse lustful desire to the point where they "present a clear and present danger of inciting antisocial or immoral action." Again tracking arguments made by Bendich, Judge Horn actually extended the protective reach of *Roth*, which nowhere demanded such a strict showing by the government. Moreover, added Horn, if the words used are "objectionable only because of coarse and vulgar language which is not erotic . . . in character, [they are] not obscene."

Not surprisingly, then, the court ruled for the defense. *Howl and Other Poems* did, indeed, have "redeeming social importance," which meant that it was no longer criminal to sell Allen Ginsberg's lyrics in San Francisco.

It was poetic justice, a major victory for the cultural outsiders. Ginsberg, then vacationing in Paris, was vindicated; Ferlinghetti and Murao were liberated; and the cause of free speech was celebrated. The elated audience in the packed courtroom welcomed the ruling with applause and cheers.

The Bible-teaching judge had done it. He had demonstrated how *Roth* could be applied in ways faithful to full First Amendment freedoms. Admirably, this municipal officer, whose daily routine was traffic offenses and other petty infractions, had developed (with the able assistance of the defense lawyers) complex points in *Roth* that would take U.S. Supreme Court Justice Brennan more than a decade to work out in a multitude of First Amendment cases.

Judge Horn's opinion would have been a memorable one, sure to be widely cited by other courts, if only it had ever been officially published.

Lawrence Ferlinghetti had quipped about his prospect of jail time as a chance to catch up on his reading. Now, he was getting no such break for relaxing literary pursuits. After hearing Judge Horn's decision, the poet-publisher did not linger outside the courthouse to be interviewed by news reporters. He graciously took in the congratulatory wishes of friends and admirers, and returned immediately to work. His very first task was to restack the front windows of City Lights Bookstore with even more copies of *Howl*.

* * *

"'HOWL' NOT OBSCENE, COURT RULES"

Howl again made front-page news. The bold banner message in the *San Francisco Chronicle* proclaimed the victory of the Beats over the censors. The article highlighted the fact that Judge Horn's "most pointed comment was in French: '*Honi soit qui mal y pense.*' So the police and public might know, he translated: 'Evil to him who evil thinks.'" While Jake Ehrlich "crowed" excitedly over the judgment, Ralph McIntosh glumly brushed it aside: "It's just another case as far as the District Attorney's office is concerned."

Three days later, the *Chronicle* delivered its editorial reflections on Judge Horn's decision. Dubbing it a "Landmark of Law," the newspaper praised Horn's opinion as "sound and clear, foursquare with the Constitution and with the letter and spirit of various courts that have heretofore found the outcries of censorship lacking virtue." The editorial ended vividly with compliments to the jurist: "For a sharp and staggering blow to the chops of prurience and censorship, we congratulate Judge Clayton Horn." The journalistic tides had turned for the man who had been mocked only two months before as the "Ten Commandments" judge.

Allen Ginsberg first learned the good news about *Howl*'s vindication while in Amsterdam. On October 10, he received a letter from Ferlinghetti containing clippings from the *Chronicle*. He was elated and relieved. But he was also eager to exploit the commercial possibilities that the trial story could create. Writing to Ferlinghetti the same day, he inquired, "Was decision news carried nationally anyway? Look up Harvey Breit on *Times*, he'll probably want to interview you."

With *Howl* no longer contraband, Ginsberg (the "PR genius of the Beat Generation") sought greater distribution of the work, and in some rather unlikely places: "If possible, . . . would like to get the single poem 'Howl' reprinted more widely, perhaps in *Time, Life, Look, Cong. Record . . . .*" Ever the solicitous son eager for his father's approval, he ended his letter to Ferlinghetti with a P.S.: "Do me a favor, phone my papa Louis G., and tell him trial news—please. He'll be proud to hear, etc."

*   *   *

Howl is the confession of faith of the generation that
is going to be running the world in 1965 and 1975—
if it's still there to run.

—Kenneth Rexroth

Time magazine billed him the "Godfather of the Beats." He denied it: "An entomologist is not a bug." Yes, Kenneth Rexroth did study the Beats. But he was also a key part of their history. After all, he did preside over the 6 Gallery readings, and testified for the defense at the *Howl* trial, among other things. He was thus both a participant in the history of the Beat movement and a chronicler of it.

"Poetry has become an actual social force." And Allen Ginsberg is "certainly a poet of revolt if there ever was one." So Rexroth put it in a 1957 essay entitled "Disengagement: The Art of the Beat Generation." And what did he make of that generation?

"It is impossible to go on indefinitely saying: 'I am proud to be a delinquent,' without destroying all civilized values." His words.

"The end result must be the desperation of shipwreck—the despair, the orgies, ultimately the cannibalism of a lifeboat." More of his words.

"I believe that most of an entire generation will go to ruin . . . voluntarily, even enthusiastically." Yet more.

And then this: "What will happen afterwards I don't know, but for the next ten years or so we are going to have to cope with the youth we, my generation, put through the atom smasher."

And finally: "Social disengagement, artistic integrity, voluntary poverty—these are powerful virtues and may pull them through, but they are not the virtues we tried to inculcate; rather they are the exact opposite."

By the end of 1957, a new generation, a rebellious one, had been launched. And there in its midst was Jack Kerouac, perched high on a stool in Goody's Bar with a pack of smokes protruding from his shirt pocket. He sat there guzzling Schlitz. Forever the rambler, Kerouac repeated an old refrain that echoed back down the corridors of time to the early days with Allen and the boys.

"Man, I can't make it. I'm cutting out."

· 10 ·

Aftermath

The Poet and the Publisher

*In their discontent with American values . . . they had restored
a sense of adventure to American culture. In their rejection
of the boring, the conventional, and the academic, in their
adoption of a venturesome lifestyle, they gave everyone the
green light to plumb their own experience.*

—Ted Morgan

So how did the stories of the great poet and publisher play out? How
did their experiments with life, literature, and law continue? Here are a
few snapshots—fast-forward, much as they lived their lives.

ALLEN GINSBERG

Although there are various lenses through which to view the life of
Allen Ginsberg, such as his great influences on the '60s and '70s counterculture and on more contemporary poets and artists, one lens that is
particularly strong is his unwavering commitment to dissent. Through
the remainder of his life, the bold poetic bard whose *Howl* made First
Amendment history raised many a lance against government censorship
of artistic and political expression. Regardless of the outcome, he never
turned down an opportunity to engage in free speech combat. On this
front, as in *Howl*, he always sided with the outsider.

After the irreverent comedian Lenny Bruce was arrested in Manhattan in April of 1964 for ribald word crimes committed in a Village coffee house, Allen circulated a petition in support of Bruce. Celebrities such as Bob Dylan, Norman Mailer, Susan Sontag, Elizabeth Taylor, Lionel Trilling, and Paul Newman signed on. Their typed press release began with the banner: "ARTS, EDUCATIONAL LEADERS PROTEST USE OF NEW YORK OBSCENITY LAW IN HARASSMENT OF CONTROVERSIAL SATIRIST LENNY BRUCE."

The body of the petition, the "manifesto," opened: "We the undersigned are agreed that the recent arrests of nightclub entertainer Lenny Bruce by the New York Police Department on charges of indecent performance constitute a violation of civil liberties as guaranteed by . . . the United States Constitution." The *New York Times* and *Herald-Tribune*, among others, ran with the story. Nonetheless, Allen's well-intentioned efforts† came to naught when Bruce was later convicted for obscenity. Similarly, Ginsberg's expert testimony on behalf of the defense in the Boston *Naked Lunch* trial did not deter the judge from finding Burroughs's bizarre book to be obscene, though it may well have contributed to the work's ultimate vindication by a higher court.

And then there was the time in August of 1968 during the Democratic Convention in Chicago, where Allen, Abbie Hoffman, Jerry Rubin, and the Youth International Party (Yippies) sponsored a Festival of Life to protest the military draft and America's involvement in the Vietnam War. "We are here," Ginsberg declared at an earlier press conference, to manifest "a desire for the preservation of the planet," to end "a long period by the war gods and the older, menopausal leaders." Setting a mood for the new planetary peace consciousness, he reached over to open a small red leather box that contained his old harmonium. Playing the one-octave keyboard, he chanted a Hindu prayer, not stopping for ten minutes: *Hare Krishna, Hare Krishna, Krishnaaaaaaa, Rama Krishna, Hare Krishna*, and on and on. Afterwards, Judy Collins summoned young people to the Windy City in late August "for a testimonial for life."

By the time Allen got to Chicago, much had happened in the explosive months from April to August of 1968 that stirred the passions

---

†One such theatrical effort was Allen's mailing of his shorn locks and beard to the prosecutor in the Bruce case, Assistant District Attorney Richard Kuh.

of disaffected and angry youth. Dr. Martin Luther King was shot at Lorraine Motel in Memphis (April 4); not long after announcing his bid for the presidency, Robert F. Kennedy was assassinated at the Ambassador Hotel in Los Angeles (June 5); the Republican National Convention nominated Richard Nixon for president and Spiro Agnew for vice-president, running on a "law and order" platform (August 23); and it appeared likely that the Democrats would nominate Senator Hubert Humphrey, a pro-war supporter, to be their presidential candidate.

Signs of unyielding tension and impending conflict were everywhere to be found in Chicago's streets and parks. Tens of thousands of young people filled with rage came to the city, a resentment ready to be ignited by the Yippies, Black Panthers, Students for a Democratic Society, and "16,000 Chicago police officers, 4,000 state police, and 4,000 National Guard troops in full battle dress armed with machine guns, bazookas, and tanks." Although Ginsberg tried to obtain a permit for peaceful protests in the parks, he was unsuccessful; with fury building all around, however, any options for nonviolent action dwindled.

The spectacle of the festival drew hordes of print and electronic reporters. Allen was one of them, as were Bill Burroughs, Norman Mailer, Terry Southern (a noted novelist and screenplay writer), and Jean Genet (the notorious French novelist, playwright, and poet). *Esquire* magazine hired them all to offer the countercultural take on what was about to happen. Bearing press credentials, beads, and love in his heart, Allen waded into an expansive sea of outraged youth, surrounded by blue-helmeted police wearing Plexiglas face-shields.

August 26, 12:20 a.m., Lincoln Park: Officers had ordered everyone to leave the park almost an hour and a half earlier, but the demand was ignored. Anticipating that the police might storm the park, protesters had erected makeshift barriers. Things escalated quickly, as the crowd of 3,000 waved Vietcong, black anarchist, and peace flags, some of them howling "kill the pigs," while police floodlights glared and bullhorns blared.

The amplified police message was clear: "This is a final warning. Please leave the park. The park is now closed. Anyone remaining in the park is in violation of the law. Everyone out of the park. This is a final notice."

The crowd's response was equally loud and clear: "Hell no, we won't go! Hell no, we won't go! Hell no, we won't go!!"

Then, from nowhere, tear gas shells hissed through the night air, as the police and National Guard, armed with shotguns, advanced into the crowd. Some protesters threw rocks, some hurtled bottles, and others ran screaming as mottled brown-and-white clouds of gas forced the panicked demonstrators to retreat. But there, in the center of the chaos, were Allen Ginsberg and 300 fellow Yippies standing their ground and chanting "Om," "Om." This was the only calmness witnessed that night.

The madness swelled a few nights later when the "Nightmare of Moloch," as Allen put it in "Howl," returned to Grand Park on the shores of Lake Michigan. After a day of tumultuous events, a mass rally was held there. In the glow of campfires burning in the summer night, young people openly smoked pot and passed hash pipes, while others sipped honey-flavored mixes spiked with acid. During the night's speech-making, Terry Southern downed tequila and took hits of "Panama Red." One reproach after another flew out from the stage: barbs were tossed at President Johnson, the war, and, of course, Chicago's contentious Mayor Richard Daley. Charged by the denunciations, a few demonstrators headed for a flagpole, and hauled down the American flag. A fight then broke out.

When Chicago's riot-ready police moved in, they were pelted with rocks and bricks. Screams of "PIG, PIG, PIG" filled the post-midnight air. Some yelled "REVOLUTION NOW!" Others shouted "THE PARK BELONGS TO THE PEOPLE!" Then a phalanx of Plexiglas-protected soldiers descended, wearing black leather gloves and wielding clubs, rifles, tear gas, and chemical mace. The fracas lasted about 10 minutes, until some semblance of order returned. At that point, Allen Ginsberg stepped onto the park's band shell to deliver his message of peace over the loudspeakers.

His voice cracked: "I lost my voice chanting in the park the last few nights." Clearing his throat, he continued: "The best strategy for you in cases of hysteria, overexcitement or fear is still to chant 'Om' together. It helps to calm fluttering of butterflies in the belly. Join me as I try to lead you."

A *New York Times* news story recounted what happened next: "So as the policemen looked in astonishment out their Plexiglas face shields, the huge throng chanted the Hindu 'Om, om,' sending deep mystic reverberations off the glass office towers along Michigan Avenue." Calmness came over the crowd.

Jean Genet, Bill Burroughs, Norman Mailer, and comedian Dick Gregory spoke next. But as at 6 Gallery, the night belonged to Allen Ginsberg. With their peace work done, Ginsberg, Burroughs, and Genet left for New York where they would write their stories for *Esquire* magazine . . . and accidentally hook up with Jack Kerouac, who was in town to appear on William F. Buckley's *Firing Line*.

* * *

Well into his 60s, Allen Ginsberg continued to rant against censorship. Ironically, his later efforts were targeted, once again, at governmental suppression of his greatest works. More than thirty years after Judge Clayton Horn ruled that *Howl* could not be banned from San Francisco bookstores as an obscene work, the Federal Communication Commission's regime of indecency regulations threatened to silence the public broadcasting of sexually explicit works, such as Ginsberg's poetry. At a meeting of the Federal Communications Bar Association, held on April 18, 1990, Allen delivered a powerful "Statement on Censorship." "In the last two decades," he explained, his "Howl," "Sunflower Sutra," "America," "Kaddish," and other poems had been "broadcast by university, public educational and listener supported stations." But now "FCC regulation could forbid broadcast of 'Howl.'" Any such "censorship of my poetry . . . is a direct violation of our freedom of expression," he rebuked. "I am a citizen. I pay my taxes and I want the opinions, the political and social ideas and emotions of my art to be free from government censorship."

Four years later, Allen railed again—this time outside the U.S. Court of Appeals in Washington, DC. Clad in a black suit (something he picked up at the Salvation Army), the poet addressed passers-by who sipped from cups of Starbucks coffee. He read "Howl" aloud, "while lawyers representing him and others stood inside, arguing in markedly less colorful language" that the FCC's indecency regulations violated the First Amendment. Pacifica, a radio station in Berkeley, had stopped broadcasting "Howl" for fear of a stiff fine. "At a recent symposium," Ginsberg explained, an FCC commissioner "pulled out a copy of *Howl* and said, 'This is perfectly fine; all Mr. Ginsberg has to do is eliminate a couple of paragraphs.' That's their idea of freedom."[†]

Death: April 5, 1997 (age 70) of liver cancer.

Two years later. It was a novel picture of America. The famous 1966 photo[††] of Allen Ginsberg was featured on the cover of a Sotheby's catalogue. Its glossy black-and-white portrait blended the yin and yang of Allen's world. Here was the face of the counterculture mixed with its commercial opposite. A paper Uncle Sam top hat perched on his head, its stars and stripes shooting skyward out of his skull. The aura of it all was reminiscent of images of Walt Whitman taken a century earlier.

On October 7, 1999, the austere Manhattan auction house swarmed with the tailored set of the famous and wealthy along with an unkempt set of aging yuppies with balding heads, bulging bellies, and beaded necklaces. They were all eager to inspect and bid upon personal property from the estates of Allen Ginsberg, Jack Kerouac, William Burroughs, and other Beat figures.

As they bid and bought, many there that day remembered Allen's famous works, public awards, and his enormous impact on things literary, political, and cultural—everything from his role in free speech struggles to his induction into the American Academy of Arts and Letters to his directorship of Naropa's Jack Kerouac School of Disembodied Poetics, and more.

Most had seen the *New York Times* front-page obituary. Remarkably, that 2,915-word story, replete with several photographs, was

---

[†]In a letter of April 4, 1995, to conservative congressman Randy "Duke" Cunningham (since convicted and sentenced for bribery, mail fraud, and tax evasion), Ginsberg again complained about censorship, this time related to funding for the National Endowment for the Arts. Alluding to FCC indecency regulations, he wrote: "The excuse is to guard the ears of minors from 'indecency,' but these same *Howl* and *Kaddish* poems of mine under ban are read in high school and college anthologies during the very hours the poems are banned off the radio." He added: "Now censorship is re-imposed on what is at present the main marketplace of ideas: radio, TV, and even now the information highway."

[††]The photograph, taken on March 26, 1966, by Fred W. McDarrah was titled "Allen Ginsberg in Fifth Avenue Peace Demonstration to End the War in Vietnam."

longer than the newspaper's obituaries for either Elvis Presley (1,076 words) or John Lennon (1,166 words), or even Allen's Beat brother Jack Kerouac (1,273 words). In that same America where the "poet laureate of the Beat Generation" once howled against military power, students at the Virginia Military Institute now studied his rebellious poem as part of their curriculum; there is even a photograph of them doing so.

The Ginsberg canon is astounding. It includes three major biographies, some 17 compilations of poetry and some 19 of prose, five photography books, some nine collections of audio-recorded materials, two DVD documentaries, and a website entitled "The Allen Ginsberg Project" and more.

* * *

One final note: On May 13, 1986, Allen wrote a letter to Lawrence Ferlinghetti, which began:

> I have been amiss in not keeping in better touch on my plans, though I wanted a part of it to be a surprise.
>
> There was little about *Howl* trial and publication, and very few footnotes to *Howl*, because I planned to cover all that extensive[ly] in [the] *Annotated Howl* which was one of the six books scheduled for Harpers in the original contract agreement [I had with them]. . . .
>
> In any case what I hadn't wanted to tell you, till the *Howl* book was out, so it be a surprise, was that the entire *Annotated Howl* book is dedicated to you anyway and has from the beginning of the work on it. So I hope this pleases you and assuages your irritation with me—partly my own negligence in keeping you abreast of progress on the *Howl* book.

Allen made good on that promise, for on the dedication page of the oversize book there were words both tender and cryptic:

To
Lawrence Ferlinghetti
Poet
Editor, Publisher, and Defender of "Howl"
in gratitude for his comradeship over three decades

Missing all our appointments
and turning up unshaven

years later
old cigarette papers
stuck to our pants
leaves in our hair.

Lawrence was touched: "thanks for the beautiful . . . dedication to the *Annotated Howl.* . . . You've done it all as no one else could," is how it put it in a February 18, 1987 letter to Allen.

* * *

LAWRENCE FERLINGHETTI

Ferlinghetti's most famous book of poetry, *A Coney Island of the Mind* (1958), was translated in over a dozen languages and sold over a million copies, making it one of the best-selling poetry collections of all time.

For more than six decades, he maintained the highly successful City Lights bookstore in San Francisco,[†] which was declared an official historical landmark in 2001. During that time, he continued as editor and publisher of City Lights Books, which could boast of 200-plus books in print. By the time of his 100th birthday, he had accumulated a bevy of honors: among others,

- San Francisco named an alley after him, Via Ferlinghetti (1994), and awarded him the title of its first poet laureate (1998);
- he received the Robert Frost Memorial Medal (2003) and membership in the American Academy of Arts and Letters (2003);
- the French Order of Arts and Letters named him Commandeur (2007);
- and the San Francisco Art Institute honored him with the Douglas MacAgy Distinguished Achievement Award (2012).

[†]Nancy Peters is the co-owner of City Lights Books. In 2007, after 23 years as City Lights' executive director, she stepped down. Today, she serves as president of the City Lights Foundation, which was formed with the "goal of advancing deep literacy, which is not only the ability to read and write but fluency in the knowledge and skills that enable us to consciously shape our lives and the life of our community."

But even awards can spark controversy when Lawrence Ferlinghetti is the designated recipient. That became evident in 2012 when Ferlinghetti was awarded the inaugural Janus Pannonius International Poetry Prize from the Hungarian division of PEN, a group that promotes freedom of speech and press and helps dissident and imprisoned writers. Ferlinghetti, however, declined the $64,000-plus award. In a letter to the organization he wrote: "Since the policies of this right-wing [Hungarian regime ruled by Prime Minister Viktor Orbán] tend toward authoritarian rule and the consequent curtailing of freedom of expression and civil liberties, I find it impossible for me to accept the Prize in the United States. Thus, I must refuse the prize in its present terms."[†] As reported in the *Daily* News, Ferlinghetti attempted to persuade the group to redirect his award money "towards causes that work to protect freedom of speech" but "was unsatisfied with the organization's efforts. In the end, despite the offer of the prize money with the government's stake withdrawn, Ferlinghetti refused outright."

* * *

Over the years, his famous Pocket Poet Series had celebrated the likes of Robert Bly, Gregory Corso, Robert Duncan, Allen Ginsberg, Jack Kerouac, Philip Lamantia, Frank O'Hara, Kenneth Patchen, and Anne Waldman.

As for himself, Ferlinghetti authored some 31 collections of poetry, three novels, four books of plays, three journals, a book of drawings, and a collection of correspondence with Allen Ginsberg, plus several audio recordings featuring his poetry. Furthermore, there are four biographies of Ferlinghetti as well as a full-length 2009 documentary about him directed by Christopher Felver.

The fighting spirit of the tall and bearded activist was well captured in *Poetry as Insurgent Art* (2007). "Be subversive, constantly questioning reality and the status quo," he counseled. "Speak up. Act out. Silence is complicity," he warned. "Be the gadfly of the state and also its firefly." Much of that fighting spirit still raged within him. His aging years notwithstanding, he would soon again fly the flag of poetic freedom.

[†]Ferlinghetti's refusal to accept the award came four months after Elie Wiesel, in 2012, returned his 2004 Order of Merit, Grand Cross award bestowed by the government of Hungary.

· 11 ·

Déjà Vu

Fighting the FCC 50 Years Later

The defense of civil liberties will always require
vigilance and courage and intelligence.

—Al Bendich, 2003

$\mathscr{B}$ack it 1988, when Allen Ginsberg lived in Los Angeles, a campaign was organized to air "Howl" on KPFK-FM, a L.A. public radio station. Here is how that matter was reported in the *Los Angeles Times* in January of that year:

> The nonprofit foundation, which operates KPFK-FM (90.7) locally and four other public radio stations throughout the United States, had originally planned to air Ginsberg, a Los Angeles resident, reading his epic on the 30th anniversary of its publication. "Howl" contains four-letter words and references to pederasty and sexual organs that might be interpreted as "patently offensive" under the FCC's April 16 guidelines.

Despite broadcaster and civil liberty groups' complaints to the FCC about the arbitrariness and vagueness of the guidelines, "an FCC spokesman said . . . there are no plans to clarify or alter the new standard which bans 'patently offensive' references on the air to sexual or excretory functions or organs." Foiled, KPFK aired a program entitled "Why Pacifica Can't Broadcast *Howl*: A Journey through 30 Years of American Censorship."

Change the focus to a purportedly far more tolerant America—fifty years after Lawrence Ferlinghetti was victorious in the *Howl* case. In 2007, Lawrence's hope was to have "Howl" aired on public radio during the daytime hours. Again, there was controversy. It began when Ferlinghetti and others[†] petitioned New York Pacifica Radio station WBAI-FM to play Allen Ginsberg's 24-minute 1959 recording of "Howl"—this in celebration of the 50th anniversary of Judge Horn's ruling in the famous case. That 1957 state-law decision notwithstanding, *federal law* in 2007 still remained another matter altogether. Seen in that light, "Howl" and its publisher were back in the news.

Here is how the story was reported in October of 2007 in the *New York Times*:

> Janet Coleman, WBAI's arts director, said that when the idea of airing the poem to test the law was proposed, "I said, 'Yes, let's try it.'" The radio station has a history of championing the First Amendment, having broadcast the comedian George Carlin's "seven dirty words" routine that resulted in a 1978 Supreme Court ruling on indecency [in the case of *Federal Communications Commission v. Pacifica Foundation*]. But after several harsh FCC rulings in 2004—against CBS for a glimpse of Janet Jackson's breast during the Super Bowl halftime show and against Fox for curse words used during the Billboard Music Awards—"our lawyer felt it was too risky," Ms. Coleman said. The commission can impose "draconian fines," she said, that could put WBAI out of business.

The fear was not without warrant since in 2005 Congress upped the penalties for indecency on the public airwaves. This empowered the FCC to fine a public radio or T.V. station (as opposed to cable) up to $325,000 for every violation of its regulations. Thus, a station could be fined heavily for any indecent language aired in the hours between 6 a.m. and 10 p.m. Part of the irony was that "Howl" had been read on public radio in the late 1950s and there was little or no controversy—the dark ages of language censorship were ending, or so it might have

---

[†]In addition to the authors, who organized the petition effort, the following signed onto a letter e-mailed to Janet Coleman of Pacifica Radio: Al Bendich (*Howl* attorney), Christopher Finan (American Booksellers Foundation for Free Expression), Peter Hale & Bob Rosenthal (Ginsberg Trust), Eliot Katz (poet and activist), Bill Morgan (archivist and biographer), and Nancy J. Peters (City Lights).

seemed. In December of 1956 at 10:30 p.m., KPFA-FM in Berkeley "broadcast a poetry reading of *Howl* . . . . Allen Ginsberg, who had recorded the tape in KPFA's studios a few months earlier, performed three poems from the book, including the long poem 'Howl.' The broadcast was Ginsberg's first appearance on radio and the first sound recording of 'Howl' to reach a public audience."

On June 12, 1957, 'Howl' was rebroadcast at an earlier hour on KPFA FM radio, though not without some word deletions as "simply a matter of taste." Still later, in 1971, "KPFA declared October 30 to be 'Allen Ginsberg Day' and gave over a fifteen-hour day of programming to recordings from a (never released) sixteen-volume set of Ginsberg's complete works read by the author."

But what about 2007? Would the poem remain outlawed from the public radio airwaves?

* * *

Lawrence's great voice spoke out, and forcefully, during a 2007 flap over airing "Howl" on broadcast radio. WBAI's Coleman favored the idea of airing the poem on their station during daylight hours. And Pacifica's attorney, John Crigler, thought that airing the poem would make for "a great test case." Still, fears remained. The FCC's fines for alleged indecency could be catastrophic. Program director Bernard White worried that the fine might be $325,000 for each of Ginsberg's dirty words, which could bankrupt the station.

What to do? WBAI opted for a safer alternative: running a program, "Howl Against Censorship," on the Pacifica.org Internet site, which is not subject to FCC regulation. The program included, among other things, Ginsberg's reading of "Howl" and a phone interview with Ferlinghetti. Even so, Coleman took exception to the need to turn to the safe harbor of Internet radio; it was anathema to the principle of poetic freedom. "Allen Ginsberg," she told NPR's Neal Conan, "throughout his life really resented this particular restriction, that his poem could only be heard after 10 o'clock. And it is a very strange archaic restriction that we still have to live by."

Ferlinghetti agreed. "I look at the present situation," Lawrence began his interview, "as a repeat in spades of what happened in the 1950s, which was also a repressive period. The current FCC policy . . . when applied to ["Howl"] amounts to government censorship of an important critique of modern civilization, especially of America and its consumerist society, whose breath is *money*, still." Responding to Coleman's question about what Ginsberg would have said today, he sighed: "Ah, well, I'm sure he'd have plenty to say about it. I often lament that he isn't around to say it."[†] Ferlinghetti asked if he could end by reciting his poem, *Pity the Nation:*

> Pity the nation whose people are sheep,
> and whose shepherds mislead them.
> Pity the nation whose leaders are liars, whose sages are silenced.

The old poet closed with lines that echoed down the halls of time, back to the words of Walt Whitman:

> Pity the nation—oh, pity the people who allow their rights to erode
> and their freedoms to be washed away.
> My country, tears of thee, sweet land of liberty.[††]

[†]In a *New York Times* editorial, entitled "A Muse Unplugged," the editors wrote: "If Ginsberg were still alive with us, he would undoubtedly pen a mocking line or two about his poem being banned from the airwaves 50 years after it was ruled not to be obscene." The piece closed by quoting Ginsberg: " 'Whoever controls the media, the images, controls the culture.' "

[††]"As recently as 2014, a program about Ginsberg on From the Vault, a series produced for podcast and radio by the Pacifica Radio Archives, played only an excerpt from the 1956 recording of *Howl*, prefacing it with the statement that 'it is still illegal to air "Howl" on American airwaves without language edits.' "

Epilogue

Onward: "Where Are Whitman's Wild Children?"

Great Oracle, sleeping through the centuries,
Awaken now at last
And tell us how to save us from ourselves
and how to survive our own rulers
who would make a plutocracy of our democracy
in the Great Divide
between the rich and the poor
in whom Walt Whitman heard America singing

—Lawrence Ferlinghetti, September 20, 2001

A brave man and a brave poet.

—Bob Dylan

$\mathcal{I}$t is an astonishing fact: a poet wrote the first major treatise on freedom of the press in the modern era. Before Benedict De Spinoza, John Locke, John Stuart Mill, Justices Oliver Wendell Holmes, Louis Brandeis, Hugo Black, William O. Douglas, and William Brennan expressed any of their thoughts on the topic of press freedom, there was John Milton and his celebrated *Areopagitica: A Speech of Mr. John Milton for the Liberty of Unlicensed Printing* (1644). Few works capture its insights in defense of freedom of the press; few works rival *Areopagitica*'s condemnations of censorship—a pamphlet addressed "To the PARLIAMENT of ENGLAND." It was a bold move coming as soon as it did on the heels of the Licensing Order of 1643 whereby Parliament compelled authors to obtain a government license in order to publish any print matter.

99

Milton, like Ferlinghetti, was a maverick. If the poet Milton was a friend of the Enlightenment, then the polemicist Milton was also an enemy of the Church and its rule over the lives of its subjects. If he helped advance the cause of truth in the marketplace, his broadminded polemics made it possible for that truth to be fiercely attacked. If his notion of a free press pointed to its use in furtherance of the rule of law, the radical in him defended the killing of the king. And if high values took refuge in his thought, what appeared to many as low ones (such as his defense of divorce†) found sanctuary in his writings. Little wonder, then, that he coined the word "pandemonium."

To be sure, the spiritual Milton was far more conservative than the spiritually unconventional Ferlinghetti. Nonetheless, both were radical for their times. And even if the author of *Areopagitica* might not countenance the gospel of *Howl*, there is something about Ferlinghetti's defense of it that would ring true to Milton. That something has to do with the imperative to contest the "corruptions of power," to be skeptical of convention, and to be free to challenge authority. Their common bond was that both poets "detested rigidity, stasis, withdrawal, timidity, small-mindedness, indecision, . . . [and blind deference] to authority." It is at that juncture that the worlds of *Areopagitica* and *Coney Island of the Mind* meet.

This point is borne out in an irony that has escaped many, though not Ferlinghetti. The case of *People v. Ferlinghetti* centered on what the Collector of Customs, Chester MacPhee, and Captain William Hanrahan found objectionable—those crude words or obscene implications let loose in Allen Ginsberg's poem. That was the charge, the so-called threat to society; that was the central issue of the trial; and that was the point that *Roth v. United States* was examined to settle. Gauged by that narrow focus, the victory for freedom of the press was one linked to the right to say in print whatever one wished when it came to so-called offensive language. What is ironic is that such objections represented the poem's *least* dangerous threats to the societal norms of the time. The real dangers posed by *Howl*, by contrast, went far beyond its colorful words and its suggested sexual indiscretions. There was much more

---

†Milton's 1643 pamphlet, titled *The Doctrine and Discipline of Divorce*, was denied a printing license when the author first applied for one. Even so, Milton published the pamphlet in violation of the law.

at stake here; there was a subterranean message far more extreme and far more objectionable to anyone who viewed *Howl* through the lens of the poet who wrote it and the publisher who printed and distributed it.

Howl was a manifesto of the powerless and the penniless and their countless attempts to restructure the evil world ordained by Moloch, the god of money, greed, exploitation, and more. The poem was a rant against capitalism, commercialism, militarism, authoritarianism, racism, and the sexual moralism of the day. It celebrated queers of all kinds coming out of their closets and into the rebellious streets to reclaim their dignity and proclaim their liberty. Ginsberg's poem pointed to nothing short of a cultural revolution, one that traced back to the poetic consciousness of Walt Whitman.

The *Howl* victory thus represented something far more significant than a triumph in the arena of the law of indecency and obscenity. Given its radical underpinnings, Ginsberg's lines were more akin to seditious messages, that is, calls to overthrow the established order. True, they were not explicit and their threat was not imminent. Still, those who first heard *Howl* read at 6 Gallery and those who thereafter celebrated its "Pocket Poet" edition probably saw in it what Ferlinghetti relished in it—its uninhibited call to redefine the codes by which we live. In 6 Gallery, Ginsberg gave voice to that call; in the "Pocket Poet" pamphlet, Ferlinghetti gave it permanence.

Dating back to antiquity, poetry has a long record of posing a threat to the established order. Plato noted as much in his *Republic*; Aristophanes revealed as much in his *Lysistrata*; William Blake confirmed as much in his *Jerusalem*; Percy Shelley demonstrated as much in his *The Masque of Anarchy*; Charles Baudelaire proved as much in his *The Flowers of Evil*; Maya Angelou disclosed as much in her *Still I Rise*; Gil Scott-Heron communicated as much in his *The Revolution Will Not Be Televised*; and Lawrence Ferlinghetti said as much in his *Poetry as Insurgent Art*. Ginsberg's *Howl* is part of that rebellious tradition, at once dangerous and inspiring.

To write such poetry is one thing; to publish it yet another. The latter, after all, requires a willingness to be held legally responsible for the messages of the former. The nexus between the two forged in *People v. Ferlinghetti* represents a triumph for the Madisonian vision of free-speech and free-press freedoms championed 228 years ago with the

ratification of the First Amendment. Even beyond that, it represents a vindication of the principle defended 375 years ago in *Areopagitica*.[†]

There is yet more in the mix of what made the victory in *People v. Ferlinghetti* the cultural landmark that it became. There was the role of the San Francisco press. Recall, as noted in Chapter 5, *San Francisco Chronicle* columnist Abe Melinkoff's attack on censorship in his "Iron Curtain on the Embarcadero." Recall, as well, that the *Chronicle*'s book review editor turned over his Sunday column, "Between the Lines," to Ferlinghetti to allow him to respond publicly to the government's attempts to censor *Howl*. Then there was the *Chronicle*'s editorial with the damning headline, "Making a Clown of San Francisco," along with a column titled "Orwell's 'Big Brother' Is Watching over Us," followed by a cartoon portraying a bulldog-faced policeman pounding a notice on a bookstore door. The caption: "Hanrahan's Law—All books must be fit for children to read—SFPD."

Think of it all from a First Amendment perspective: A poet dared to write a poem condemning the guardians of the societal canon, a publisher dared to print that poem, a bookseller dared to sell and circulate that poem and then defend it in court, a newspaper dared to rally to the cause of the poet, publisher, and bookseller, and finally a god-fearing judge dared to protect the poem and the publisher in the name of the law. For those several months in 1956 and 1957, the cultural and constitutional stars aligned in a way to give staying power to a principle boldly embraced by a poet, a publisher, a bookseller and his clerk, a civil liberties organization, a local newspaper, and a municipal judge. It was a Madisonian moment if ever there were one.

But there is yet more to the story.

* * *

Censorship struggles to persist when the will of courageous men and women place it beyond the bounds of the acceptable. That was the creed of Whitman and Emerson, poets who celebrated the howls of the

---

[†]Vincent Blasi has noted that it is possible that Milton "wrote the *Areopagitica* at the behest of the journeymen printers of the City of London. This politically active group, with whom Milton was in contact, saw its livelihood threatened by the prospect of strict enforcement of the Licensing Order [of 1643] for the benefit of the limited number of master printers favored by the Parliament with monopoly privileges."

nonconformist, the iconoclast, the dissident, and the sexual outlaw who from time immemorial have been the foes of bluenose orthodoxy. "If the First Amendment is to have an organizing principle," Steven Shiffrin wrote, "let it be [the symbol] of the dissenter." Let it feed on the poetic spirit, the spirit of the romantic that struggles to break out of the captivity that cabins it. Al Bendich, the young ACLU lawyer who raced to *Howl*'s defense, pointed to that spirit in the memorandum he prepared for Judge Horn. In it, Bendich quoted from a 1943 Supreme Court opinion by Justice Hugo Black:

> The authors of the First Amendment knew that novel and unconventional ideas might disturb the complacent, but they chose to encourage a freedom [that] they believed essential if vigorous enlightenment was ever to triumph over slothful ignorance. This freedom embraces the right to distribute literature and necessarily the right to receive it.

Did the authors of the First Amendment actually strike that balance in their constitutional command to government? Perhaps. Then again, it is just as likely that Justice Black took poetic license, which is where Whitman and Ferlinghetti and their literary like come into play. The lesson that poets teach us is that the freedom vouchsafed by the First Amendment cannot be left to black letter lawyers and robed judges, important as they can be in safeguarding our liberties. If it is to realize its ideal, the law of the First Amendment must be rooted in the *spirit* of liberty, in the soil in which the seeds of dissent stir. Law and poetry, reason and romance—they came together in *People v. Ferlinghetti* in a mixture as unusual as it was essential.

Ferlinghetti, however, was no street-fighting starry-eyed radical, no Allen Ginsberg maniac, no Jack Kerouac hypochondriac. True, he hung with them, supported them, and published them. But he was also something they never were—a successful *businessman*. Strange portrayal of someone who has long had socialist blood in his veins. Make of it what one will, but remember this: Lawrence Ferlinghetti launched a profitable bookstore, started a successful publishing house, placed both in jeopardy in the *Howl* case, and in the process became an example (albeit a rare one) of a fearless businessman who stood firmly and proudly on his rights. It is easy to overlook the fact that Ferlinghetti's stand could have gone south; he could have lost the case, his liberty, and his business. How many business people would follow his example?

To raise such a question is to point to the psyche of the poet, painter, publisher, and bookstore owner known as Lawrence Ferlinghetti —the calm rebel, the outspoken businessman, the spirited poet, the daring publisher, and the quiet bookstore owner who refused to silence the voices of his authors.

* * *

1855: In that year Walt Whitman first published his *Leaves of Grass*. He penned his poetic words, designed the cover and interior, and even "set some of the type for it in a Brooklyn printing office." Poet, printer, and bookseller, too, Whitman came to be defined by his great work. Over time, Whitman refined and expanded it. One of the poems in that collection is titled "In Paths Untrodden." It is as good as any a window into the mind of the man and his life view. Here is how it opens:

> *In paths untrodden,*
> *In the growth by margins of pond-waters,*
> *Escaped from the life that exhibits itself,*
> *From all the standards hitherto publish'd, from the pleasures, profits, conformities,*
> *Which too long I was offering to feed my soul,*
> *Clear to me now standards not yet publish'd, clear to me that my soul*

Those "untrodden paths" await freethinkers, skeptics, and non-conformists. Those future travelers yearn to live life free of "standards hitherto publish'd." They are the ones destined to remove themselves "from the clank of the world." Little wonder that Ralph Waldo Emerson was so taken with *Leaves* when his eyes first rested on its text: "I greet you at the beginning of a great career." Recall, it was that passage from Emerson's July 21, 1855 letter to Whitman that Ferlinghetti echoed in his telegram to Ginsberg after hearing "Howl" performed at 6 Gallery.

Much of the same Whitmanic thinking finds expression, though reconfigured a bit, in Ferlinghetti's "Populist Manifesto #1" poem, which opens with these words:

Poets, come out of your closets,
Open your windows, open your doors,
You have been holed-up too long
in your closed worlds

Ferlinghetti's poets do not retreat from the world; nay, they launch themselves into it with vigor. In this manifesto, there is the same Whitmanesque skepticism, the same nonconformity associated with the bearded poet with the wide brim hat. But in Ferlinghetti's hands, that nonconformity points outwards to social action—toward political justice, racial justice, gender justice, "queer" justice, economic justice, and environmental justice. It is in that spirit that later in the poem Ferlinghetti asks: "Where are Whitman's Wild Children, where [are] the great voices speaking out?"

Indeed, where are such voices in these times of our American crisis? In that crisis (the kind that tries our souls), one of Whitman's wild children continues to speak softly but forcefully: Lawrence Ferlinghetti, painter, poet, publisher, bookstore owner, and social activist—a most unusual man, an American maverick.

Addenda[†]

People v. Ferlinghetti
(1957 Unpublished Opinion)

IN THE MUNICIPAL COURT OF THE CITY AND COUNTY
OF SAN FRANCISCO, STATE OF CALIFORNIA

HONORABLE CLAYTON W. HORN, JUDGE

PEOPLE OF THE STATE OF CALIFORNIA
Plaintiff

vs.

LAWRENCE FERLINGHETTI, NO. B27585
Defendant

Thomas C. Lynch, District Attorney
Ralph McIntosh, Deputy District Attorney
for the People

[†]Originally, the case name read *People of the State of California, Plaintiff vs. Shigeyoshi Murao, No. B27083 and Lawrence Ferlinghetti, No. B27585, Defendants.* The case against Murao was dismissed before Judge Horn issued his opinion in the matter of *People v. Ferlinghetti*. None of the surviving and incomplete versions of *People v. Ferlinghetti* contain authoritative citations within the body of the opinion. After much original research and analysis, the authors inserted citations and quotations in all of the appropriate places. Hence, this is the sole definitive version of the opinion.

108

J. W. Ehrlich
Lawrence Speiser
Albert Bendich
for the Defendants

HORN, CLAYTON W., J. The defendant is charged with a violation of Section 311.3 of the Penal Code of the State of California. Defendant pleads Not Guilty. The complaint alleged that the defendant did willfully and lewdly print, publish and sell obscene and indecent writings, papers and books, to wit: "Howl and Other Poems."

It is to be noted that the statute requires proof of criminal intent, namely, that the defendants did willfully and lewdly commit the acts specified. It should also be noted that no reference to minors is made in the statute.

It must be borne in mind that the prosecution has the burden of proving beyond a reasonable doubt and to a moral certainty two things: first, that the book is obscene and, second, that the defendants willfully and lewdly committed the crime alleged. It is elementary that where a statute makes a specific intent an element of an offense, such intent must be proved. People v. Wepplo, 78 Cal. App. 2d Supp. 959, 965, 178 P.2d 853, 857 (1974). The proof may be circumstantial; but if so, the circumstances must be such as reasonably to justify an inference of the intent. Id. at 857–58.

The prosecution has advanced the theory that the word "indecent" means something less than obscene.

In their broadest meaning the words indecent and obscene might signify offensive to refinement, propriety and good taste. A penal statute requiring conformity to some current standard of propriety defined only by statutory words would make the standard in each case, *ex post facto.*

Unless the words used take the form of dirt for dirt's sake and can be traced to criminal behavior, either actual or demonstrably imminent, they are not in violation of the statute. Indecent as used in the Penal Code is synonymous with obscene, and there is no merit in the contention of the prosecution that the word indecent means something less than obscene.

The evidence shows that "Howl" was published by the defendant and therefore it remains to be seen whether said book is obscene and if so, whether this defendant willfully and lewdly published it. The prosecution contends that having published the book defendant had knowledge of the character of its contents and that from such knowledge a lewd intent might be inferred.

The mere fact of knowledge alone would not be sufficient. The surrounding circumstances would be important and must be such as reasonably to justify an inference of the intent. To illustrate, some might think a book obscene, others a work of art, with sincere difference of opinion. The bookseller would not be required to elect at his peril. Unless the prosecution proved that he acted lewdly in selling it, the burden would not be met.

Written reviews of "Howl" were admitted in evidence on behalf of the defendants, over the objection of the District Attorney. One was from the *New York Times Book Review*, dated September 2, 1956; one from the San Francisco Chronicle, dated May 19, 1957, which included a statement by Ferlinghetti; one from the Nation dated February 23, 1957. All of the reviews praised "Howl."

The practice of referring to reviews in cases of this nature has become well established. Opinions of professional critics publicly disseminated in the ordinary course of their employment are proper aids to the court in weighing the author's sincerity of purpose and the literary worth of his effort. These are factors which, while not determining whether a book is obscene, are to be considered in deciding that question.

Over the objection of the prosecution the defense produced nine expert witnesses, some of them with outstanding qualifications in the literary field. All of the defense experts agreed that "Howl" had literary merit, that it represented a sincere effort by the author to present a social picture, and that the language used was relevant to the theme. As Professor Mark Schorer put it: "'*Howl*,' like any work of literature, attempts and intends to make a significant comment on, or interpretation of, human experience as the author knows it."

The prosecution produced two experts in rebuttal, whose qualifications were slightly less than those of the defense. One testified that "Howl" had some clarity of thought but was an imitation of Walt Whitman, and had no literary merit; the other and by far the most voluble, that it had no value at all. The court did not allow any of the experts to express an opinion on the question of obscenity because this was the very issue to be decided by the court.

Experts are used every day in court on other subjects and no reason presents itself justifying their exclusion from this type of case when their experience and knowledge can be of assistance. The court also read many of the books previously held obscene or not for the purpose of comparison.

In determining whether a book is obscene it must be construed as a whole. Wepplo, 78 Cal. App. 2d Supp. at 961, 178 P.2d at 855. The courts are agreed that in making this determination, the book must be construed as a whole and that regard shall be had for its place in the arts.

The freedoms of speech and press are inherent in a nation of free people. These freedoms must be protected if we are to remain free, both individually and as a nation. The protection for this freedom is found in the First and Fourteenth Amendments to the United States Constitution, and in the Constitution of California, Art. I, sec. 9 which provides in part:

> Every citizen may freely speak, write, and publish his sentiments on all subjects, being responsible for the abuse of that right; and no law shall be passed to restrain or abridge the liberty of speech or of the press . . .

The Fourteenth Amendment to the Federal Constitution prohibits any State from encroaching upon freedom of speech and freedom of the press to the same extent that the First Amendment prevents the Federal Congress from doing so. Commonwealth v. Gordon, 66 Pa. D. & C. 101, 138–39 (1949).

These guarantees occupy a preferred position under our law to such an extent that the courts, when considering whether legislation infringes upon them, neutralize the presumption usually indulged in favor of constitutionality. Id. at 139.

Thomas Jefferson in his bill for establishing religious freedom wrote that "to suffer the Civil Magistrate to intrude his powers into the field of opinion, and to restrain the profession or propagation of principles on supposition of their ill tendency, is a dangerous fallacy which at once destroys all religious liberty . . . it is time enough for the rightful purposes of civil government for its officers to interfere when principles break out into overt acts against peace and good order." Id. at 139–40 (quoting Thomas Jefferson, "A Bill for Establishing Religious Freedom," 12 June 1779).

The now familiar "clear and present danger" rule represents a compromise between the ideas of Jefferson and those of the judges, who had in the meantime departed from the forthright views of the great statesman. Under the rule the publisher of a writing may be punished if the publication in question creates a clear and present danger that there will result from it some substantive evil which the legislature has a right to proscribe and punish. Id. at 140.

Mr. Justice Brandeis maintained that free speech may not be curbed where the community has the chance to answer back. He said: "those who won our independence by revolution were not cowards. They did not fear political change. They did not exalt order at the *cost* of liberty. To courageous, self-reliant men, with confidence in the power of free and fearless reasoning applied through the processes of popular government, no danger flowing from speech can be deemed clear and present, unless the incidence of the evil apprehended is so imminent that it may befall before there is opportunity for full discussion. If there be time to expose through discussion the falsehood and fallacies, to avert the evil by the processes of education, the remedy to be applied is more speech, not enforced silence. Only an emergency can justify repression. Such must be the rule if authority is to be reconciled with freedom. Such, in my opinion, is the command of the Constitution. It is therefore always open to Americans to challenge a law abridging free speech and assembly by showing that there was no emergency justifying it." Whitney v. California, 274 U.S. 357, 377, 47 S.Ct. 641, 648–49 (1927) (Brandeis, J., concurring). "Moreover, even imminent danger cannot justify resort to prohibition of these functions essential to effective democracy, unless the evil apprehended is relatively serious. Prohibition of free speech and assembly is a measure so stringent that it would be inappropriate as the means for averting a relatively trivial harm to society—the fact that speech is likely to result in some violence or in destruction of property is not enough to justify its suppression. There must be the probability of serious injury to the State. Among free men, the deterrents ordinarily to be applied to prevent crime are education and punishment for violations of the law, not abridgment of the rights of free speech and assembly." <u>Gordon</u>, 66 Pa. D. & C. at 140–42.

The authors of the First Amendment knew that novel and unconventional ideas might disturb the complacent, but they chose to encourage a freedom which they believed essential if vigorous enlightenment was ever to triumph over slothful ignorance. <u>Id</u>. at 143 (quoting Martin v. Struthers, 319 U.S. 141, 143 (1943)).

I agree with the words of Macaulay who finds it "difficult to believe that in a world so full of temptations as this, any gentleman, whose life would have been virtuous if he had not read Aristophanes and Juvenal, will be made vicious by reading them." <u>Id</u>. at 155.

I do not believe that "Howl" is without redeeming social importance. The first part of "Howl" presents a picture of a nightmare world; the second part is an indictment of those elements in modern society destructive of the best qualities of human nature; such elements are predominantly identified as materialism, conformity, and mechanization leading toward war. The third part presents a picture of an individual who is a specific representation of what the author conceives as a general condition.

"Footnote to Howl" seems to be a declamation that everything in the world is holy, including parts of the body by name. It ends in a plea for holy living.

The poems, "Supermarket," "Sunflower Sutra," "In the Baggage Room at Greyhound," "An Asphodel," "Song," and "Wild Orphan" require no discussion relative to obscenity. In "Transcription of Organ Music" the "I" in four lines remembers his first sex relation at age 23 but only the bare ultimate fact and that he enjoyed it. Even out of context it is written in language that is not obscene, and included in the whole it becomes a part of the individual's experience "real or imagined," but lyric rather than hortatory and violent, like "Howl."

The theme of "Howl" presents "unorthodox and controversial ideas." Coarse and vulgar language is used in treatment and sex acts are mentioned, but unless the book is entirely lacking in "social importance" it cannot be held obscene. This point does not seem to have been specifically presented or decided in any of the cases leading up to <u>Roth v. United States</u>, 354 U.S. 476 (1957).

No hard and fast rule can be fixed for the determination of what is obscene, because such determination depends on the locale, the time, the mind of the community and the prevailing mores. Even the word itself has had a chameleon-like history through the past, and as Mr. Justice [Holmes] said: "A word is not a crystal, transparent and unchanged. It is the skin of living thought and may vary greatly in color and content according to the circumstances and the time in which it is used." Towne v. Eisner, 245 U.S. 418, 425 (1918). The writing, however, must have a substantial tendency to deprave or corrupt its readers by inciting lascivious thoughts or arousing lustful desires. Commonwealth v. Isenstadt, 318 Mass. 543, 550, 62 N.E.2d 840, 844 (1945).

The effect of the publication on the ordinary reader is what counts. The Statute does not intend that we shall "reduce our treatment of sex to the standard of a child's library in the supposed interest of a salacious few." United States v. Roth, 237 F.2d at 812 (1956). This test, however, should not be left to stand alone, for there is another element of equal importance—the tenor of the times and the change in social acceptance of what is inherently decent.

The modern rule is that obscenity is measured by the erotic allurement upon the average modern reader; that the erotic allurement of a book is measured by whether it is sexually impure—i.e., pornographic, "dirt for dirt's sake," a calculated incitement to sexual desire—or whether it reveals an effort to reflect life, including its dirt, with reasonable accuracy and balance; and that mere coarseness or vulgarity is not obscenity. Gordon, 66 Pa. D. & C. at 136.

Sexual impurity in literature (pornography, as some of the cases call it) is any writing whose dominant purpose and effect is erotic allurement; a calculated and effective incitement to sexual desire. It is the effect that counts, more than the purpose, and no indictment can stand unless it can be shown. Id. at 151.

In the Roth case no question of obscenity was involved or considered by the court. The sole question was whether obscenity as such was protected by the constitution and the court held it was not. Roth v. United States, 354 U.S. at 481 (1957). In the appeals involved the material was obviously pornographic, it was advertised and sold as such. The United States Supreme Court refers to the various rules on obscenity by stating that: "sex and obscenity are not synonymous. Obscene material is material which deals with sex in a manner appealing to prurient interest. The portrayal of sex, e.g., in art, literature and scientific works is not itself sufficient reason to deny material the constitutional protection of freedom of speech and press." Id. at 486–87.

The following instruction, given in the Alberts case, is approved in Roth: "The test is not whether it would arouse sexual desires or sexual impure thoughts in those comprising a particular segment of the community, the young, the immature or the highly prudish, or would leave another segment, the scientific or highly educated or the so-called worldly-wise and sophisticated indifferent and unmoved. The test in each case is the effect of the book, picture or publication considered as a whole, not upon any particular class, but upon all those whom it is likely to reach. In other words, you determine its impact upon the average person in the community. The books, pictures and circulars must be judged, as a whole, in their entire context, and you are not to consider detached or separate portions in reaching a conclusion. You judge the circulars, pictures and publications which have been put in evidence by present-day standards of the community. You may ask yourself does it offend the common conscience of the community by present-day standards. In this case, ladies and gentlemen of the jury, you and you alone are the exclusive judges of what the common conscience of the community is, and in determining that conscience you are to consider the community as a whole, young and old, educated and uneducated, the religious and the irreligious, men, women and children." Id. at 490

Mr. Chief Justice Warren, concurring in the result in the Roth case, stated: "I agree with the result reached by the court in these cases, but the line dividing the salacious or pornographic from literature or science is not straight and unwavering, the personal element in these cases is seen most strongly in the requirement of scienter. Under the California law, the prohibited activity must be done 'willfully and lewdly.'" Id. at 494.

There are a number of words used in "Howl" that are presently considered coarse and vulgar in some circles of the community; in other circles such words are in everyday use. It would be unrealistic to deny these facts. The author of "Howl" has used those words because he believed that his portrayal required them as being in character. The People state that it is not necessary to use such words and that others would be more palatable to good taste. The answer is that life is not encased in one formula whereby everyone acts the same or conforms to a particular pattern. No two persons think alike; we were all made from the same mold but in different patterns. Would there be any freedom of press or speech if one must reduce his vocabulary to vapid innocuous euphemism? An author should be real in treating his subject and be allowed to express his thoughts and ideas in his own words.

In People v. Viking Press, the court said: "The Courts have strictly limited the applicability of the statute to works of pornography and they have consistently declined to apply it to books of genuine literary value. If the statute were construed more broadly than in the manner just indicated, its effect would be to prevent altogether the realistic portrayal in literature of a large and important field of life . . . The Court may not require the author to put refined language into the mouths of primitive people," 174 Misc. 813, 814–816, 264 N.Y.S. 534 (1933), and in People v. Vanguard Press, the court observed: "The speech of the characters must be considered in relation to its setting and the theme of the story. It seems clear that use of foul language will not of itself bring a novel or play within the condemnation of the statute." 192 Misc. 127, 129, 84 N.Y.S.2d 427 (1947). "As I have indicated above, all but one of these books are profoundly tragic, and that one has its normal quota of frustration and despair. No one could envy or wish to emulate the characters that move so desolately through these pages. Far from inciting to lewd or lecherous desires, which are sensorially pleasurable, these books leave one either with a sense of horror or of pity for the degradation of mankind. The effect upon the normal reader, l'homme moyen sensuel (there is no such deft precision in English), would anything but what the vice hunters fear it might be. We are so fearful for other people's morals; they so seldom have the courage of our own convictions." Gordon, 66 Pa. C. & D. at 109.

In Commonwealth v. Gordon: "the test for obscenity most frequently laid down seems to be whether the writing would tend to deprave the morals of those into whose hands the publication might fall by suggesting lewd thoughts and exciting sensual desires." Id. at 113. "The statute is therefore directed only at sexual impurity and not at blasphemy or coarse and vulgar behavior of any other kind. The word in common use for the purpose of such statute is 'obscenity.'" Id. The "familiar four-letter words that are so often associated with sexual impurity are, almost without exception, of honest Anglo-Saxon ancestry, and were not invented for purely scatological effect. The one, for example, that is used to denote the sexual act is an old agricultural word meaning "to plant" and was at one time a wholly respectable member of the English vocabulary. The distinction between a word of decent etymological history and one of smut alone is important; it shows that fashions in language change as expectably as do the concepts of what language connotes. It is the old business of semantics again, the difference between word and concept. But there is another distinction. The decisions that I cite have sliced off vulgarity from obscenity. This has had the effect of making a clear division between the words of the bathroom and those of the bedroom; the former can no longer be regarded as obscene, since they have no erotic allurement, and the latter may be so regarded, depending on the circumstances of their use. This reduces the number of potentially offensive words sharply." Id. at 114.

"The law does not undertake to punish bad English, vulgarity, or bad taste, and no matter how objectionable one may consider the book on those grounds, there is no right to convict on account of them." Id. at 122 (citing Commonwealth v. Dowling, 14 Pa. C. C. 607 (1894)). The dramatization of the song 'Frankie and Johnnie' caused much furor, but the court there held that "the language of the play is coarse, vulgar and profane; the plot cheap and tawdry. As a dramatic composition it serves to degrade the stage where vice is thought by some to lose 'half its evil by losing all its grossness.'" Id. at 134. "That it is indecent from every consideration of propriety is entirely clear, but the court is not a censor of plays and does not attempt to regulate manners. One may call a spade a spade without offending decency, although modesty may be shocked thereby. The question is not whether the scene is laid in a low dive where refined people are not found or whether the language is that of the bar room rather than the parlor. The question is whether the tendency of the play is to excite lustful and lecherous desire." Id. (internal citations omitted).

"To determine whether a book falls within the condemnation of the statute, an evaluation must be made of the extent to which the book as a whole would have a demoralizing effect on its readers, specifically respecting sexual behavior. Various factors must be borne in mind when applying the judicially accepted standards used in measuring that effect. Among others, these factors include the theme of the book, the degree of sincerity of purpose evidenced in it, its literary worth, the channels used in its distribution, contemporary attitudes toward the literary treatment of sexual behavior and the types of readers reasonably to be expected to secure it for perusal." <u>People v. Creative Age Press</u>, 192 Misc. 188, 190–191, 79 N.Y.S. 198 (1948).

Material is not obscene unless it arouses lustful thoughts of sex and tends to corrupt and deprave l'homme moyen sensuel by inciting him to anti-social activity or tending to create a clear and present danger that he will be so incited as the result of exposure thereto.

If the material is disgusting, revolting or filthy, to use just a few adjectives, the antithesis of pleasurable sexual desires is born, and it cannot be obscene.

In <u>United States v. Roth</u>, a footnote to the concurring opinion of Judge Frank is of interest: "The very argument advanced to sustain the statute's validity, so far as it condemns the obscene, goes to show the invalidity of the statute so far as it condemns 'filth,' if 'filth' means that which renders sexual desires 'disgusting.' For if the argument be sound that the legislature may constitutionally provide punishment for the obscene because, anti-socially, it arouses sexual desires by making sex attractive, then it follows that whatever makes sex disgusting is socially beneficial." <u>United States v. Roth</u>, 237 F.2d at 801.

"To date there exist, I think, no thoroughgoing studies by competent persons which justify the conclusion that normal adults reading or seeing of the 'obscene' probably induces anti-social conduct. Such competent studies as have been made do conclude that so complex and numerous are the causes of sexual vice that it is impossible to assert with any assurance that 'obscenity' represents a ponderable causal factor in sexually deviant behavior. Although the whole subject of obscenity censorship hinges upon the unproved assumption that 'obscene' literature is a significant factor in causing sexual deviation from the community standard, no report can be found of a single effort at genuine research to test this assumption by singling out as a factor for study the effect of sex literature upon sexual behavior. What little competent research has been done, points definitely in a direction precisely opposite to that assumption." <u>Id</u>. at 812.

While the publishing of "smut" or "hard core pornography" is without any social importance and obscene by present-day standards, and should be punished for the good of the community, since there is no straight and unwavering line to act as a guide, censorship by Government should be held in tight rein. To act otherwise would destroy our freedoms of free speech and press. Even religion can be censored by the medium of taxation. The best method of censorship is by the people as self-guardians of public opinion and not by government. So we come back, once more, to Jefferson's advice that the only completely democratic way to control publications which arouse mere thoughts or feelings is through non-governmental censorship by public opinion.

From the foregoing certain rules can be set up, but as has been noted, they are not inflexible and are subject to changing conditions, and above all each case must be judged individually.

1. If the material has the slightest redeeming social importance it is not obscene because it is protected by the First and Fourteenth Amendments of the United States Constitution, and the California Constitution.
2. If it does not have the slightest redeeming social importance it may be obscene.
3. The test of obscenity in California is that the material must have a tendency to deprave or corrupt readers by exciting lascivious thoughts or arousing lustful desire to the point that it presents a clear and present danger of inciting to anti-social or immoral action.
4. The book or material must be judged as a whole by its effect on the <u>average adult</u> in the community.
5. If the material is objectionable only because of coarse and vulgar language which is not erotic or aphrodisiac in character it is not obscene.
6. Scienter must be proved.
7. Book reviews may be received in evidence if properly authenticated.
8. Evidence of expert witnesses in the literary field is proper.
9. Comparison of the material with other similar material previously adjudicated is proper.
10. The people owe a duty to themselves and to each other to preserve and protect their constitutional freedoms from any encroachment by government unless it appears that the allowable limits of such protection have been breached, and then to take only such action as will heal the breach.
11. I agree with Mr. Justice Douglas: I have the same confidence in the ability of our people to reject noxious literature as I have

in their capacity to sort out the true from the false in theology, economics, politics, or any other field.

12. In considering material claimed to be obscene it is well to remember the motto: *"Honi soit qui mal y pense."* (Evil to him who evil thinks.)

Therefore, I conclude the book "Howl and Other Poems" does have some redeeming social importance, and I find the book is not obscene.

The defendant is found not guilty.

2007 PACIFICA INTERVIEW WITH
LAWRENCE FERLINGHETTI AND
COMMENTARY

As noted in Chapter 11, in October of 2017 Ferlinghetti hoped to have "Howl" aired on public radio during the daytime hours. Again, there was controversy. It began when Ferlinghetti and others[†] petitioned New York's Pacifica Radio station WBAI-FM to play Allen Ginsberg's 24-minute 1959 recording of "Howl"—this in celebration of the 50th anniversary of Judge Horn's ruling in the famous case. Pacifica's lawyers counseled against airing the reading on broadcast radio. In order to circumvent FCC broadcast regulations, Pacifica aired the reading along with an interview with Ferlinghetti, follow by commentary, on Internet radio. That interview and commentary follow.

* * *

Janet Coleman: Welcome to WBAI's webcast for Pacifica, celebrating this October 3rd the 50th anniversary of the landmark verdict in the obscenity trial of Allen Ginsberg's great poem, "Howl." I'm Janet Coleman, arts director of WBAI Pacifica's New York station.

In the years since Judge Clayton Horn's milestone decision declaring "Howl" a work of literary merit, and not obscene, "Howl" has been read several times only by the author on daytime broadcast television. Oddly, with the passage of time, there has been more reservation about broadcasting the poem due to increasingly strict rules of indecency enforced by the FCC.

We were approached late this summer by a consortium of First Amendment activists, including poet and "Howl" publisher Lawrence Ferlinghetti, with an entreaty to broadcast live a reading of the Ginsberg poem without regard for the FCC's safe harbor, the hours between 10:00 p.m. and 6:00 a.m. when there are milder language restrictions than the daylight hours when children supposedly might listen. After consultation with Pacifica's lawyer, John Crigler, it was

---

[†]In addition to the authors, who organized the petition effort, the following signed onto a letter e-mailed to Janet Coleman of Pacifica Radio: Al Bendich (*Howl* attorney), Christopher Finan (American Booksellers Foundation for Free Expression), Peter Hale & Bob Rosenthal (Ginsberg Trust), Eliot Katz (poet and activist), Bill Morgan (archivist and biographer), and Nancy J. Peters (City Lights).

decided that this Internet rendition of "Howl," available throughout the Pacifica stations and affiliates, would be the best way to honor the anniversary of the "Howl" decision, short of risking draconian FCC fines that would bankrupt Pacifica and take us off the air.

Our program today includes a reading of "Howl" by Allen Ginsberg, a conversation with poet and "Howl" publisher Lawrence Ferlinghetti, and a panel discussion with poet and poetry entrepreneur Bob Holman, First Amendment scholar Ron Collins, and Beat Generation scholar Regina Weinreich on the importance and ramifications of "Howl," its publication, its public readings, its obscenity trial, and the questions of censorship that concern us now.

To begin with, I'd like to introduce WBAI program director Bernard White, whose dedication and commitment to the "Howl" 50th anniversary celebration was, from the first mention, enthusiastic and unsparing. Bernard?

Bernard White: Thank you, Janet. WBAI has historically been in the forefront of challenging restrictions to freedom of speech and freedom of expression. In fact, the so-called "seven dirty words" that you can't say in media came out of a 1975 Supreme Court ruling in the case of the *FCC v. Pacifica*.

Over the past several US administrations, the Federal Communications Commission has continued to tighten its control over certain kinds of speech under the rubric of protecting the public from indecent, unwholesome language. The FCC has actually been used as a weapon to silence dissenting voices, to limit broadcasts that question US foreign and domestic policy, while the real obscenities in U.S. culture are embodied in those very same policies. It is with this sensitivity and a belief in the sanctity of the freedom of expression that we present award-winning poet Allen Ginsberg's celebrated epic poem "Howl."

JC: Next, Allen Ginsberg reading uncensored his poem "Howl" as recorded in January 1959 at the Big Table Reading at the Shaw Festival in Chicago. The title was then and until the City Lights publication "Howl for Carl Solomon," and it was released in 1959 as part of the album, "Howl." It was reissued by Fantasy Records shortly after Ginsberg's death as "Howls, Raps and Roars: Recordings from the San Francisco Poetry Renaissance." This is Allen Ginsberg.

[The recording of "Howl" is played in its entirety.]

JC: Lawrence Ferlinghetti is a bookseller who in 1953 founded with Peter D. Martin the first bookstore in America for literary paperbacks, City Lights in San Francisco. He's also a poet, most famously of *Pictures of the Gone World* and *A Coney Island of the Mind*, a painter, a pacifist, and a publisher of City Lights Books, who brought to print works by such writers as Kenneth Rexroth, Kenneth Patchen, Marie Ponsot, as well as writers associated with the Beat Generation including Jack Kerouac, William Burroughs, Michael McClure, Gary Snyder, Diane di Prima, and of course, Allen Ginsberg.

In the fall of 1956, Ferlinghetti published Allen Ginsberg's first collection of poetry, *Howl and Other Poems*, as the fourth in a 75-cent series called the City Lights Pocket Poet Series. Because of its frank language and observations, Ginsberg's great *cri de coeur* about self and society was impounded for obscenity—first by the U.S. Customs Office then by the San Francisco Police.

In a landmark decision the following year, October 3, 1957— fifty years ago, following Ferlinghetti's arrest and long legal wrangling in a trial involving the ACLU and many distinguished literary figures testifying as witnesses in defense of *Howl*—Judge Clayton Horn ruled that *Howl* was not obscene, and that ruling cleared the way for the poem's publication continuing to this day. Ironically, because of language restrictions imposed on broadcasters by the FCC, we're still not able to broadcast a reading of "Howl," although the poem was first presented in public readings, something that Ginsberg always intended for his poems.

Along with Nancy J. Peters, Ronald K. L. Collins, ACLU defense co-counsel Albert Bendich, and several other poets and First Amendment advocates, Lawrence Ferlinghetti was one of the signers of a letter entreating WBAI to challenge the FCC's language rules by airing a reading of "Howl" in the daylight hours in what has become known as the "unsafe harbor"—before 10:00 p.m. Well, we haven't done that, but we have provided this Pacifica-wide Internet broadcast, Mr. Ferlinghetti, for you to make a statement commemorating this anniversary.

Lawrence Ferlinghetti: Yes, as Allen Ginsberg's original publisher and editor, editor for most of his life, I look at the present situation as a repeat in spades of what happened in the 1950s, which was also a repressive period. The current FCC policy wasn't conceived just for poetry, but when applied to the case of Allen Ginsberg's poem "Howl," it amounts to government censorship of an important critique of modern civilization and especially of America and its consumer society, whose breath is money still. It's such a hypocritical concept of American culture in which children are regularly exposed to adult programming in the mass media with subjects ranging from the sexual to criminal to state-sponsored terrorism while at the same time they are not allowed to hear poetry far less explicit. I suggest the FCC ban all television newscasts until after 10:00 p.m. when children won't be listening.

JC: Hear, hear. Mr. Ferlinghetti, what are the consequences if language censorship can be considered a part of a free society?

LF: I have an email from Ronald Collins and his website Freedom Forum.org. In his letter to me, he's quoted Clayton Horn, who was the God-fearing Sunday school teacher judge who ruled on "Howl" and determined that it wasn't obscene. Horn says in an unpublished opinion, "Would there be any freedom of the press or speech if one must reduce his vocabulary to vapid innocuous euphemism?"

JC: Right. Allen Ginsberg talked about the chilling effect of language censorship—these seven words, and if they can't be used what other concepts and ideas are shut down because of the words that lead to these ideas.

LF: Yes, of course. At the time that "Howl" was busted in the 1950s, it wasn't really the four-letter words that the government didn't like. It was that the poem directly attacked American society and the American way of life. An attack on corporate monoculture, etc.

JC: Oddly enough, before you even published "Howl," before it was your idea, you heard it read in a public setting at the 6 Gallery. Is that correct?

LF: That was in a remodeled garage and they made so much of that reading. It was just maybe thirty people passing around a jug of wine.

JC: But nevertheless, that's the way it came to your ear.

LF: I had read the poem. Allen had given me the manuscript before that, and I didn't know the Beats well enough to hang out with them, really. I was leading a perfectly conventional life, married on Potrero Hill, San Francisco. I went home by myself, or with my wife at the time, to Potrero Hill and I sent a Western Union telegram—this before there was any Internet or fax, and the way people communicated in emergencies was Western Union. I copied what I had heard Emerson had written to Walt Whitman upon reading the first copy of his *Leaves of Grass*. So, I wrote to Allen, "I greet you at the beginning of a great career dot dot dot dot when do I get the manuscript?" That's how that went.

JC: And how long did it take? It was a handshake deal?

LF: That's right, we never had a written contract.

JC: And did you publish the first thousand copies?

LF: Well, the first printing was 1,500 copies. Then it was seized by U.S. Customs, and Customs released it when the government refused to prosecute. And then the local police seized the book. The San Francisco Juvenile Department came into the store and arrested my partner Shigeyoshi Murao and me for publishing and selling it. That's how we got into a trial.

The trial lasted maybe six weeks in the summer of '57 in the old San Francisco municipal courthouse, which no longer exists. It was only a municipal court, and yet the precedent set by Judge Clayton Horn's opinion has held up all these years. It opened the floodgates, allowing the Grove Press in New York, for instance, to publish Henry Miller's *Tropics*, *Lady Chatterley's Lover*, and many others. Of course with their own lawsuits in each case where they had to defend them.

JC: So it was very costly to be a First Amendment activist, as it continues to be.

LF: Yes, well, it certainly could have been. Thank God for the American Civil Liberties Union. We would have been out of business in no time because we're just a little one-room bookstore. We didn't have any money for lawyers. And, of course, the government realized that was a good way to drive us out of business.

JC: Did you consult with the ACLU before you published the poem?

LF: We did. I sent the manuscript to the San Francisco ACLU, and they actually committed themselves to defending it before we sent it to the press. The main defense lawyer on the ACLU team was Al

Bendich. It was his first case in court, just a couple of years out of law school and he won the case on the constitutional grounds.

JC: Who were the literary figures that came to defend "Howl" on literary grounds?

LF: It was a famous criminal lawyer named Jake Erlich who associated himself with the case. And he spent most of the defense time reading from books like *Moll Flanders* to prove that dirty words had been published before, and left but ten minutes on the last day for Al Bendich to make the constitutional points upon which the case was won. And we had a long string of eminent literary scholars and critics and professors from the University of California, Berkeley. People like Kenneth Rexroth, who was an early KPFA Pacifica programmer, and Alan Watts. Many, many—I would say all the important literary figures in San Francisco. And the prosecution had a couple of very lame witnesses from the University of San Francisco.

JC: English teachers?

LF: [Chuckles.] Yes.

JC: Talk a little bit about the connection between the Pacifica station of that era and the San Francisco literary flowering.

LF: I came to San Francisco in 1951. I'd been in Paris on the G.I. Bill because I'd been in the Navy four years—never had a desk job—one ship to another. As such, I had a good American boy background. I'd been in the Navy and never questioned anything about the war. I even was at Nagasaki six weeks after the bomb was dropped. And being totally naive politically (and you might say illiterate politically when I came to San Francisco), listening to the early KPFA, the first 10 years of KPFA, it was a total political, social education for me.

People like Kenneth Rexroth, he had a books program, but he didn't just review poetry or anything like that, he addressed every subject you could think of. He was a real polymath in philosophy, theology, you name it. And he considered himself a philosophical anarchist. I never heard such a term back east. I could say listening to the early KPFA is how I got wise to what was going on in this country as far as capitalism masquerading as democracy.

JC: It is sort of stupefying now that, despite its progressive ambitions and exercise of those ambitions, Pacifica is really strangulated by this particular language restriction, in my opinion. What is yours?

LF: I think the FCC is only giving lip service to the First Amendment and to the U.S. Constitution because it is the servant of a government in which capitalism masquerades as democracy.

JC: Have you been following any of the current FCC trials in the various courts of appeals? CBS's Janet Jackson case, and the fleeting expletive on Fox?

LF: I really don't have time to watch cable television. I don't have cable, but I must say, I'm listening to Amy Goodman's *Democracy Now* practically every morning.

JC: So you haven't been following the ins and outs of it, but neither of these cases really seems to focus on actual First Amendment issues. They are focused more on community standards, you know, broadcast standards—whether these words will offend or not—but the root cause here, the First Amendment violation, does not seem to be a part of either these trials.

Let's talk a little bit about the history of the rare readings of "Howl" that have been presented on the radio. Do you recall a few?

LF: Yes, KPFA broadcast it more than once in the 1960s, but it's been a long time you know, that's a half a century ago, I don't remember the details.

JC: So we're rolling backwards? After this wave of literary censorship victories, where are we going with this?

LF: It's still very hard for a prosecutor to get a conviction on a printed book. For some reason the safeguards seem to hold up much better when it comes to print as opposed to the spoken word. I suppose that's because the spoken word is heard by more people, and it's heard by people who don't necessarily expect to hear it or want to hear it.

JC: Whom do you think gets shut out of the general conversation—the radio, the broadcasting conversation—because of being silenced in their vocabulary?

LF: Well, I don't know. It seems to me some days listening to dissident voices on the dissident radio stations in San Francisco, for instance—there are stations that don't swallow the party line completely, such as KALW and of course KPFA. It seems to me sometimes that we're all talking to ourselves and the total intellectual population of the United States is about 1% of the television viewing audience and it's a pathetic situation, so that anyone with a dissident opinion has no power whatever.

JC: Why do you suppose that in the 1950s—what was the energy, what was the good luck that made it possible for so many First Amendment heroes to be able to exercise actual power and effect over the law? You, Barney Rosset, many other publishers, booksellers?

LF: The huge corporate state hadn't really gotten organized to the point it is today. Today it's more like the early days of Italian fascism under Mussolini where there's complete cooperation between the government and corporations, hand-in-hand. In the 1950s, they hadn't really gotten it all together yet. The Beats came up in the 1950s in San Francisco particularly because with the Second World War, the huge displacement of the population, a lot went home after they'd been in the Armed Services but they didn't stay long, and then many took off for the West. It was as if the whole continent had tilted westward, the population slid westward. It took that long for a new synthesis of a new post-war culture to come together, and it came together in San Francisco, which in a way was still the last frontier.

When "Howl" was published in 1956, this was really the first cry of what became the counterculture. It was a youth revolt against the industrialization and the corporate monoculture and the war machine—the youth could sense it was coming down on them. The Beat writers articulated most of the themes that became the main shibboleths of the 1960s hippie counterculture—the anti-war activism, the turning toward Far Eastern philosophies, the first articulation of ecological consciousness, many other things like that.

JC: Judith Malina, the leading actress and artistic director of The Living Theater, was here at WBAI the other day. They have been doing a revival of "The Brig."

LF: I saw it in New York the first time.

JC: It was scary, wasn't it?

LF: Yes.

JC: She says that young people are still coming, flooding the theater. And she said that the problem with the people today, as opposed to the kids in the 1960s, they have the spirit of change but they don't have any strategies.

LF: I don't see where their motivation is. It seems to me, everyone who might do something about it—in other words, those who aren't on the bottom rung of society, and ones who have some education and jobs—they're all too well fed to do anything. And in the universities these days, there doesn't seem to be much revolt. They're too intent on their own private pursuits.

JC: Right. What distinguished the Beat Generation writers was their lack of connection with the universities. They departed from universities at the first opportunity to go on the road.

LF: It definitely was a non-academic generation, even though Allen Ginsberg loved teaching.

JC: He certainly did it well, too. How many copies would you say of "Howl" have so far been disseminated?

LF: It's getting up towards four-fifths of a million.

JC: Really? And it's published in how many languages?

LF: I don't know, maybe two dozen.

JC: Really? So everyone has it, everyone knows it?

LF: Oh, yes.

JC: And how many countries have broadcasted it?

LF: I have no idea.

JC: I wonder if it's really out there in Pacifica-like stations?

LF: Allen was known in every country in the world, it seemed, and he traveled extensively—he went everywhere.

JC: What do you suppose he would have done had he been present on this 50th anniversary? What sort of statement would he be making today because his poem still cannot be read?

LF: Well, I'm sure he'd have plenty to say about it, and I often lament that he isn't around to say it, but he never was ingested by the system. You know, the famous quote by Herbert Marcuse about the enormous capacity of the dominant society to ingest its own most dissident elements has happened to so many prominent people, and rock stars, and others in the 1960s—it never happened to Allen Ginsberg. He remained totally un-ingested; he was still buying his suits in the Salvation Army.

JC: That is a symptom, isn't it, of not being ingested? No Armani suits?

LF: In Allen's last ten years, he began to look more and more like his father, and also more and more like a rabbi.

JC: You published his father, did you not?

LF: No, we didn't. But I loved Louie. He was a real human being and that's not so easy to say these days.

JC: I'm afraid you're right.

LF: You know, without Allen I think there probably wouldn't have been any Beat Generation recognized as such. It would have been just various great writers scattered about the landscape, but he's the one that really pulled it all together.

JC: In the book *"Howl" on Trial*, there's correspondence between you and Ginsberg. He was in Europe or in Tangier during the "Howl" trial, right? He wasn't even in the States?

LF: No, he was never arrested.

JC: Was that deliberate for him to stay out of the United States during that time? So he wouldn't be?

LF: I have no idea, but that's what he was doing before any legal action came up. So, I mean, he didn't just drop everything and come back to the States. For one thing, you've got to realize that poets didn't have any money. None of us had any money.

JC: So it wasn't so easy to take a plane back at the drop of the trial?

LF: They could live in a place like Tangier on $30 a month; that's why so many American expatriates stayed in Europe for so many years. After the Second World War, we were the conquerors, we set the exchange rate. It was extraordinarily cheap for Americans over there. There's a whole generation of wartime Americans who became expatriates.

JC: Right. Ginsberg himself was very fastidious about the publishing details of "Howl" and all his other materials. What was the sort-of simultaneous publication in the *Evergreen Review*, how did that happen? And what were the questions about whether it would hurt or help the City Lights edition?

LF: That was Don Allen and the *Evergreen Review* No. 2, which was a San Francisco issue. And we gave permission, of course, to publish the main part of "Howl"—although not the "Footnote to 'Howl,'" which was very important. And I won't quote it here or you'll be off the air with a $25 million fine.

JC: Well, we're on the Internet, you can quote away!

LF: It did a great service for San Francisco poets, it sort of put them on the map. Barney Rosset is probably the second most important publisher in America, as far as getting Beat writers and that whole generation published.

JC: You were so courageous to do this, as if you didn't even think twice. Did you think twice about publishing "Howl"?

LF: Well, I thought twice enough to send it to the ACLU ahead of time to see whether they would support us.

JC: Okay, so you thought twice.

LF: You know, I was young and foolish, and I figured: Well, I wouldn't get treated too badly in jail and I'd get a lot of reading done.

JC: You don't seem totally nostalgic that it has been 50 years; you sound as feisty as you were 50 years ago. Do you feel that way?

LF: Not necessarily, it's the kind of an old fogey term. I'm only 88, after all.

JC: You're a kid.

LF: Could I end by reading my poem, "Pity the Nation"?

JC: I wish you would.

LF: This is after a poem by Khalil Gibran that he wrote early in the 20th century. "Pity the Nation":

> *Pity the nation whose people are sheep, and whose shepherds mislead them.*
> *Pity the nation whose leaders are liars, whose sages are silenced, and whose bigots haunt the airwaves. . . .*

> *Pity the nation whose breath is money and sleeps the sleep of the too well fed.*
> *Pity the nation—oh, pity the people who allow their rights to erode and their freedoms to be washed away.*
> *My country, tears of thee, sweet land of liberty.*

JC: Well, it sounds like you could do it all over again. I want to thank you so much, Lawrence Ferlinghetti, for joining us on this 50th anniversary celebration of the "Howl" trial—not the publication, but the verdict ruling that the poem was not obscene. What can we do, besides cross our fingers that the FCC . . .

LF: You send me a CD of this program and people should wake up and speak up. I have a new book just out from New Directions called

Poetry as Insurgent Art. It really urges people to wake up, the world's on fire.

JC: Sorry to say you are right, so we should all be writing poems then or at least reading them.

LF: Right.

JC: Thank you.

LF: Thanks a lot.

* * *

The following comments aired on Pacifica Internet radio and followed the Ferlinghetti interview. Joining Janet Coleman were Ronald Collins, Bob Holman, and Regina Weinreich.

JC: As promised on this 50th anniversary celebration of the "Howl" verdict, now we will have a panel discussion on the importance and ramifications of "Howl," its publication, its public readings, its obscenity trial, and the questions of censorship that concern us now.

I'd like to introduce Ron Collins who was a scholar at the First Amendment Center. He is the coauthor with David Skover of *The Trials of Lenny Bruce*, and through their imagination and persistence they persuaded former New York Governor George Pataki to post-humously pardon Lenny Bruce. It is through Ron Collins's efforts that this 50th anniversary celebration of the "Howl" verdict came to fruition. Due in the fall 2008 is his next book with David Skover, entitled *Mania*, about Allen Ginsberg and the Beats. Welcome, Ron.

Ronald Collins: Thank you.

JC: Bob Holman has been called this generation's Ezra Pound. He has been a central figure in the re-emergence of poetry as a vital force in our culture. For seven years he was a curator of the Poetry Project at St. Mark's Church in New York, and is a co-founder of the Nuyorican Poets Cafe and a major figure in presentations of its poetry slams. For television, he produced the PBS series "The United States of Poetry," with readings by 60 poets including rappers, songwriters, cowboy poets, and slammers in street settings reflective of their poems. As founder and artistic director of the Bowery Poetry Club in New York, he has created a vibrant new and centrifugal center for the performance and perpetuation of poetry in the arts. Bob Holman's new CD is *The Awesome Whatever*. Hello, Bob.

Bob Holman: Hi. I'm not a fascist, nor anti-Semite.

JC: Well, that's very good!

BH: I always get that out there.

Regina Weinreich: I'm glad. I was worried.

JC: That's good for a Pacifica panel.

Regina Weinreich, the voice you just heard, teaches The Beat Generation in the Department of Arts and Humanities of the School of Visual Arts, is the author of *Kerouac's Spontaneous Poetics: A Study of the Fiction*, is a writer on the documentary *The Beat Generation: An American Dream*, and editor of Jack Kerouac's *Book of Haikus*. She is producer with Catherine Hiller Warnow of *Paul Bowles: The Complete Outsider*, featuring Allen Ginsberg—a film now out in DVD.

Well, all of you had some special connection to Allen Ginsberg and to the "Howl" poem. I want to ask Bob Holman first—because you have such dedication to the public performance of poetry—whether Allen Ginsberg was an inspirational force for your commitment.

BH: Absolutely. You know, I was just trying to stay alive in a little river town in Ohio when I came across Ginsberg's poetry. The nice thing about the Pocket Poets Series is they literally would fit in your pockets, and so I would carry "Howl" around with me. And it was a primary reason why I came to Columbia, which was Allen's alma mater.

Hearing him read for the first time was to discover the bard—that there is such a thing as a poet who is alive and changing. The first time I met Allen was at a party where he was doing the dishes, and that was as impressive as any of the poems had been. A life of service and, you know, he could get those plates clean so that we could get the next servings served up. Coming up through the Lower East Side was to live in the Holy Land where Allen's poets still litter the streets. It's great to be here, and of course, this whole idea of the censorship trials is so American and so continuing, to the point where now 50 years later you still can't hear the damned thing on the radio.

JC: Did you say damned thing? You can say that.

BH: I think it's not one of the seven. I'm going to be very careful about which are the seven.

RC: Bob, if you need a lawyer I'm right here.

BH: Thank you, Ron.

JC: Ron, you are a First Amendment specialist and activist. What are the consequences to a society that deals in language censorship?

RC: Well, where do you begin? How about with the poets in antiquity. Remember, Plato wanted to send them all packing—Aristophanes wasn't too big on Plato either. But putting dead Greeks aside, I'd like to say how Allen Ginsberg came into my world—someone who's trained in the law. Some of my best friends are poets, and I aspire to be one myself some day.

Back in the late 1990s when I was researching a book with David Skover on Lenny Bruce, we were just about done and we had interviewed one of Bruce's lawyers, a guy named Al Bendich. Al started talking to us about this other client he had, this fellow named Lawrence Ferlinghetti, and how in 1957 he had represented him, along some other lawyers, in a case called *People v. Ferlinghetti* involving Allen Ginsberg's "Howl."

He shared with us some legal documents that had been lost at the time. I went home that night, started looking at them, and thought, "Wow." The next day, I went to the bookstore, bought "Howl," and while reading it said "Wow" once again. I called David the next day and I said, "Our San Francisco chapter needs to start with "Howl," and we should think about doing a totally separate book focusing on the "Howl" trial.

Here we are, almost a decade later, and we've spent the last five or six years reading about Allen Ginsberg, his life, and what happened on October 7th, 1955 when this incredible man came onto a stage at 6 Gallery and recited his incredible poem. One more thing—and we could talk a lot about this—but there's something about the orality of "Howl"; as magnificent as its print version is, there's something about the orality of that poem that touches the soul—at least it deeply touched my soul. There was almost something rabbinical that happened on that October night, if you can put it that way.

JC: Or cantorial, you might say?

RC: That's true, yes. I will say more about censorship. I don't want to take time from my colleagues here, so I'll put that on hold for a second and just emphasize again the importance of the orality.

One of the things about hearing "Howl"—and we have a CD version of it here, a later recording, not the original reading done in

1955 which was not recorded. To have been in that room, with all of those folks (including Jack Kerouac) chanting "Go! Go! Go!," and to experience the enthusiasm. At the end of the reading, people cried, people applauded, people stomped their feet, people clicked their fingers—it was just an incredible emotive experience. And to think that such a moment could not be shared with Americans on broadcast television or radio is an outrage—it is a cause for howling today, more loudly than ever. To think that broadcasters might be fined millions and millions of dollars.

One last point: In 1957, Lawrence Ferlinghetti liberated the word—that is, in *People v. Ferlinghetti* the court ruled that it was permissible for children's eyes to read "Howl"—and yet today, a half-century later, it is unlawful for their ears to hear it—it is an incredible irony, an incredible injustice. Sooner or later, if liberty under the First Amendment means anything, "Howl" must be read—and read loudly on our broadcast airwaves, radio and television.

JC: Children's ears that censors wish to protect—I want to get back to my question about what it does to a society to have a censorship environment. That was a passionate concern of Allen Ginsberg, that the chilling effect of censorship be broken down. So, I'll ask Regina Weinreich what you, as a teacher of literature, think about keeping language from children's ears?

RW: Part of what Allen was doing with "Howl" was saying, "Okay, listen to these words." And when a society censors it, they're clearly distracting people from something else; I think that's the political nature of "Howl," from a language point of view. I mean, Allen was saying, "Well, wait a minute, you think this is obscene? Well what about poverty? What about racism? What about all these other things in our culture that you're not thinking are obscene?"

JC: Bob Holman, you give a stage to hundreds of young poets of color, and rappers, and hip-hop artists who use the language of the streets freely. What does the censorship mean to their work?

BH: Of course, it means that if they get to beep 50 Cent, they don't have to worry about having all their words be heard, there'll be plenty of beeps on the radio. I think that there is an environment of censorship that the FCC is a part of.

I was just thinking about what Ron was saying, and how what this says about the division of orality and literature. You know, that you can buy the book and that it can be in a library—and I assume that "Howl" is not allowed in, and is banned in certain libraries—but that there are no legal repercussions for anyone to take this book out of the library or to buy it or to give it to anybody of any age; and yet, nobody is allowed to hear it on broadcast radio or television.

This prejudice—the idea that a written text somehow can pass a test, that there is a certain kind of intelligence inherent in one's ability to read and decipher print, versus the animalistic immediacy and impact of orality—must be stopped. If you think about it, it becomes a really damning piece of analysis of this country's appreciation of different cultures. There's a can of worms that Ron was opening there.

As part of the field of censorship that's going on in the country right now, you know that the NEA is now under conservative leadership and able to get its funding raised at the same moment that the varieties of art that it sponsors, and especially the individual artists who used to be funded through the federal government, are no longer. All this results in a type of self-censorship that I think is one of the greatest dangers that's going on right now. If an artist wants to get a grant, from the starting line it has to be a certain kind of art in order to be approved. And so, even to get on to *Def Poetry Jam* on HBO, you are going to have to limit yourself to a certain kind of poetry; in order to have your poem heard on the radio, certain words aren't going to be used there. So what happens is you begin with the mindset of censorship as an implicit part of creation. Now let me tell you, when the government rules your mind like that, I think you are in a dangerous fascist state.

JC: Well, you opened up another can of worms that maybe Ron can talk to and that is visual censorship. Rudy Giuliani tried that with the Brooklyn Museum. Are there any other instances?

RC: For those that are listening, I just want them to know that this room is filled with worms. They're all around, they're crawling, we've opened up more cans of them. Well, yes, let me answer that and piggyback on something Bob just said. We have entered an era where in some respects, not all, government censorship is at an alarming high. Let me give an example. The FCC fines prior to 2006—the minimum fines for broadcasters who aired a single objectionable or indecent form of expression, be it audio or visual, including Janet Jackson's nipple—9/16, 9/16th of a second, mind you—

JC: They didn't anticipate the visual would be part of the censorship.

RC: And even if the eye could catch it, one wonders if the game was worth the candle. But be that as it may, the fine was increased ten times—that's the minimum fine: $325,000 for each word, all right, and then $3 million for each additional day. So to read "Howl" could cost literally millions and millions, and if it were broadcast on various stations across the country, you could be talking hundreds of millions of dollars.

JC: Multiple millions. Each word?

RC: That's right.

JC: $325,000 per indecent word?

RC: That's the minimum. And that's not the end of it. For example, Clear Channel Communications has decided that if you go on their show or if you're a radio producer, you must indemnify them. So, if I go on their show and read "Howl" and they are thereafter fined, I must pay the fine. So you see, it's not just the station's fine anymore. What's happening is that some comedians are even taking out indecency policies to protect them. Do you know that it costs $22,000 to get a million dollars' worth of coverage? If you need fifty millions of dollars, think about what that costs you a year.

So, the censorial impact of this is absolutely enormous. And when it comes to visual censorship—in 2004 Janet Jackson and Justin Timberlake did a musical number during the Super Bowl in which they had a bustier malfunction for 9/16th of a second, which CBS didn't know about, and now CBS was fined—and the FCC case goes to the United States Court of Appeals for the Third Circuit. For 9/16ths of a second!

One final point if I may: only the American mind could be this schizophrenic. I don't know about you, but as I surf through the channels I don't know the difference between broadcast and cable. And yet cable and satellite are not regulated, as evidenced by *The Sopranos*. You can say or show pretty much anything you want—something that's clearly obscene can't be. So there's this dichotomy, one standard for broadcasters on radio and television and another standard for cable and satellite.

JC: Well, I think the theory is that you pay for cable and satellite. And if you pay you can listen to whatever language can be delivered. And it is an interesting contrast because in the reruns of *The Sopranos* on not-pay-for-cable A&E, the language is omitted. The obscene or harmful or anti-community standards language is just omitted, and it looks crazy, you know? Because if you heard it the first time, you know that the substitution is for the "F" word, which I say here quite casually, even though we're not on broadcast radio. There we have to really watch our step. I remember once Allen doing a radio interview with me, I think was probably my first live interview, and he was going to read his poem about the bones . . .

BH: "Father Death Blues?"

JC: Yes, "Father Death Blues"—to which he had written some new stanzas. And I said, "read the new stanzas, but please if there are any of the seven dirty words, please do not read those words." He was not agreeable to the idea that he should be his own censor. And finally he said, "You see what the chilling effect is? I haven't even spoken these words and you are afraid I'm going to say them and that's the chilling effect." So here, now, Pacifica, in its fear that it will be fined these gigantic sums has now gone kind of overboard, I think, even on the safe harbor, the hours between 10 p.m. and 6 a.m. when supposedly, with disclaimers and so forth, you can say these seven words. We really can't say them anymore.

RW: Well, you know what's kind of funny about all of this? If you get certain editions of William Burroughs' *Naked Lunch*, you have the trial transcript. Because *Naked Lunch* was also censored, as you might remember, and in those transcripts you have someone saying, "Well, certain words that are unmentionable are mentioned 242 times within this text." And the court says, "Would you mention them then?" And there you are, reading in the transcript mega times all of these seven words.

RC: Regina makes an excellent point. And just to show you how the past repeats itself, Regina, when *Fox v. FCC*—incredible, *Fox v. FCC*. Think about that.

JC: Fox was the good guy there.

RC: And Fox is challenging the FCC—this is recently—for some allegedly indecent expressions on its television station. And when that case was argued in the United States Court of Appeals for the Second Circuit several months ago, it was covered by cable television.

JC: On C-Span.

RC: On C-Span. And the lawyers in the course of their argument mentioned the words time and time and time again. The court ruled against the Federal Communications Commission. And just yesterday, I understand, the Federal Communications Commission has decided to take that case to the Supreme Court. Now, isn't it amazing? At a time when we're talking about shock jocks, and Janet Jackson, and what-have-you—isn't it amazing, in light of all of that, that one of America's great poems—one of the great traditions left to us . . . . you know, it's almost as if we couldn't read *Leaves of Grass* on the radio—query whether or not we can.

JC: We might not be able.

RC: It is a great and grave injustice, whatever one thinks about indecency, wherever one draws the line or doesn't draw the line. By the way, this was something that concerned Allen Ginsberg right to the end. Right to the end, he fought very hard against censorship, made some very strong statements, and we can talk about those in a moment. But wherever one draws the line on indecency, if "Howl" by Allen Ginsberg cannot be read on the American airwaves there is something terribly wrong about our system of justice in this country.

JC: As a legal scholar, have you observed a sea change in legal confrontation over the First Amendment in these FCC cases? They assume that this decency regulation is implicit to their behavior. I mean, it's not about the First Amendment, is it?

RC: Well, in a sense it's all about the First Amendment.

JC: Well, it's about ignoring the First Amendment. What is the difference here?

RC: If you consider the Pacifica case in 1978—that's when a divided Supreme Court with a plurality opinion by Justice John Paul Stevens, who should have known better (but he had other wonderful decisions thereafter)—it was in 1978 when the Justices ruled that indecency could be regulated in broadcasts.

Though "Howl" had been read on broadcast in the late '70s, in the '80s, and as late as 1997, by 2004 when Janet Jackson had her 9/16ths of a second clothing malfunction we were in a completely different regulatory era with draconian fines. And the Federal Communications Commission has made it clear that it has a zero tolerance policy when it comes to anything that it deems indecent, in language or in images, and so we really are in a completely new era. Were Lenny Bruce alive today, he certainly could not appear on any broadcast TV or radio station. There's no doubt about that.

JC: Well, he could on cable TV. Just like all the other comedians who use the words he couldn't.

RC: He'd be on HBO with Larry David and his gang.

JC: Right. That's better than he got, isn't it? A better chance than he got to be heard?

RC: Ironically, we have a way of honoring our great poets and comedians when they're dead, you know? I mean, as wonderful as it was to posthumously pardon Lenny Bruce, it would have been a lot better if in 1968 the New York justice system had gotten it right. And the same thing with Judge Clayton Horn, the Sunday school teacher who ruled in favor of the First Amendment and "Howl" a half-century ago; yet a half-century later, you know, that precedent has been undermined significantly by what's happening with FCC regulation of television and radio.

JC: It's incredible, yes. Bob Holman, what's the genie in the bottle that the censors don't want to let out? There was a genie in Allen Ginsberg's bottle—it was probably sex, homosexuality, society, and war.

BH: The poets who are listened to so little and who have so little power, why are the great forces of government lined up against them with all of their catapults and human-sized glue traps? That's a good question. I think it's because when you hear the poem (and that's why for a lot of kids these days poetry is like rock-and-roll was, why they are adamant that hip-hop is another genre of poetry in the American vein), when you do hear the words of a single human slicing through the years of wax collection and the momentous detritus of advertising commercials and political lies that seem to be what we hear as language most of the time these days, the liberation that's set in is the same kind of liberation that Allen found, both in sex and in poetry, and in a whole way of life that I think still is celebrated in his great neighborhood of the Lower East Side.

In fact, it was in Tompkins Square Park just about a month ago at the "Howl" Festival where 20 poets collected and read "Howl" in its entirety during the holy hours when you can't say dirty words on the radio and spoke those words over the loudspeaker to whoever happened to be wandering through Tompkins Square Park. And the effect on the audience was totally remarkable. To be able to hear every word, to be able to listen to a 24-minute poem with no commercial breaks was—it was meaningful. The clouds of meaning were let loose with the rains of understanding, and it was happening live in front of you at Tompkins Square Park.

When you see that sense of playful understanding of humanity being able to relax with itself, with citizens seeing themselves as citizens instead of consumers—which is what we appeared to be, the end product of the horrific triumph of capitalism—then you begin to sense the power that poetry may have. And in the great battlefields these days, when communism and socialism seem to be looked on as simply failed experiments, the gift of the poetic economy seems to be about all we've got left to stand up to the system that has turned us all into non-thinking eaters of existence.

JC: The poetic economy.

RW: You know, Allen intones the word "Moloch" in one section of "Howl." Moloch is the God who eats children, and it stands for the kind of industry that really doesn't regard human life as important compared to economic gain. And we see that all the time in our culture, and in many cultures actually. What are we doing in Afghanistan right now, for example? We are disregarding a whole lot of things that are human, and I'm sure that if Allen were here today he would want to howl even louder.

JC: No question about it. I'm curious because I know this is pre-Vietnam—The Beat Generation has so much appeal, I assume, for a young generation of students. You teach at a school of visual arts, teach The Beat Generation. What's there for college students now? What appeals to them and what sense of individuality and rebellion is stirred by these works, if at all and which in particular?

RW: Well, I think that "Howl," *On the Road, Naked Lunch*, are a rude awakening for a lot of students these days. I think that people have been moving along and largely accepting things as they are; and what these great works of literature do is open people's eyes: "Wait a minute, maybe you ought to look at language," "Maybe you ought to see what's being rammed down your throats," "Maybe you should be more alert." And I think that students are galvanized by reading "Howl," *On the Road*, and *Naked Lunch*.

JC: Galvanized to do what?

RW: Galvanized to pay attention, and emboldened to speak up if things are not quite right for them. They don't have to become major consumers in our culture. They don't have to buy into what the culture is giving them. They can think about it and decide. And that, I think, is the essence of democracy.

BH: The irony is that the reason why we're here today, and the reason why *On the Road* and "Howl" are getting a lot of play is because it just happens to be the 50th anniversary. You know? Two years ago we were thrilled to be celebrating the publication of "Howl" and today I'm overjoyed to be celebrating the fact that it won in a court case!

RC: It's amazing what time does. Add a half century to something, and it's amazing what it does. First, *On the Road*: it wasn't until really this year, 2007, that the American public discovered that there's something incredibly spiritual about *On the Road*. Same thing.

JC: The American critic. I don't know about the American public.

RC: Well, the American public, they're buying *On the Road*, the scroll version. Whether or not they're reading it remains to be seen. But there is something very old-fashioned about "Howl." I mean, old-fashioned values. About right and wrong, about humanity. It's so touching, those lines in "Howl" where Allen writes about Carl Solomon. Carl Solomon took objection, understandably, and Allen's intentions were mostly noble, but there's something incredibly humanitarian about those passages. As you read the poem, there's a sense of injustice that he talks about—it's almost as if his hand comes and touches your soul. I would defy any critic of reading that poem on the radio or television to say what is it in the poem, taken as a whole, that corrupts the youth.

Athens gave Socrates hemlock for that, and of course Athens got it wrong. And we're getting it wrong now. All right? If you really do believe in humanitarian values, if you really do believe that there's something wrong with the moneychangers in the temple, if those old-fashioned values appeal to you, as radical as "Howl" is there is, nonetheless, something very old-fashioned about it that should appeal to you. And I would think that properly understood "Howl" really has the potential to instill values long lost. If you want to call them Whitmanesque values, all right—values that are certainly a great part of the American tradition: Whitman, Paine, Madison, what have you. And it's just beyond me how because of certain words we can stamp the poem as indecent and prevent children from hearing it. If nothing else, I think children should hear more of "Howl."

JC: Regina?

RW: Ron, do you think that the people who are censoring "Howl" have actually read it?

RC: No, in fact, but this is typical of censors. Their defense: "It's so disgusting that I can't read it or I can't see it." The same thing was said with Burroughs. It took Burroughs forever and a day to get *Naked Lunch* published—with the help, by the way, of Allen Ginsberg, which leads to another important point. Allen was an incredibly wonderful, kind soul. He helped everybody get published, everybody—Jack Kerouac, Burroughs, all of them. He was always there and he was fighting the censorship battles.

Had the original version of *On the Road* been published as Kerouac had written it, it may well have found its way to an obscenity challenge—because there were objectionable things in the original version of *On the Road*, as well. Those were altered or dropped. By the way, I think it was "Old Midnight Angel"—

RW: "Old Angel Midnight."

RC: I defer to my esteemed colleague. "Old Angel Midnight" was originally dedicated to Lucien Carr. And there's a number of very objectionable things in there that you could not read on the radio today—and to think that this great work cannot be shared with the public on broadcast radio. I don't think our young people would be corrupted beyond repair if they lived out some of the values of *On the Road* and "Howl."

JC: I don't think any of us here does. I think that's why we're here. Bob, you laughed when Ron mentioned the old fashionedness of "Howl." What caused you to laugh?

BH: I think what Ron is referring to is a kind of romantic notion of democracy, what we think of as a romantic notion. You know, the true rights of the individual which may be looked on as the originating ideas of the fathers of the Constitution. Not to mention the mothers of the Constitution and those who were enslaved under the

Constitution.

Well, it was just a few years ago where this battle of censorship fell on the head of Amiri Baraka, previously known as LeRoi Jones, one of the Beats with Ginsberg who was appointed the poet laureate of New Jersey and whose poem "Somebody Blew Up America" was deemed obscene in that it made some references to the World Trade Tower bombing and alternate theories to those that the government had proposed.

This resulted in the New Jersey Legislature trying to fire Baraka. But they discovered that, in the speed of creating the job of poet laureate, they had forgotten to create a way that you could "unhire" the guy. So what they did was a very simple and clever legislative trick: they outlawed the job. They said, "Okay, we just won't have a poet laureate."

But the response is exactly as Ron said. If they had bothered to read the whole poem, they would see that the postulation that Baraka was making was in line with a lot of other outrageous and marvelously imaginative possibilities that he had laid out, and he was in no way meaning to say, "I'm giving you a definitive answer." Just as in "Howl," the ecstatic panoply of realities that Ginsberg lays out, both in joy and in horror, presents possible ways of living that would provide those in a democracy with wealth. Here's a lot of different routes I can take. Routes, many of which are blocked off now by the censors.

JC: It occurs to me that a lot of this censorship of any spontaneous off-the-cuff natural response to the human condition is a cause for alarm. If you think of the little off-the-cuff expletives or expressions that politicians use that can be repeated over and over again and cause punishment to the politicians. Similar idea isn't it?

BH: But poets, you know—these guys work really hard at having a work that appears spontaneous that in fact is carefully crafted.

JC: Well, right.

BH: Part of the genius of the Beats was to do that, you know? So what you have here is a carefully crafted poem that has great operatic crescendos and emotional arcs going on within it that's being picked apart by the censors to say which word it is that we're finding offensive. What we really have here is a symphony of the human spirit.

JC: Anybody have anything to add to that idea of a symphony of the human spirit?

RC: Well, I certainly want to make a case for romanticism, being a card-carrying romantic myself with photographs of Percy Shelley in my wallet. Now, I think it's—

JC: Is he dressed?

RC: [Laughs.] If you do study Allen's life—obviously he was radical, obviously he was rebellious, but there was something (only go to his poem "Kaddish")—there was something terribly old-fashioned about him as well.

I think Bob hit the nail on the head with romanticism, because we're brought back to Whitman and his vision of America. It may have not have been the America founded in 1787, when we signed the Constitution, but it represented an ideal. And that ideal you could hear echoing through Whitman, through others.

Even through Justice Hugo Black, who in 1961 ended a dissent in a First Amendment case with the incredible line, "We must not be afraid to be free." And if anything, I think what's happened is just extraordinary timidity that has taken over the American mind, and because of that we fear freedom. We somehow fear that if these particular words are heard, our children will be corrupted and we ignore the larger message.

I'd like to read just a couple of lines that Allen stated in 1990 about his commitments to free speech values. This is the sort of thing that Hugo Black could have written. "Censorship of my poetry and the work of my peers is a direct violation of our freedom of expression. I am a citizen. I pay my taxes and I want the opinions, the political and social ideas and emotions of my art to be free from government censorship. I petition for my right to exercise liberty of speech guaranteed me by the Constitution." That's something that someone could have said in 1787.

JC: I think that we might even end there. I want to thank you all so very much—Regina Weinreich, Ron Collins, Bob Holman. If you have another P.S. here, let's add it now because I don't want to censor you.

RW: I have a P.S. I want to say that Allen was almost like a barometer of what was going on in the culture. And when he talks about what galvanized him or what was a catalyst for him, even to become a poet, even to want to express himself, it had to do with wanting to express a tenderness that he found was missing in the culture. I think that speaks for all of us, really. That we need to recognize what is tender and caring and human in ourselves that cannot be expressed in any other way but for us to take a chance, to be free.

JC: You've been listening to the 50th anniversary celebration of the "Howl" verdict. Today, you heard "Howl" publisher and poet Lawrence Ferlinghetti, poet Bob Holman, Beat Generation scholar Regina Weinreich, and First Amendment scholar Ronald Collins. This program was assembled with the generous help of David Dozer, Chante Mouton of City Lights Publishing, Jon Almeleh, Nathan Moore, and Ursula Ruedenberg of Pacifica, and Pacifica legal counsel John Crigler. For permission to use the recording of "Howl," thank you Bill Belmont of Fantasy Records. For WBAI, I'm Janet Coleman.

BOOKS BY LAWRENCE FERLINGHETTI:
1955–2019

Poetry

1. *Pictures of the Gone World* (City Lights, 1955, enlarged, 1995)
2. *A Coney Island of the Mind* (New Directions, 1958)
3. *Tentative Description of a Dinner Given to Promote the Impeachment of President Eisenhower* (Golden Mountain Press, 1958)
4. *One Thousand Fearful Words for Fidel Castro* (City Lights, 1961)
5. *Starting from San Francisco* (New Directions, 1961)
6. *Where Is Vietnam?* (Golden Mountain Press, 1963)
7. *Two Scavengers in a Truck, Two Beautiful People in a Mercedes* (1968)
8. *Tyrannus Nix?* (New Directions, 1969)
9. *The Secret Meaning of Things* (New Directions, 1970)
10. *Back Roads to Far Towns After Basho* (City Lights, 1970)
11. *Love Is No Stone on the Moon* (ARIF, 1971)
12. *Open Eye, Open Heart* (New Directions, 1973)
13. *Who Are We Now?* (New Directions, 1976)
14. *Northwest Ecolog* (City Lights, 1978)
15. *Landscapes of Living and Dying* (W. W. Norton, 1980)
16. *Over All the Obscene Boundaries* (W. W. Norton, 1986)
17. *These Are My Rivers: New & Selected Poems, 1955–1993* (New Directions, 1993)
18. *A Buddha in the Woodpile* (Atelier Puccini, 1993)
19. *City Lights Pocket Poets Anthology* (City Lights, 1995)
20. *A Far Rockaway of the Heart* (New Directions, 1998)
21. *How to Paint Sunlight: Lyrics Poems & Others, 1997–2000* (New Directions, 2001)
22. *San Francisco Poems* (City Lights Foundation, 2001)
23. *Americus: Part I* (New Directions, 2004)
24. *A Coney Island of the Mind* (Arion Press, 2005), with portraiture by R. B. Kitaj
25. *Poetry as Insurgent Art* (New Directions, 2007)
26. *A Coney Island of the Mind: Special 50th Anniversary Edition* (with a CD of the author reading his work) (New Directions, 2008)

27. *50 Poems by Lawrence Ferlinghetti 50 Images by Armando Milani* (Rudiano, 2010)
28. *Time of Useful Consciousness* (Americus, Book II) (New Directions, 2012)
29. *City Lights Pocket Poets Anthology: 60th Anniversary Edition* (City Lights, 2015)
30. *Pictures of the Gone World: 60th Anniversary Edition* (City Lights, 2015)
31. *Ferlinghetti's Greatest Poems* (New Directions, 2017)

Novels

1. *Her* (New Directions, 1960)
2. *Love in the Days of Rage* (E.P. Dutton, 1988; City Lights, 2001)
3. *Little Boy* (Doubleday, 2019)

Plays

1. *Unfair Arguments with Existence: Seven Plays for a New Theatre* (New Directions, 1963)
2. *Routines* (New Directions, 1964)
3. *Street Kids and Other Plays* (with Brio Burgess) (Jacob's Ladder Books, 1996)
4. *Routines, Expanded Edition* (New Directions, 2001)

Journals

1. *Journal for the Protection of All Beings* (City Lights, 1961)
2. *On the Barracks: Journal for the Protection of All Beings* (City Lights, 1968)
3. *The Mexican Night* (New Directions, 1970)

Correspondence

1. *I Greet You at the Beginning of a Great Career: The Selected Correspondence of Lawrence Ferlinghetti and Allen Ginsberg 1955–1997* (City Lights, 2015)

Drawings

1. *Life Studies, Life Stories* (City Lights, 2003)

Timeline

1919

March 24   Lawrence Monsanto Ferlinghetti born in Yonkers, New York.

1925–1937

Orphaned and abandoned by his aunt, Emily Monsanto, Ferlinghetti is adopted by Presley and Anna Bisland, a wealthy couple living in an exclusive neighborhood in Bronxville, NY. Presley encouraged him to read, educated him in the ancient classics, and placed him in a series of private and public schools. When young Ferlinghetti is arrested for shoplifting as part of his gang of "Parkway Road Pirates," he is sent to Mount Hermon, a private boy's high school on a farm near Greenfield, MA, where he received an excellent education while learning self-discipline. On his 16th birthday, Ferlinghetti receives a gift from the Bislands of his first book of poetry, a French-English edition of Baudelaire poems. It inspired him to begin writing poems himself.

1941

Ferlinghetti graduates from the University of North Carolina in Chapel Hill with a B.A. in Journalism. During college he was the circulation manager of *The Daily Tar Heel*, the campus newspaper.

1942–1944

After the Japanese attack on Pearl Harbor, Ferlinghetti attended midshipmen's school in Chicago and shipped out as ensign on J. P. Morgan III's yacht, retrofitted for submarine patrol off the East

Coast. As commander of the submarine chaser USS *SC1308*, he screened the beaches during the Normandy invasion on D-Day. After VE Day, he was transferred to the Pacific Theater, where he was navigator of the troop ship USS *Selinur*. Thereafter, he became a life-long pacifist after visiting the ruins of atom-bombed Nagasaki.

1947–1951

Enrolled under the G.I. Bill, Ferlinghetti graduates in 1947 from Columbia University with a master's degree in English literature. His thesis focused on John Ruskin and the British painter J. M. W. Turner.

Continuing his studies in Paris at the Sorbonne from 1948–1951, Ferlinghetti earns a Doctorat de l'Université de Paris ("mention très honorable") with a dissertation on the city as a symbol in modern poetry.

Returning to Bronxville in the summer of 1949 to visit "Mother Bisland" after the death of her husband, Ferlinghetti meets his future wife, Selden Kirby-Smith, aboard a ship en route to France in September. "Kirby," as she was called, was on her way to the Sorbonne to study courses on French civilization. After hemming and hawing, Ferlinghetti proposes to Kirby in the summer of 1950.

1951

January 5   Ferlinghetti first arrives in Oakland, CA, and settles in San Francisco. He teaches French in an adult education program, paints, and writes art criticism.

April 10   Marries Kirby in Jacksonville, Florida.

July   Publishes his first book review—an analysis of six recent collections of poetry—in the *San Francisco Chronicle*. Thereafter, he becomes a regular contributor of book reviews.

October   Ferlinghetti first meets noted literary figure and cultural critic Kenneth Rexroth at one of his soirées. Rexroth's beliefs in philosophical anarchism influenced Ferlinghetti's political development. In time, Rexroth became one of Ferlinghetti's most steadfast supporters.

1952

September   *Inferno*, a well-respected San Francisco literary magazine with a radical bent, publishes Ferlinghetti's translations of eight surrealistic poems by Jacques Prévert, along with the first of his own poems to be published, an early verse titled "Brother, Brother." More of his Prévert translations appear the next year in the prestigious *Contact* and *California Quarterly* magazines.

1953

After the Ferlinghettis moved to an apartment at 339 Chestnut Street, Lawrence begins writing the "painter" poems that eventually constituted the core of his first collection of poems, *Pictures of the Gone World*.

Spring   The popular culture magazine *City Lights*, published by Peter D. Martin, features six of Ferlinghetti's translations of Prévert poems.

June   Ferlinghetti and Martin launched City Lights Pocket Book Shop, America's first all-paperback bookstore.

1954

Winter   Allen Ginsberg introduces himself to Ferlinghetti at City Lights Pocket Books. Although Ferlinghetti is not interested in publishing Ginsberg's first collection of poems, *Empty Mirror*, the two strike up a friendship based on common interests in literature and politics.

1955

January   When Peter Martin returns to the East Coast, Ferlinghetti becomes the sole proprietor of City Lights Pocket Book Shop.

August 10   Ferlinghetti inaugurates the publishing arm of City Lights with his own first book of poems, *Pictures of the Gone World*, issued as "Pocket Poet Number One."

August   Working in his cottage at 1010 Montgomery Street, Allen Ginsberg composes the first part of "Howl."

October 7   At the 6 Gallery, 3119 Fillmore Street, Ginsberg gives his first public reading of Part I of "Howl."

October 8   Lawrence Ferlinghetti sends Ginsberg a telegram congratulating him on "Howl"—"I greet you at the beginning of a great literary career"—and offers to publish the manuscript.

1956

March 18	Ginsberg gives the first reading of the completed text of "Howl" at the Town Hall Theater in Berkeley, California.
March	Ferlinghetti prevails on the ACLU to defend him if he is prosecuted for publishing *Howl and Other Poems.*
November 1	Official publication date for *Howl and Other Poems.* With a first printing of 1,500 copies, the book is the fourth number in the City Lights Pocket Poet Series.
December	KPFA-FM in Berkeley broadcasts, during a 10:30 p.m. program, a recorded tape of Ginsberg reading "Howl."

1957

March 25	Chester MacPhee, the San Francisco Collector of Customs, seizes 520 copies of the second printing of *Howl and Other Poems* on the basis of obscenity. An additional 1,000 copies go through Customs without detection.
April 3	The ACLU informs MacPhee that it will challenge the seizure of the book and the charge of obscenity.
May	To avoid further seizures by Customs, Ferlinghetti arranges for 2,500 copies of *Howl* to be printed within the United States.
May 29	Customs releases the copies of *Howl* after the U.S. Attorney in San Francisco refuses to initiate condemnation proceedings.
June 3	After selling a copy of *Howl* to two local undercover police officers, Russell Woods and Thomas Pagee, the bookstore manager Shigeyoshi Murao is arrested. Subsequently, a warrant is issued for the arrest of Ferlinghetti by Captain William A. Hanrahan of the San Francisco Police Department's Juvenile Bureau.
June 6	Returning from Big Sur, Ferlinghetti turns himself in to the police and is released after the ACLU posts $500 bail.
June 12	"Howl" is rebroadcast at 9:30 pm on KPFA-FM, though some words were deleted "simply as a matter of taste."
August 8	Trial in *People v. Ferlinghetti and Murao* is scheduled to begin at the Municipal Court of the City and County of San Francisco, at 750 Kearny Street, with Judge Byron Arnold presiding. Ferlinghetti is defended by Jake Ehrlich and the ACLU lawyers Lawrence Speiser and Albert Bendich.

August 16   Trial by jury is waived and the case is transferred to the court of Judge Clayton W. Horn, a Sunday school teacher who once sentenced five female shoplifters to watch *The Ten Commandments* movie and to write essays on its moral lessons.

August 22   Charges against Shigeyoshi Murao are dismissed, since the prosecution could not prove that he had read the publication.

September 5   Nine defense witnesses testify as to the literary, artistic, political, and social merits of *Howl*. Beyond the police witnesses, the prosecution relies on two expert witnesses.

September 19   Closing arguments are given in the trial.

October 3   Judge Horn renders his opinion and verdict. Ferlinghetti is found not guilty of publishing and selling obscene writings, on the basis that *Howl* was not without redeeming social importance. The landmark First Amendment case established a key legal precedent for publication of other controversial literary works.

October   With increased public interest in *Howl*, a fourth printing of 5,000 copies is ordered.

1958

A Coney Island of the Mind, Ferlinghetti's most famous book of poetry, is released. With more than a million copies sold and translated in more than a dozen languages, it became over the years one of the best-selling modern poetry collections.

1962

Jack Kerouac's autobiographical novel, *Big Sur*, characterizes Ferlinghetti as the amiable and generous Lorenzo Monsanto, whose coastal cabin is the site of Dionysian revelries for Kerouac and his Beat friends.

1971

October 30   KPFA-FM declares "Allen Ginsberg Day" with 15 hours of programming featuring Ginsberg's complete works as read by him.

1986

May 13   Ginsberg writes a letter to Ferlinghetti informing him that the "Annotated Howl" will be dedicated to him.

1987

February 18   Ferlinghetti writes to Ginsberg to thank him for the dedication of "Annotated Howl"—"You've done it all as no one else could."

April 16   The Federal Communications Commission rules that radio and television stations risk penalty if they broadcast indecent material. Eventually, the FCC permits such material to be broadcast only between midnight and 6 a.m.

1988

January 6   Although "Howl" was to be broadcast on several radio stations as part of a series on censorship called *Open Ears / Open Minds*, five Pacifica stations choose not to air the poem fearing FCC fines.

1990

April 18   At a meeting of the Federal Communications Bar Association, Ginsberg delivers a speech, "Statement on Censorship," complaining about the FCC's indecency regulation as applied to "Howl."

1994

                While lawyers challenged FCC indecency regulations in a District of Columbia federal courts of appeals, Ginsberg reads "Howl" aloud outside on the sidewalk.

                San Francisco names an alley—Via Ferlinghetti—after the poet-publisher.

1997

April 5   Allen Ginsberg dies of liver cancer at 70 years of age.

April 7   *New York Times* publishes a front-page 2,915-word obituary of Ginsberg, replete with several photographs.

1998

                Ferlinghetti is inaugurated as Poet Laureate of San Francisco. In his public address, he urges San Franciscans to vote to remove the earthquake-damaged Central Freeway and replace it with a boulevard, decrying automobiles for destroying "the poetry of a city."

2001

City Lights Bookstore is declared an official historical landmark.

2003

Ferlinghetti is elected to the American Academy of Arts and Letters.

2007

Ferlinghetti is named Commandeur, French Order of Arts and Letters.

August   Ferlinghetti and others petition New York Pacifica Radio station WBAI-FM to play Allen Ginsberg's 1959 recording of "Howl" in celebration of the 50th anniversary of the victory in *People v. Ferlinghetti*. Despite initial interest, fears of catastrophic FCC fines for "indecency" ultimately prevailed. Instead, WBAI ran a program "Howl against Censorship," on the Pacifica.org Internet site, which included Ginsberg's reading of "Howl" and a phone interview with Ferlinghetti, who ended by reciting excerpts from his poem "Pity the Nation."

2010

60 Years of Painting, a retrospective of Ferlinghetti's artwork, is staged in Rome and Reggio Calabria.

Andrew Rogers portrays Ferlinghetti in the film *Howl*.

2012

Ferlinghetti declines to accept an award of the inaugural Janus Pannonius International Poetry Prize from the Hungarian PEN organization after learning that the Hungarian government under Prime Minister Viktor Orbán was a partial sponsor of the prize of 50,000 Euros. He expresses his opposition to the "right wing regime" of the Prime Minister.

2013

Christopher Felver's documentary, *Lawrence Ferlinghetti: A Rebirth of Wonder*, is released.

2017

October   The recipient of many American and Italian awards for his contributions to arts and blletters, Ferlinghetti is conferred with the

Career Award at the XIV edition of the *Premio di Arti Letterarie Metropoli di Torino.*

2019

March   Lawrence Ferlinghetti's experimental new book, *Little Boy*—
                     blending autobiography, literary criticism, poetry, and philoso-
                     phy—is published in honor of the author's centenary.

March 24   Ferlinghetti's 100th birthday, which is celebrated nationally and
                     internationally.

Sources

BOOKS

Amburn   Ellis Amburn. *Subterranean Kerouac: The Hidden Life of Jack Kerouac.* New York: St. Martin's Griffin, 1999.

Averbusch & Knoble   Bernard Averbusch & John Wesley Knoble. *Never Plead Guilty.* Farrar, Straus & Cudahy, 1955.

Burroughs—1   William S. Burroughs. *The Letters of William S. Burroughs, 1945—1959.* Edited by Oliver Harris. New York: Viking, 1993.

Burroughs—2   William S. Burroughs. *Junky.* New York: Penguin, 1977. Rpt. *Junky: The Definitive Text of 'Junk.'* Edited with an introduction by Oliver Harris. New York: Penguin, 2003.

Burroughs—3   William S. Burroughs. *Naked Lunch.* New York: Grove Press, 1959 (1990 ed).

Burroughs—4   William S. Burroughs. *Word Virus: The William S. Burroughs Reader.* Edited by James Grauerholz & Ira Silverberg. New York: Grove Press, 1998.

Burroughs—5   William S. Burroughs. *The Job: Interviews with William S. Burroughs.* Edited by Daniel Odier. New York: Penguin, 1989.

Burroughs—6   William S. Burroughs. *Exterminator!* New York: Penguin, 1986.

Burroughs—7   William S. Burroughs. *My Education: A Book of Dreams.* New York: Penguin, 1996.

Burroughs—8   William S. Burroughs. *Burroughs Live: The Collected Interviews of William S. Burroughs, 1960–1997.* Edited by Sylvère Lotringer. Los Angeles: Semiotext(E), 2001.

Burroughs—9   William S. Burroughs. *Last Words.* Edited and Introduction by James Grauerholz. Fort Lauderdale, FL: Flamingo Press, 2001.

Burroughs—10   William S. Burroughs. *Queer: A Novel.* New York: Penguin, 1995.

Burroughs—11   William S. Burroughs. *Interzone.* Edited by James Grauerholz. New York: Viking, 1989.

Burroughs—12   William S. Burroughs. *Naked Lunch: The Restored Text.* Edited by James Grauerholz & Barry Miles. New York: Grove Press, 2001.

Burroughs—13   William S. Burroughs. *Rub Out the Words LP: The Letters of William S. Burroughs 1959–1974.* Edited by James Grauerholz. New York: Harperluxe, 2012.

Burroughs & Ginsberg   William S. Burroughs and Allen Ginsberg. *The Yage Letters Redux.* Edited with an introduction by Oliver Harris. San Francisco: City Lights Books, 2006.

Burroughs & Kerouac   William S. Burroughs and Jack Kerouac. *And the Hippos Were Boiled in Their Tanks.* With an afterword by James W. Grauerholz. New York: Grove Press, 2009.

Burroughs, Jr.   William S. Burroughs, Jr. *Cursed from Birth: The Short, Unhappy Life of William S. Burroughs, Jr.* Edited by David Ohle. New York: Soft Skull Press, 2006.

C. Cassady—1   Carolyn Cassady. *Off the Road: My Years with Cassady, Kerouac, and Ginsberg.* New York: William Morrow, 1990.

C. Cassady—2   Carolyn Cassady. *Heart Beat: My Life with Jack and Neal.* Berkeley: Creative Arts Press, 1976.

Caveney   Graham Caveney. *Screaming with Joy: The Life of Allen Ginsberg.* New York: Broadway Books, 1999.

Charters—1   Ann Charters. *Kerouac: A Biography.* San Francisco: Straight Arrow Books, 1973. Rpt. New York: St. Martin's Press, 1974.

Charters—2   Ann Charters, ed. *Beat Down to Your Soul: What Was the Beat Generation?* Introduction by Ann Charters. New York: Penguin, 2001.

Charters—3   Ann Charters, ed. *The Portable Beat Reader.* New York: Penguin, 1992.

Charters—4   Jack Kerouac. *On the Road.* Introduction by Ann Charters. New York: Penguin, 1991.

Charters—5   Ann Charters, ed. *The Beats: Literary Bohemians in Postwar America.* Detroit: Gale Research Company, 1983, 2 vols.

Cherkovski   Neeli Cherkovski. *Ferlinghetti: A Biography.* New York: Doubleday, 1979.

Ciuraru   Carmela Ciuraru. *Beat Poets.* New York: Alfred A. Knopf, 2002.

Collins & Skover—1   Ronald K. L. Collins & David M. Skover. *The Trials of Lenny Bruce: The Fall and Rise of an American Icon.* Naperville, IL: Source Books, 2002.

Collins & Skover—2   Ronald K. L. Collins & David M. Skover. *Mania: The Story of the Outraged and Outrageous Lives That Launched a Cultural Revolution.* Oak Park, IL: Top Five Books, 2013.

Davidson   Michael Davidson. *The San Francisco Renaissance: Poetics and Community at Mid-century.* New York: Cambridge University Press, 1989.

Day   John Day. *Molech: A God of Human Sacrifice in the Old Testament.* New York: Cambridge University Press, 1989.

de Grazia   Edward de Grazia. *Girls Lean Back Everywhere: The Law of Obscenity and the Assault on Genius.* New York: Random House, 1992.

Ehrlich—1   J. W. Ehrlich. *Howl of the Censor: The Four-Letter Word on Trial.* San Carlos, CA: Nourse Publishing, 1961.

Ehrlich—2   J. W. Ehrlich. *A Life in My Hands: An Autobiography.* New York: G.P. Putnam's Sons, 1965.

Ehrlich—3   J. W. Ehrlich. *The Holy Bible and the Law.* New York: Oceana Publications, 1962.

Ehrlich—4   J. W. Ehrlich. *A Reasonable Doubt.* Cleveland: World Publishing Co., 1964.

Ehrlich—5   J. W. Ehrlich, ed. *Ehrlich's Blackstone.* New York: Capricorn, 1959.

Eisler   Kim Eisler. *A Justice for All.* New York: Simon & Schuster, 1993.

Emerson   Thomas I. Emerson. *The System of Freedom of Expression.* New York: Random House, 1970.

Feldman   Gene Feldman, ed. *The Beat Generation and the Angry Young Men.* New York: Dell, 1960.

Felver—1   Christopher Felver. *Ferlinghetti Portrait.* Salt Lake City, UT: Gibbs-Smith, 1998.

Felver—2   Christopher Felver. *Beat.* San Francisco: Last Gasp Books, 2007.

Felver—3   Christopher Felver. *The Late Great Allen Ginsberg: A Photo Biography.* New York: Thunder Mouth Press, 2002.

Felver—4   *Beat: Photographs/Commentary.* San Francisco: Last Gasp, 2007.

Ferlinghetti—1   Ferlinghetti, Lawrence and Nancy J. Peters. *Literary San Francisco: A Pictorial History from Its Beginnings to the Present Day.* San Francisco: City Lights Books and Harper & Row, 1980.

Ferlinghetti—2   Lawrence Ferlinghetti. *These Are My Rivers: New and Selected Poems: 1955–1993.* New York: New Directions Books, 1994.

Ferlinghetti—3   Lawrence Ferlinghetti. *A Coney Island of the Mind.* New York: New Directions Books, 1958.

Ferlinghetti—4   Lawrence Ferlinghetti, ed. *City Lights Pocket Anthology*. San Francisco: City Lights Books, 1995.

Ferlinghetti—5   Lawrence Ferlinghetti. *The Canticle of Jack Kerouac*. Boise, Idaho: Limberlost Press, 1993.

Ferlinghetti—6   Lawrence Ferlinghetti. *Poetry as Insurgent Art*. New York: New Directions, 2007.

Ferlinghetti—7   Lawrence Ferlinghetti, *San Francisco Poems*. San Francisco: City Lights Foundation, 2001.

Ferlinghetti—8   *Wild Dreams of a New Beginning*. New York: New Directions Books, 1974.

French   Warren French. *Jack Kerouac*. New York: Macmillan, 1986.

Friedman   Leon Friedman, ed. *Obscenity: The Complete Oral Arguments before the Supreme Court in the Major Obscenity Cases*. New York: Chelsea House Publishers, 1970.

George-Warren   Holly George-Warren, ed. *The Rolling Stone Book of the Beats*. New York: Hyperion, 1999.

Ginsberg—1   Allen Ginsberg. *Howl: Original Draft Facsimile, Transcript & Variant Versions, Fully Annotated by Author, with Contemporary Correspondence, Account of First Public Reading, Legal Skirmishes, Precursor Texts & Bibliography*. Edited by Barry Miles. New York: Harper & Row, 1985. Rpt. New York: Harper Perennial, 1995, 2006. *Howl* was originally published in 1956 by City Lights Book, San Francisco, CA; see Ginsberg—9.

Ginsberg—2   Allen Ginsberg. *The Fall*. Unpublished memorandum held at Department of Special Collections, Stanford University Libraries, "Allen Ginsberg" Journals, Box 3.

Ginsberg—3   Allen Ginsberg. *Spontaneous Mind: Selected Interviews, 1958–1996*. Edited by David Carter. Preface by Václav Havel and Introduction by Edmund White. New York: HarperCollins, 2001. Rpt. New York: Perennial, 2002.

Ginsberg—4   Allen Ginsberg. *Deliberate Prose: Selected Essays, 1952–1995*. Edited by Bill Morgan. Foreword by Edward Sanders. New York: HarperCollins, 2000. Rpt. New York: Perennial, 2001.

Ginsberg—5   Allen Ginsberg. *Journals: Early Fifties, Early Sixties*. Edited by Gordon Ball. New York: Grove Press, 1977.

Ginsberg—6   Allen Ginsberg. *The Book of Martyrdom and Artifice: First Journals and Poems, 1937–1952*. Cambridge, MA: Da Capo Press, 2006.

Ginsberg—7   Allen Ginsberg & Neal Cassady. *As Ever: The Collected Correspondence of Allen Ginsberg and Neal Cassady*. Edited by Barry Gifford. Berkeley: Creative Arts, 1977.

Ginsberg—8   Allen Ginsberg. *Photographs*. Altadena, CA: Twelve Trees Press, 1990.

Ginsberg—9 Allen Ginsberg. *HOWL and Other Poems.* San Francisco: City Lights Books, 1956.

Ginsberg—10 Allen Ginsberg. *Kaddish and Other Poems, 1958–1960.* San Francisco: City Lights Books, 1961.

Ginsberg—11 Allen Ginsberg. *The Fall of America: Poems of These States, 1965–1971.* San Francisco: City Lights Books, 1972.

Ginsberg—12 Allen Ginsberg. *Psychiatric Record, New York Psychiatric Institute, June 2, 1949–February 27, 1950.* On file at Allen Ginsberg Archives, New York, New York.

Ginsberg—13 *Poems for the Nation: A Collection of Contemporary Political Poems.* Edited by Allen Ginsberg with Andy Clausen and Eliot Katz. Introduction by Eliot Katz and Bob Rosenthal. New York: Seven Stories Press, 2000.

Ginsberg—14 Allen Ginsberg. *Journals: Mid-Fifties.* Edited by Gordon Ball. New York: HarperCollins, 1995.

Ginsberg—15 Allen Ginsberg. *Snapshot Poetics: A Photographic Memoir of the Beat Era.* San Francisco: Chronicle Books, 1993.

Ginsberg—16 Allen Ginsberg. *Collected Poems: 1947–1957.* New York: HarperCollins, 2006.

Ginsberg—17 Allen Ginsberg. *The Letters of Allen Ginsberg.* Edited by Bill Morgan. Cambridge, MA: Da Capo Press, 2008.

Ginsberg & Ginsberg Allen & Louis Ginsberg. *Family Business: Two Lives in Letters and Poetry.* Edited by Michael Schumacher. London: Bloomsbury Publishing, 2001.

Ginsberg & Snyder Allen Ginsberg & Gary Snyder. *The Selected Letters of Allen Ginsberg and Gary Snyder, 1956–1991.* Edited by Bill Morgan. Berkeley, CA: Counterpoint, 2008.

Hamalian Hamalian, Linda. *A Life of Kenneth Rexroth.* New York: W. W. Norton & Co., 1991.

Hemmer Kurt Hemmer. *Encyclopedia of Beat Literature.* New York: Facts on File, 2006.

Hipkiss Robert A. Hipkiss. *Jack Kerouac: Prophet of the New Romanticism.* Lawrence, KS: Regents Press, 1976.

Hitchens Christopher Hitchens. *Letters to a Young Contrarian.* New York: Basic Books, 2001.

Holmes—1 John Clellon Holmes. *Nothing More to Declare.* New York: E. P. Dutton, 1967.

Holmes—2 John Clellon Holmes. *Go: A Novel.* New York: Thunder's Mouth Press, 1952. Rpt. New York: Thunder's Mouth Press, 1997.

Holmes—3 John Clellon Holmes. *Representative Men: The Biographical Essays.* Fayetteville: University of Arkansas Press, 1988.

Holmes—4	John Clellon Holmes. *Passionate Opinions: The Cultural Essays*. Fayetteville: University of Arkansas Press, 1988.
Holmes—5	John Clellon Holmes. *Displaced Person: The Travel Essays*. Fayetteville: University of Arkansas Press, 1987.
Hrebeniak	Michael Hrebeniak. *Action Writing: Jack Kerouac's Wild Form*. Carbondale, IL: Southern Illinois University Press, 2008.
Hyde	Lewis Hyde, ed. *On the Poetry of Allen Ginsberg*. Ann Arbor, MI: The University of Michigan Press, 1984.
Kerouac—1	Jack Kerouac. *Selected Letters, 1940–1956*. Edited by Ann Charters. New York: Viking, 1995.
Kerouac—2	Jack Kerouac. *Windblown World: The Journals of Jack Kerouac, 1947–1954*. Edited and with an introduction by Douglas Brinkley. New York: Viking, 2004.
Kerouac—3	Jack Kerouac. *The Portable Jack Kerouac*. Edited by Ann Charters. New York: Penguin, 1995.
Kerouac—4	Jack Kerouac. *Vanity of Duluoz*. New York: Coward-McCann, 1968. Rpt. New York: Penguin, 1994.
Kerouac—5	Jack Kerouac. *Selected Letters, 1957–1969*. Edited by Ann Charters. New York: Viking, 1999.
Kerouac—6	Jack Kerouac. *The Dharma Bums*. Introduction by Ann Douglas. New York: Viking Press, 1958. Rpt. New York: Penguin Books, 2006.
Kerouac—7	Jack Kerouac. *Desolation Angels*. Introduction by Seymour Krim. New York: Coward-McCann, 1965.
Kerouac—8	Jack Kerouac. *The Town and the City*. New York: Harcourt, 1950. Rpt. Fort Washington, PA: Harvest Books, 1970.
Kerouac—9	Jack Kerouac. *Visions of Cody*. New York: McGraw-Hill, 1972. Rpt. New York: Penguin, 1993.
Kerouac—10	Jack Kerouac. *Desolation Angels*. Introduction by Joyce Johnson. New York: Riverhead Books, 1995.
Kerouac—11	Jack Kerouac. *On the Road*. Introduction by Ann Charters. New York: Penguin Books, 2003.
Kerouac—12	Jack Kerouac. *Old Angel Midnight*. Edited by Donald Allen with prefaces by Ann Charters & Michael McClure. San Francisco: Grey Fox Press, 2001.
Kerouac—13	Jack Kerouac. *Book of Haikus*. Edited with an introduction by Regina Weinreich. New York: Penguin Poets, 2003.
Kerouac—14	Jack Kerouac. *Big Sur*. Foreword by Aram Saroyan. New York: Penguin Books, 1992.
Kerouac—15	Jack Kerouac. *On the Road: 50th Anniversary Edition*. New York: Viking, 2007.

Kerouac—16   Jack Kerouac. *On the Road: The Original Scroll.* Edited by Howard Cunnell with introductions by Howard Cunnell, Penny Vlagopoulos, George Mouratidis and Joshua Kupetz. New York: Viking, 2007.

Kerouac—17   Jack Kerouac. *Road Novels 1957–1960.* Edited by Douglas Brinkley. New York: Library of America, 2007.

Kerouac—18   Jack Kerouac. *Mexico City Blues.* New York: Grove Press, 1990.

Kerouac—19   Jack Kerouac. *Good Blonde & Others.* Edited by Donald Allen with preface by Robert Creeley. San Francisco: Grey Fox Press, 1993.

J. H. Kerouac   Joan Haverty Kerouac. *Nobody's Wife: The Smart Aleck and the King of Beats.* Introduction by Jan Kerouac. Foreword by Ann Charters. Berkeley, CA: Creative Art Books, 1995.

Kramer   Jane Kramer. *Allen Ginsberg in America.* New York: Random House, 1969. Rpt. with a new introduction by the author. New York: Fromm International, 1997.

Krim   Seymour Krim. *The Beats.* Greenwich, CT: Fawcett Publications, 1960.

Kurlansky   Mark Kurlansky. *1968: The Year That Rocked the World.* New York: Ballantine Books, 2004.

Leland   John Leland. *Why the Beats Matter: The Lessons of* On the Road *(They're not what you think).* New York: Viking Press, 2007.

Maher—1   Paul Maher, Jr. *Kerouac: The Definitive Biography.* Foreword by David Amran. Lanham, MD: Taylor Trade Publishing, 2004.

Maher—2   Paul Maher, Jr., ed. *Empty Phantoms: Interviews and Encounters with Jack Kerouac.* New York: Thunder Mouth Press, 2005.

Maher—3   Paul Maher, Jr. *Kerouac: His Life and Work: Revised and Updated.* Foreword by David Amran. Lanham, MD: Taylor Trade Publishing, 2007.

Maher—4   Paul Maher, Jr. *Jack Kerouac's American Journey: The Real-Life Odyssey of* On the Road. Berkeley, CA: Thunder's Mouth Press, 2007.

McClure—1   Michael McClure. *Passage.* Big Sur, CA: Jonathan Williams, 1956.

McClure—2   Michael McClure. *Huge Dreams: San Francisco and Beat Poems.* New York: Penguin Books, 1999.

McClure—3   Michael McClure. *Scratching the Beat Surface: Essays on New Vision from Blake to Kerouac.* New York: Penguin Books, 1994.

McClure—4   Michael McClure. *Rebel Lions.* New York: New Directions, 1991.

McNally   Dennis McNally. *Desolate Angel: Jack Kerouac, the Beat Generation, and America.* New York: Random House, 1979. Rpt. New York: McGraw-Hill, 1980.

Meltzer　David Meltzer, ed. *San Francisco Beat: Talking with the Poets.* San Francisco: City Lights Books, 2001.

Merrill　Thomas F. Merrill. *Allen Ginsberg.* New York: Twayne Publishers, 1969.

Miles—1　Barry Miles. *Ginsberg: A Biography.* New York: Simon & Schuster, 1989. Rpt. revised edition. London: Virgin Books, 2001.

Miles—2　Barry Miles. *The Beat Hotel: Ginsberg, Burroughs, and Corso in Paris, 1957–1963.* New York: Grove Press, 2000.

Miles—3　Barry Miles, ed. *The Beat Collection.* London: Virgin Books, 2005.

Miles—4　Barry Miles. *William Burroughs, El Hombre Invisible: A Portrait.* New York: Hyperion, 1993.

Morgan—1　Bill Morgan. *I Celebrate Myself: The Somewhat Private Life of Allen Ginsberg.* New York: Viking Press, 2006.

Morgan—2　Bill Morgan. *The Beat Generation in New York: A Walking Tour of Jack Kerouac's City.* San Francisco: City Lights Books, 1997.

Morgan—3　Bill Morgan. *The Beat Generation in San Francisco: A Walking Tour of Jack Kerouac's City.* San Francisco: City Lights Books, 2003.

Morgan—4　Bill Morgan. *The Response to Allen Ginsberg, 1926–1994: A Bibliography of Secondary Sources.* Westport, CT: Greenwood Press, 1996.

Morgan—5　Bill Morgan. *Beat Atlas: A State by State Guide to the Beat Generation in America.* San Francisco: City Lights Books, 2011.

Morgan—6　Bill Morgan. *The Typewriter Is Holy: The Complete, Uncensored History of the Beat Generation.* Counterpoint, 2011.

Morgan—7　Bill Morgan, ed., *I Greet You at the Beginning of a Great Career: the Selected Correspondence of Lawrence Ferlinghetti and Allen Ginsberg, 1955–1997.* San Francisco: City Lights Books, 2015.

Morgan & Peters　Bill Morgan & Nancy Peters, eds. *Howl on Trial: The Battle for Free Expression.* San Francisco: City Lights Books, 2006.

T. Morgan　Ted Morgan. *Literary Outlaw: The Life & Times of William S. Burroughs.* New York: Henry Holt, 1998.

Nicosia　Gerald Nicosia. *Memory Babe: A Critical Biography of Jack Kerouac.* New York: Grove Press, 1983.

Nicosia & Santos　Gerald Nicosia & Anne Marie Santos. *One and Only: The Untold Story of* On the Road. Berkley, CA: Viva Editions, 2011.

Noble & Averbuch　John Wesley Noble & Bernard Averbuch. *Never Plead Guilty: The Story of Jake Ehrlich.* New York: Farrar, Straus & Cudahy, 1955.

Parkinson　Thomas Parkinson, ed. *A Casebook on the Beat.* New York: Thomas Y. Crowell, 1961.

Patchen   Kenneth Patchen. *Poems of Humor and Protest*. San Francisco: City Lights Books, 1955.

Plimpton   George Plimpton, ed. *Beat Writers at Work: The Paris Review*. New York: The Modern Library, 1999.

Raskin   Jonah Raskin. *American Scream: Allen Ginsberg's* Howl *and the Making of the Beat Generation*. Berkeley: University of California Press, 2005.

Reynolds   David S. Reynolds. *Walt Whitman's America: A Cultural Biography*. New York: Knopf, 1995.

Sanders—1   Ed Sanders. *The Poetry and Life of Allen Ginsberg*. New York: Scribner, 2002.

Sanders—2   Ed Sanders. *The Tales of Beatnik Glory*. New York: Carol Publishing, 1990.

Sandison & Vikers   David Sandison & Graham Vikers. *Neal Cassady: The Fast Life of a Beat Hero*. Chicago: Chicago Review Press, 2006.

Schumacher   Michael Schumacher. *Dharma Lion: A Critical Biography of Allen Ginsberg*. New York: St. Martin's Press, 1992.

Shinder   Jason Shinder, ed. *The Poem That Changed America: "Howl" Fifty Years Later*. New York: Farrar, Straus and Giroux, 2006.

Silesky   Barry Silesky. *Ferlinghetti: The Artist in His Time*. New York: Warner Books, 1990.

Smith   Larry Smith. *Lawrence Ferlinghetti: Poet-at-Large*. Southern Illinois University Press, 1983.

Solomon—1   Carl Solomon. *Mishaps, Perhaps*. Edited by Mary Beach. San Francisco, CA: City Lights Books, 1966.

Solomon—2   Carl Solomon. *Emergency Messages: An Autobiographical Miscellany*. Edited and with a foreword by John Tytell. New York: Paragon House, 1989.

Sotheby's—Ginsberg   Sotheby's. *Allen Ginsberg and Friends, including property from the Estates of Allen Ginsberg, Jack Kerouac and William S. Burroughs*. October 7 1999. New York Auction Catalogue. Introductory Note by Peter Hale, foreword by Bill Morgan.

Sova   Dawn B. Sova. *Banned Books: Literature Suppressed on Social Grounds*. New York: Facts On File, 1988.

Theado—1   Matt Theado, ed. *The Beats: A Literary Reference*. New York: Carroll & Graf, 2001.

Theado—2   Matt Theado. *Understanding Jack Kerouac*. Columbia: University of South Carolina Press, 2000.

Tytell—1   John Tytell. *Naked Angels: Kerouac, Ginsberg, Burroughs*. New York: Grove Press, 1976. Rpt. Chicago: Ivan R. Dee, 1991.

Tytell—2   John Tytell. *Paradise Outlaws: Remembering the Beats*. New York: William Morrow & Company, 1999.

Waldman	Anne Waldman, ed. *The Beat Book: Writings from the Beat Generation.* Foreword by Allen Ginsberg. Boston: Shambhala Publications, 2007.
Watson	Steve Watson. *The Birth of the Beat Generation: Visionaries, Rebels, and Hipsters, 1944–1960.* Afterword by Robert Creeley. New York: Pantheon Books, 1998.
Whitman	Walt Whitman. *Leaves of Grass.* Introduction by Justin Kaplan. New York: Bantam Classics, 2004.
Zott	Zott, Lynn M. *The Beat Generation: A Critical Companion.* 3 vols., foreword by Anne Waldman. Detroit: Thompson/Gale, 2003.

LIBRARY COLLECTIONS

Burroughs—Papers	Ohio State University.
Ferlinghetti—Papers	University of California (Berkeley), University of Connecticut, Columbia University, Southern Methodist University, Washington University (St. Louis).
Ginsberg—Papers	Stanford University and University of North Carolina.
Holmes—Papers	Kent State University.
Kerouac—Papers	University of Massachusetts (Lowell) and New York Public Library.
T. Morgan—Papers	Arizona State University.

LEGAL OPINIONS AND RELATED DOCUMENTS

Alberts v. California, 354 U.S. 476 (1957).
Memoirs v. Massachusetts, 383 U.S. 413 (1966).
Roth v. United States, 354 U.S. 476 (1957).
Speiser v. Randall, 357 U.S. 513 (1958).
Torcaso v. Watkins, 367 U.S. 488 (1961).
Big Table v. Schroeder, 186 F. Supp. 254 (N.D. IL, 1960).
In the Matter of the Complaint that BIG TABLE Magazine is nonmailable under 18 U.S. Code 1461 (Post Office Department, Docket No. 1/150) (12 August 1959).
Attorney General v. A Book Named Naked Lunch, 351 Mass. 298 (1959).
Attorney General v. A Book Named Tropic of Cancer, 345 Mass. 11 (1958).
People v. Ferlinghetti, unpublished opinion, October 3, 1957. Printed in Ehrlich—1 (without citations).
Speiser v. Randall, 48 Cal. 2d 903, 311 P.2d 546 (Cal. 1958).
Attorney General Edward W. Brooke v. A Book Named Naked Lunch, Massachusetts Superior Court, docket # 83001, January 12–13, 1965 (trial transcript).

SCHOLARLY ARTICLES, MONOGRAPHS, DISSERTATIONS, REPORTS, AND PROCEEDINGS

Benas, Betram B. "The Holy Bible and the Law by J. W. Ehrlich." 26 *Modern Law Review* 6 (November, 1963), pp. 731–733.

Caplan, Gerald M. "A Reasonable Doubt by Jacob W. Ehrlich." 73 *Yale Law Journal* 8 (July 1964), pp. 1508–1512.

Charters, Ann. "The Beats, Literary Bohemians in Postwar America." In *Dictionary of Literary Biography*, vol. 16. Detroit: Gale, 1983.

Hunt, Tim. *Off the Road: The Literary Maturation of Jack Kerouac.* Cornell University, PhD Thesis, 1975.

Report *of the Special Committee of the Student Government Organization in re: The Chicago Review, University of Chicago*, 1959.

Sigler, S. A. "Customs Censorship." 15 *Cleveland Law Review* (January 1966), p. 63.

SELECT MAGAZINE, NEWSPAPER, AND INTERNET ARTICLES

"300 Police Use Tear Gas to Breach Young Militant's Barricade in Chicago." *New York Times*, 27 August 1968, p. 29.

"A Howl of Protest in San Francisco." *New Republic*, 16 September 1957, p. 26.

"A Muse Unplugged." *New York Times*, 8 October 2007, sec. A, p. 22.

Anspacher, Carolyn. " 'Battle of Books Is On: 'Howl' Trial Starts Big Crowd." *San Francisco Chronicle*, 17 August 1957, p. 1.

———. " 'Obscene' Book Trial: Dismissal for 'Howl' Clerk Indicated." *San Francisco Chronicle*, 23 August 1957, p. 4.

"At 99, the Poet Lawrence Ferlinghetti Has a New Novel." *New York Times*, 6 June 2018.

Barber, David. "The Legend of 'Howl'." *Boston Globe*, 30 April 2006, sec. E, p. 2.

Bess, Donovan. "Poetic Justice: Court Rules on Biblical Essays—1 Wins, 1 Loses." *San Francisco Chronicle*, 7 August 1957, p. 1.

"Big Day for Bards at Bay: San Francisco Muse Thrives in Face of Trial over Poems." *Life*, 9 September 1957, p. 105.

Bohm, Dan. "The Murals of Rincon Center in San Francisco," *Collectors Weekly*, 4 August 2010, www.collectorsweekly.com/articles/the-murals-of-rincon-center-in-san-francisco/.

"Bookmen Ask Mayor to Ban Cop Censors." *San Francisco Chronicle*, 16 August 1957, p. 1.

"Bookshop Owner Surrenders." *San Francisco Chronicle*, 7 June 1957, p. 2.

Brame, Gloria G. "An Interview with Poet Allen Ginsberg." *Eclectic Literary Forum*, Summer, 1996.

Brechin, Gray. "Trial of the Rincon Annex Murals." *FoundSF.org*, www.foundsf.org/index .php?title = Trial_of_the_Rincon_Annex_Murals.

Brinkley, Douglas. "In the Kerouac Archive." *The Atlantic Monthly*, November 1998, pp. 49–76.

Bruckner, D. J. R. "Chicago Police Use Tear Gas to Rout Thousands." *Los Angeles Times*, 28 August 1968, p. 1.

"Buyers Howl for Ginsberg Poetry and Other Stuff He Loved." *The Star-Ledger*, 8 October 1999, p. 35.

Ciardi, John. "The Book Burners and Sweet Sixteen." *Saturday Review*, 27 July 1959, p. 22.

———. "Writers as Readers of Poetry." *Saturday Review*, 23 November 1957, p. 33.

Clarke, Terence. "'Howl,' Your Morals, and the FCC." *Blogcritics Culture*, 6 October 2007.

Cohen, Noam S. "Lawrence Speiser, 68, a Civil Liberties Lawyer," *New York Times*, September 12, 1991, p. 38.

Cohen, Patricia. "'Howl' in an Era That Fears Indecency." *New York Times*, 4 October 2007.

Collier, Peter. "Lawrence Ferlinghetti: Doing His Own Thing." *New York Times Book Review*, 21 July 1968, p. 4.

"Cops Don't Allow No Renaissance Here." *San Francisco News*, 4 August 1957, p. 17.

"Court Rules on Biblical Essays—1 Wins, 1 Loses." *San Francisco Chronicle*, 7 August 1957, p. 1.

"Creative Writing in Horn's Court." *San Francisco Chronicle*, 8 August 1957, p. 20.

Dickey, James. "From Babel to Byzantium." *Sewanee Review*, 65: July–September 1957, p. 510.

Douglas, Ann. "On the Road Again." *New York Times Book Review*, 9 April 1995, p. 1.

Dreisinger, Baz. "'Howl,' Ginsberg's Time Bomb, Still Setting Off New Explosions." *New York Observer*, 10 April 2006.

Eberhart, Richard. "West Coast Rhythms." *New York Times Book Review*, 2 September 1956.

Eckman, Frederick. "Neither Tame nor Fleecy." *Poetry*, September 1957, p. 387.

Edidin, Peter. "The Sound of 'Howl.'" *New York Times*, 16 February 2008, sec. B, p. 10.

Ellison, Michael. "The Beat Goes on at Ginsberg Auction." *The Guardian* (London), 8 October 1999, p. 19.

Ferlinghetti, Lawrence. "Horn on 'Howl'." *Evergreen Review* 2: 1957, p. 145.

———. "Love & War." *Minnesota Street Project*, 20 August 2016.

———. "To the Oracle at Delphi." *The Nation*, 20 September 2001.

Fink, John. "Who Is Jack Kerouac?" *Chicago Tribune*, 28 September 1968, p. 13.

Fox, Sylvan. "300 Police Use Tear Gas to Breach Young Militants Barricade in Chicago Park." *New York Times*, 27 August 1968, p. 29.

Garofoli, Joe. "'Howl' Too Hot to Hear: 50 Years after Poem Ruled Not Obscene, Radio Fears to Air It." *San Francisco Chronicle*, 3 October 2007.

"Ginsberg Enters Hall After Startling Police." *New York Times*, 29 August 1968, p. 23.

"Ginsberg's Belongings Auctioned Off at Sotheby's: Poet's Lover, Nephews, Nieces Likely to Get Money." *Globe and Mail* (Toronto, Canada), 8 October 1999, sec. A, p. 19.

Hall, Molly. "In the Spirit of Kerouac; School Is Born from the Beat Generation." *Chicago Tribune*, 4 August 1994, p. 8.

Hampton, Wilborn. "Lucien Carr, a Founder and a Muse of the Beat Generation, Dies at 79." *New York Times*, 30 January 2005, p. 35.

———. "Allen Ginsberg, Master Poet of Beat Generation, Dies at 70." *New York Times*, 6 April 1997.

Held, Jr., John. "In Conversation: Lawrence Ferlinghetti with John Held, Jr." SFAQ, 22 December 2014, sfaq.us/2014/12/in-conversation-lawrence-ferlinghetti-with-john-held-jr/.

Henry III, William A. "In New York, *Howl* Becomes a Hoot." *New York Times*, 7 December 1981, p. 8.

Hogan, William. "Between the Lines." *San Francisco Chronicle*, 19 May 1957, p. 34.

Hollander, John. "Poetry Chronicle." *Partisan Review*, 24: Spring 1957, p. 298.

Hollenbach, Lisa. "Broadcasting *Howl*." *M/M*, 12 July 2018.

Holmes, John Clellon. "This Is the Beat Generation," *New York Times Magazine*, 16 November 1952, p. 10.

———. "The Philosophy of the Beat Generation." *Esquire*, February 1958, p. 35.

Honan, William H. "Ferlinghetti Reflects on Glow of City Lights." *New York Times*, 29 July 1993.

"'Howl' Decision Landmark of Law." *San Francisco Chronicle*, 7 October 1957, p. 18.

"Jake Ehrlich, Criminal Lawyer Who Won Murder Cases, Dies." *New York Times*, 25 December 1971, p. 20.

"Jake Ehrlich Sr. Quotes." www.neverpleadguilty.com.

Kellogg, Carolyn. "Lawrence Ferlinghetti Declines Hungarian Award over Human Rights." *Los Angeles Times*, 11 October 2012.

King, Lydia Hailman. "'Howl' Obscenity Prosecution Still Echoes 50 Years Later." First Amendment Center, at www.firstamendmentcenter.org/news.aspx?id = 19132.

Landauer, Susan and Carl. "Open Eye, Open Palette: The Art of Lawrence Ferlinghetti." *Confrontation*, 117: 2015, p. 93.

Latham, Aaron. "The Columbia Murder that Gave Birth to the Beats." *New York Magazine*, 19 April 1976, p. 41.

———. "The Lives They Lived: Allen Ginsberg; Birth of a Beatnik." *New York Times*, 4 January 1998.

Lauderman, Connie. "The Broad Reach of the Beats: Generations Later, the Literary Rebels Still Have a Cause." *Chicago Tribune*, 24 October 1999, sec. C, p. 5.

Lelyveld, Joseph. "Jack Kerouac, Novelist, Dead; Father of the Beat Generation." *New York Times*, 22 October 1969.

Lippman, Laura. "Ginsberg 'Howls' Again as Lawyers Battle FCC Ruling." *Baltimore Sun*, 20 October 1994.

Lukas, J. Anthony. "Police Battle Demonstrators in Streets." *New York Times*, 29 August 1968, p. 1.

Lurvey, Ira. "Beatniks Fight for Banned Verse." *Daily Defender*, 28 January 1959, sec. A, p. 4.

"Making a Clown of San Francisco." *San Francisco Chronicle*, 6 June 1957, p. 22.

Margolick, David. "An Unlikely Home for Ginsberg's Archive." *New York Times*, 20 September 1994, sect. C, p. 15.

McDougal, Dennis. "FCC Firm on Decency Code; 'Howl' Muffled." *Los Angeles Times*, 8 January 1988, pt. 6, p. 1.

———. "Obscenity Issue Still Unresolved." *Los Angeles Times*, 4 January 1988, pt. 6, p. 1.

Melinkoff, Abe. "Morning Report: Iron Curtain on the Embarcadero." *San Francisco Chronicle*, 28 March 1957.

Millstein, Gilbert. "Books of the Times." *New York Times*, 5 September 1957, p. 27.

Musetto, V.A. "'Ferlinghetti: A Rebirth of Wonder' Review." *New York Post*, 8 February 2013.

"New Test for Obscenity." *The Nation*, 9 November 1957, p. 314.

Older, Julia. "Poetry's Eternal Graffiti: Late-Night Conversations with Lawrence Ferlinghetti." *Poet's & Writers*, March–April, 2007, pp. 38–46.

Onishi, Norimitsu. "Free Spirits Flock to Park to Hear Ginsberg Poetry." *New York Times*, 29 September 1997.

Onwuemezi, Natasha. "Faber Signs Lawrence Ferlinghetti's 'Last Word.'" *The Bookseller*, 18 July 2018.

Paton, Fiona. "Banned Beats." lib.newpaltz.edu/events/bannedbooks.html.

Patterson, Robert. "'Jake'—One of Famed Line of Men Who Symbolized SF." *San Francisco Examiner*, 24 December 1971.

Perlman, David. "How Captain Hanrahan Made 'Howl' a Best-Seller." *The Reporter*, 12 December 1957, pp. 37–39.

———. "'Howl' Not Obscene, Judge Rules." *San Francisco Chronicle*, 4 October 1957, p. 1.

Podhoretz, Norman. "A Howl of Protest in San Francisco." *New Republic*, 16 September 1957, p. 26.

"Post Office Morals." *The Nation*, 30 May 1959, p. 486.

Raskin, Jonah. "Still Howling after 50 Years." *Columbia Spectator*, 21 April 2006.

Rexroth, Kenneth. "Discordant and Cool." *New York Times Book Review*. 29 November 1959, p. 14.

———. "It's an Anywhere Road for Anybody Anyhow." *San Francisco Chronicle*, 1 September 1957, p. 18.

———. "San Francisco Letter." *Evergreen Review*. Summer, 1957.

———. "San Francisco's Mature Bohemians." *The Nation*, 23 February 1957, p. 159.

———. "The Voice of the Beat Generation Has Some Square Delusions." *San Francisco Chronicle* (This World Magazine), 16 February 1958, p. 23.

Rosen, Jonathan. "Return to Paradise." *The New Yorker*, 2 June 2008.

Rosenthal, M. L. "Poet of the New Violence." *The Nation*, 23 February 1957, p. 162.

Rothschild, Matthew. "Allen Ginsberg: 'I'm Banned from the Main Marketplace of Ideas in My Own Country.'" *The Progressive*, August 1994.

Rumaker, Michael. "Allen Ginsberg's *Howl*." *Black Mountain Review* 7: Fall 1957.

Shaboy, Benny. Studio Notes, No. 26, August–October 1999. www.studionotes.org/26/ferlinghetti.html.

Shattuck, Kathryn. "Sotheby's to Auction Ginsbergiana." *New York Times*, 7 October 1999, sec. E, p. 3.

Smith, Dinitia. "Chanting in Homage to Allen Ginsberg." *New York Times*, 16 May 1998.

———. "How Allen Ginsberg Thinks His Thoughts." *New York Times*, 8 October 1996.

Smith, J. Y. "Lawrence Speiser Dies: Championed Civil Rights." *Washington Post*, 31 August 1991.

Suiter, John. "When the Beats Came Back." *Reed Magazine*, Winter 2008, p. 20.

"They'll 'Howl' over Ginsberg Sale." *New York Post*, 5 October 1999, p. 9.

"Thou Shalt Not Miss." *San Francisco Chronicle*, 8 August 1957, p. 20 (political cartoon).

Trott, William C. "Poet Howls about Censorship." *United Press International*, 7 January 1988.

Usborne, David. "Sotheby's Sells Off Allen Ginsberg Estate." *Hamilton Spectator* (Ontario, Canada), 8 October 1999, sec. F, p. 11.

"U.S. Court to Rule on State Loyalty Oath." *Los Angeles Times*, 26 November 1957, p. 14.

von Hoffman, Nicholas. "Yippies Unveil 'Politics of Ecstasy.'" *Washington Post*, 20 March 1968, sec. A, p. 3.

Well, Martin. "Jake Ehrlich, Criminal Lawyer, Dies." *The Washington Post*, 25 December 1971.

Will, George W. "Along Via Ferlinghetti, the Beat Goes On." *Washington Post*, 14 June 2002, sect. A, p. 31.

Williamson, Eric Miles. "He Saw the Best Minds of His Generation." *Washington Post Book World*, 16 April 2006, p. 4.

Yarrow, Andrew L. "Allen Ginsberg's 'Howl' in a New Controversy." *New York Times*, 6 January 1988, sec. C, p. 22.

Young, Christopher. "Beat This: Lawrence Ferlinghetti Refuses Hungarian Cash Award." *Daily News*, 12 October 2012.

INTERVIEWS

Al Bendich Interview. Berkeley, CA: Fantasy Studios. 27 August 2001.
Lawrence Ferlinghetti Interview. San Francisco: City Lights Bookstore. 27 July 2001.

RECORDS, CDs, FILMS, AND DVD DOCUMENTARIES

Aronson, Jerry. *The Life and Times of Allen Ginsberg*. New York: New York Video, 2006.
Burroughs, William. *Call Me Burroughs*. Santa Monica, CA: Rhino /World Beat, 1995.
Burroughs, William & Kurt Cobain. *The 'Priest' They Called Him*. Portland. OR: Tim Kerr Records, 1993.
Ginsberg, Allen. *Holy Soul Jelly Roll: Poems and Songs, 1949–1993*. Los Angeles: Rhino, 1994.
Howls, Raps & Roars: Recordings from the San Francisco Poetry Renaissance. Berkeley, CA: Fantasy Studios, 1993 (CD).
Kerouac, Jack. *The Jack Kerouac Collection*. Santa Monica, CA: Rhino/World Beat, 1993.
On the Road with Jack Kerouac: King of the Beats. Active Home Video, 1990 (VHS).
The Allen Ginsberg Audio Collection. Caedmon, HarperCollins, 2006.
The Beat Generation. Santa Monica, CA: Rhino Records, 1992 (CD).
The Best of William Burroughs from Giorno Poetry Systems. New York: Mercury, 1998 (4 CD box).
The Life and Times of Allen Ginsberg: A Film by Jerry Aronson. New York: New Yorker Video, 2007 (DVD).
The Source. Written, directed and produced by Chuck Workman. New York: Fox Lorber, 2000 (VHS).
What Happened to Kerouac? New York: Shout! 1986 (DVD).

Notes

PROLOGUE

- "Self-made man": Ferlinghetti—3 at 64.
- Name changes: Silesky at 14, 58.
- Footnote re Sterling Lord: Morgan—7 at 48, 224.
- Footnote re Lord representing Ferlinghetti for his 2019 novel, *Alexandra Alter*: "At 99, the Poet Lawrence Ferlinghetti Has a New Novel," *New York Times*, 6 June 2018.
- Footnote re Lord representing Ferlinghetti on his *Love in the Days of Rage* novel: *ibid*.
- *Little Boy*: Natasha Onwuemezi, "Faber Signs Lawrence Ferlinghetti's 'Last Word,'" *The Bookseller*, 18 July 2018.
- Impressionistic cues from Thomas Wolfe: Silesky at 13.

CHAPTER 1

- Dickensian: Silesky at 1–2.
- "Corporate monoculture": Hitchens at 16; Ferlinghetti—7 at 26.
- Tumultuous youth: "Lawrence Ferlinghetti," *The Poetry Foundation*, www.poetry foundation.org/poets/lawrence-ferlinghetti.
- Most of his formative years: Silesky at 127.
- Footnote re communication by telegrams: *Ibid* at 38, 66.
- "he was a quiet man": *Ibid.* at 43.

CHAPTER 2

- City Lights Books: Cherkovski at 80–82; Miles—1 at 180–181; Morgan—3 at 1 ("head, heart, and undersoul"), 2–4, 6–7; Schumacher at 221; Silesky at 56–57.

- Common man: Silesky at 14, 17, 20–23.
- Intellectual side: *Ibid.* at 2–15, 21–22, 24–25, 34, 45–48, 50–51, 55–56.
- Artistic side: Benny Shaboy, Studio Notes, No. 26, August–October 1999, www.studionotes.org/26/ferlinghetti.html; Susan and Carl Landauer, "Open Eye, Open Palette: The Art of Lawrence Ferlinghetti," *Confrontation*, 117: 2015, p. 93; Silesky at 35, 48, 53–55.
- Footnote re poems and painting: Lawrence Ferlinghetti, "Love & War," *Minnesota Street Project*, 20 August 2016.
- Political side: Miles—1 at 181.
- Rincon Annex Post Office murals: Dan Bohm, "The Murals of Rincon Center in San Francisco," *Collectors Weekly*, 4 August 2010, at www.collectorsweekly.com/articles/the-murals-of-rincon-center-in-san-francisco/; Gray Brechin, "Trial of the Rincon Annex Murals," *FoundSF.org*, at www.foundsf.org/index.php?title = Trial_of _the_Rincon_Annex_Murals; Silesky at 59–60.
- Lawrence Ferlinghetti: Cherkovski at 45–46, 49–60, 67, 77–79, 82; Julia Older, "Poetry's Eternal Graffiti: Late-Night Conversations with Lawrence Ferlinghetti," *Poets & Writers*, March–April 2007, pp. 38, 40; Schumacher at 221, 223; Silesky at 1–2, 25–29, 34–35, 42–45, 47, 57–58, 66, 92.
- "I was the last of the Bohemian generation": Julia Older, "Poetry's Eternal Graffiti: Late-Night Conversations with Lawrence Ferlinghetti," *Poets & Writers*, March–April 2007, p. 40. See also Silesky at 82–83.
- John Held, Jr., "In Conversation: Lawrence Ferlinghetti with John Held, Jr.," *SFAQ* , 22 December 2014, at faq.us/2014/12/in-conversation-lawrence-ferlinghetti -with-john-held-jr/.
- Business side: Silesky at 56–58; William H. Honan, "Ferlinghetti Reflects on Glow of City Lights," *New York Times,* 29 July 1993.
- "It seemed like the logical thing to do": Silesky at 57.

CHAPTER 3

- Epigraph quote: Allen Ginsberg, "Notes Written on Finally Recording *Howl*," in Ginsberg—4 at 229 ("There was something wonderfully subversive").
- "I am no closer": Schumacher at 200 (quoting Allen Ginsberg's journal entry of 10 June 1955).
- "Money problems of reality": Schumacher at 199 (quoting Allen Ginsberg).
- Boyfriend problems: Miles—1 at 180; Schumacher at 199.
- Girlfriend problems: Miles—1 at 181–182 (quoting Sheila Williams).
- Vollmer dream: Ginsberg—14 at 136; Watson at 180. See also Ginsberg's poem titled "Dream Record: June 8, 1955" in Allen Ginsberg—16 at 125.
- Writer's block: Schumacher at 197, 705 note 197.
- "Rules for Spontaneous Prose": Morgan—3 at 25. When published, the "Rules" were given the formal title of "Essentials of Spontaneous Prose" in Charters—3 at 484–485.
- "trouble deaf heaven": Schumacher at 199 (letter of Allen Ginsberg to Jack Kerouac, 5 June 1955).

- Appearance of 1010 Montgomery Street room: Ginsberg—14 at 147 (photograph of 1010 Montgomery Street bedroom/study taken in August of 1955); Miles—1 at 180; Morgan—3 at 25.
- Peter in New York: Morgan—1 at 202–203.
- "I saw the best minds": Ginsberg—1 at 13.
- Footnote re journal entry: Ginsberg—14 at 159.
- "*come* from within, out": "Essentials of Spontaneous Prose" in Charters—3 at 485.
- Strophes from first typewritten draft: Ginsberg—1 at 12, 14, 16, 20.
- Typing into darkness: Raskin at 163.
- "bardic breath": Allen Ginsberg, "Notes Written on Finally Recording *Howl*," in Ginsberg—4 at 229.
- Seven pages: Ginsberg—1 at 12–25.
- Footnote re Kerouac and Burroughs: Miles—1 at 186; Schumacher at 202.
- "I'd thought the poem": Allen Ginsberg, "Reintroduction to Carl Solomon," in Ginsberg—1 at 111.
- "Carl Solomon!": Ginsberg—1 at 89; Miles—1 at 187; Schumacher at 202–203.
- "Your HOWL FOR CARL SOLOMON": Kerouac—1 at 508 (letter of Jack Kerouac to Allen Ginsberg, 19 August 1955).
- "I realize how right you are": Morgan & Peters at 33 (letter of Allen Ginsberg to Jack Kerouac, 25 August 1955). See also Miles—1 at 188; Schumacher at 203–204.
- "saw him as another": Lawrence Ferlinghetti, "Introduction: 'Howl' at the Frontiers," in Morgan & Peters at xii.
- Ferlinghetti & Ginsberg relationship: Cherkovski at 97; Schumacher at 204, 224; Silesky at 62.
- "the most significant single long poem": "Between the Lines," *San Francisco Chronicle*, 19 May 1957, in Morgan & Peters at 107 (publishing statement of Lawrence Ferlinghetti in defense of *Howl*).
- "City Lights Bookstore here": Miles—1 at 190 (quoting Allen Ginsberg).
- Lafcadio Orlovsky: Morgan—1 at 204; Schumacher at 204–205.
- 1624 Milvia Street: Ginsberg—14 at 160 (journal entry of 1 September 1955); Raskin at 141; Schumacher at 205.
- "$35 per mo.": Ginsberg—17 at 119–120, Morgan & Peters at 31 (letter of Allen Ginsberg to Eugene Brooks, 16 August 1955). See also Ginsberg—17 at 123 (letter of Allen Ginsberg to John Allen Ryan, mid-September 1955).

CHAPTER 4

- Kerouac & crucifixion: Douglas Brinkley, "In the Kerouac Archive," *Atlantic Monthly*, November 1998, at 52.
- Columbia college days: Maher—3 at 78.
- Kerouac on Bach: See Jack Kerouac, "On the Origins of a Generation," in Kerouac—19 at 56.
- Listening to *St. Matthew Passion*: Miles—1 at 191; Schumacher at 213.
- Kerouac images: Amburn at 220–221; McNally at 201–202; Nicosia at 490–491; C. Cassady—1 at 262–267 ("We never really slept, so afraid were we to miss a minute of being together; we only dozed now and then, clinging to each other's

warmth and our hopeless dreams. A little before dawn [Jack] took his sleeping bag and went outside so the children wouldn't find him in my bed.'"). Amburn's and Nicosia's accounts do not mention any visit to Neal and Carolyn Cassady in advance of arriving in San Francisco.

- Michael McClure conversation re 6 Gallery: Amburn at 224; Miles—1 at 190–191; Schumacher at 211–212; Silesky at 63.
- Kerouac declines to read: Miles—1 at 192; Morgan—1 at 297; Schumacher at 213.
- Gary Snyder: Miles—1 at 190–191; Raskin at 1–2; Schumacher at 212–213; Silesky at 63–64.
- Philip Whalen: Miles—1 at 191–192; Schumacher at 214; Silesky at 64.
- Kerouac's description of Snyder: Kerouac—6 at 7. For consistent characterizations, see also Amburn at 223; Allen Ginsberg, "The Six Gallery Reading," in Ginsberg—4 at 241.
- Kerouac's description of Whalen: Kerouac—6 at 7. For consistent characterizations, see also Amburn at 223–224; Allen Ginsberg, "The Six Gallery Reading," in Ginsberg—4 at 240.
- Kerouac's description of Rexroth: Kerouac—6 at 7, 11. For consistent characterization, see Nicosia at 492.
- *Pure Land Sutra* scenario: Nicosia at 491.
- Philip Lamantia: Nicosia at 366. See also Miles—1 at 192; Raskin at 2; Silesky at 52, 64.
- Kerouac's description of Lamantia: Kerouac—6 at 7.
- Postcard: Liner Notes to CD Collection, *Howls, Raps & Roars: Recordings from the San Francisco Poetry Renaissance* (Berkeley, CA: Fantasy Studios, 1993), at 13; Theado at 63.
- Epigraph quote: Mikal Gilmore, "Allen Ginsberg: 1926–1997," in George-Warren at 235.
- 6 Gallery event: Our narrative sketches derive from Amburn at 225–228; Frank Bidart, "A Cross in the Void," in Shinder at 246–254; Cherkovski at 99; Charters—1 at 240–241; Laszlo Géfin, "Ellipsis: The Ideograms of Ginsberg," in Hyde at 272–287; Allen Ginsberg, "Reading at the Six Gallery, October 7, 1955," in Ginsberg—1 at 165–166; Kerouac—1 at 524 (letter of Jack Kerouac to John Clellon Holmes, 12 October 1955); Kerouac—6 at 9–11; Michael McClure, *Scratching the Beat Surface*, reprinted in Ginsberg—1 at 168; McNally at 203–204; Miles—1 at 192–194; Morgan—1 at 208–209; Morgan—3 at 109–110; Nicosia at 492–493; "Peter Orlovsky & Allen Ginsberg Interview, 1975," reprinted in Ginsberg—1 at 167; Raskin at 17–18; Michael Rumaker, "Allen Ginsberg's 'Howl'," in Hyde at 36–40; Sandison & Vickers at 241–242; Schumacher at 214–217; Silesky at 64–65; Theado at 61–64. See generally Hyde at 1–84, 221–370, 401–454; Shinder at 19–58, 143–214, 260–272.
- Footnote re 6 Gallery: Miles—1 at 192; Morgan—3 at 109–110; Schumacher at 214; Silesky at 60–61.
- Footnote re performance of Part I: Barry Miles, "A Note on the Manuscript," in Ginsberg—1 at xiii.
- Sam Wo: Miles—1 at 194; Schumacher at 216; Silesky at 65.
- "We had gone beyond a point of no return": Michael McClure, *Scratching the Beat Surface*, reprinted in Ginsberg—1 at 168.

- Ferlinghetti telegram: Cherkovski at 99; Lawrence Ferlinghetti, "Introduction: 'Howl' at the Frontiers," in Morgan & Peters at xii; Miles—1 at 194; Raskin at 19–20; Schumacher at 216; Silesky at 54, 65–66.
- Footnote re Ferlinghetti telegram: Morgan—1 at 209; Letter of Allen Ginsberg to Fernanda Pivano, 30 July 1964 (Treviso, Italy: Fernanda and Riccardo Pivano Library); E-mail of Bill Morgan to authors, 31 July 2007 (establishing 30 July 1964 letter as basis for statement in his text); E-mail of Michael Schumacher to authors, 26 July 2007 (re interviews with Allen Ginsberg and Lawrence Ferlinghetti); Justin Kaplan, "Introduction" in Walt Whitman, *Leaves of Grass* (New York: Bantam Dell, 2004) at xxi (letter of Ralph Waldo Emerson to Walt Whitman, 21 July 1855).
- Moloch: See generally Day; *Leviticus* 18:21 in Bruce M. Metzger & Ronald E. Murphy, eds., *The New Oxford Annotated Bible* (New York: Oxford University Press, 1991).
- Moloch viewing: Allen Ginsberg, "Notes Written on Finally Recording *Howl*," in Ginsberg—4 at 230; Ginsberg—14 at 61, 63 (journal entry of 18 October 1954); Morgan & Peters at 31; Schumacher at 205–206.
- "We wandered on Peyote all downtown": Morgan & Peters at 34 (quoting letter of Allen Ginsberg to Jack Kerouac, 25 August 1955).
- Writing of Part II: Miles—1 at 189–190, 194–195; Schumacher at 206–207, 217; Raskin at 138–139, 141–142, 168–172.
- "No 'spontaneous' poem was more thoroughly rewritten": Raskin at 168.
- 17 subsequent typewritten drafts: Ginsberg—1 at 56–87.
- Part II excerpts: Ginsberg—1 at 6–7.
- "Moloch who reaches up at night": Ginsberg—1 at 56 (quoting Gary Snyder).
- Writing of Part III: Allen Ginsberg, "Notes Written on Finally Recording *Howl*," in Ginsberg—4 at 230; Miles—1 at 195–196; Raskin at 139–140.
- Part III excerpts: Ginsberg—1 at 7–8.
- "a little rose-covered cottage": Kerouac—6 at 11–12.
- Footnote re Solomon: Ginsberg—3 at 489 ("sympathetic attentiveness"); Raskin at 156–157 (derived from Ellen Pearlman, "Biography, Mythology and Interpretation," *Vajradhatu Sun*, April—May 1990, p. 17, quoting Allen Ginsberg). See also Morgan—1 at 318 (noting Solomon's anger with Ginsberg re use of his name).
- Writing of Part IV (later called Footnote to *Howl*): Allen Ginsberg, "Notes Written on Finally Recording *Howl*," in Ginsberg—4 at 230–231; Miles—1 at 196; Schumacher at 217–218; *Isaiah* 6:7 in Bruce M. Metzger & Ronald E. Murphy, eds., *The New Oxford Annotated Bible* (New York: Oxford University Press, 1991).
- Excerpts of Part IV (later called Footnote to *Howl*): Ginsberg—1 at 8.

CHAPTER 5

- City Lights Books: Cherkovski at 80–82; Miles—1 at 180–181; Morgan—3 at 1 ("head, heart, and undersoul"), 2–4, 6–7; Schumacher at 221; Silesky at 56–57.
- Lawrence Ferlinghetti: Cherkovski at 45–46, 49–60, 67, 77–79, 82; Miles—1 at 181 ("left-leaning, libertarian, anarchistic political philosophy"); Julia Older, "Poetry's Eternal Graffiti: Late-Night Conversations with Lawrence Ferlinghetti,"

Poets & Writers, March–April 2007, pp. 38, 40; Schumacher at 221, 223; Silesky at 1–2, 25–29, 34–35, 42–45, 47, 57–58, 66, 92.

- "It seemed like the logical thing to do": Silesky at 57.
- "I was the last of the Bohemian generation": Julia Older, "Poetry's Eternal Graffiti: Late-Night Conversations with Lawrence Ferlinghetti," *Poets & Writers*, March–April 2007, p. 40. See also Silesky at 82–83.
- "would be busted": Lawrence Ferlinghetti, "Introduction: 'Howl' at the Frontiers," in Morgan & Peters at xiii.
- "We were just a little" & ACLU: Lawrence Ferlinghetti interview with authors, San Francisco: City Lights Bookstore, 27 July 2001; Schumacher at 252.
- "Civil Liberties Union here": Ginsberg—1 at 151 (quoting letter of Allen Ginsberg to Louis Ginsberg, March 1956); Schumacher at 288.
- Revisions & selections of poems: Miles—1 at 201; Silesky at 66–67.
- "call it simply "Howl": Lawrence Ferlinghetti, "Introduction: 'Howl' at the Frontiers," in Morgan & Peters at xii.
- Footnote re Ferlinghetti statement on omission of one-page section: Andrew P. Madden, "Interview with Lawrence Ferlinghetti, 1998," in Plimpton at 44 (interview originally published in *The Paris Review*).
- "Footnote to 'Howl'": Cherkovski at 99–100; Silesky at 66.
- Williams's introduction: William Carlos Williams, "Introduction," in Ginsberg—9 at 7–8. See also Cherkovski at 100; Miles—1 at 201–202; Silesky at 67.
- *Song of Myself*: Whitman at 43.
- Dedication: Ginsberg—9 at 3. See also Miles—1 at 204, 207; Schumacher at 238–239.
- Re Lucien Carr: Ginsberg—1 at 159 (letter of Lucien to Allen Ginsberg, 21 September 1956); Morgan & Peters at 52–53 (letter of Allen Ginsberg to Lawrence Ferlinghetti, 15 January 1957).
- Ginsberg to Ferlinghetti: Morgan—7 at 14 ("My friend Lucien Carr") (Jan. 15, 1957 letter from AG to LF)
- Ferlinghetti reply: Morgan—7 at 15 (*"Howl* will be delayed") (5 February 1957 letter from LF to AG)
- Solomon footnote: Morgan—7 at 36, 38 ("As fate would have it")
- Ditto copies: Felver—4 at 5; Miles—1 at 201; Schumacher at 238; Silesky at 69.
- "beautiful gentleness": Schumacher at 238 (quoting letter of John Clellon Holmes to Allen Ginsberg, 26 September 1956).
- "Thought your *Howl*": Ginsberg—1 at 150 (letter of Lucien Carr to Allen Ginsberg, 13 February 1956).
- Berkeley reading: Amburn at 226; Miles—1 at 199–200; Schumacher at 228; Silesky at 68. A recent discovery of a reel-to-reel tape recording of Allen Ginsberg reciting "Howl" establishes that the first recorded performance of the first part of the poem occurred on Valentine's Day in 1956 in a student hostel at Reed College in Portland, Oregon, three months before the Berkeley reading. Nevertheless, the March 1956 recording made in Berkeley is the earliest known recording of the entire poem. John Suiter, "When the Beats Came Back," *Reed Magazine*, Winter 2008, pp. 20–25; Peter Edidin, "The Sound of 'Howl,'" *New York Times*, 16 February 2008, sec. B, p. 10.
- "You have no idea": Morgan & Peters at 38 (letter of Allen Ginsberg to Louis Ginsberg, late March 1956).

- Eberhart letter: Ginsberg—17 at 130–139, Charters—2 at 208–221 (letter of Allen Ginsberg to Richard Eberhart, 18 May 1956).
- "I'm afraid I have to tell you": Ginsberg—1 at 156 (letter of Lionel Trilling to Allen Ginsberg, 29 May 1956).
- Villiers: Cherkovski at 100–101; Lawrence Ferlinghetti interview with authors, San Francisco: City Lights Bookstore, 27 July 2001; Lawrence Ferlinghetti, "Introduction: 'Howl' at the Frontiers," in Morgan & Peters at xii–xiii; Schumacher at 252; Silesky at 68–69.
- Gallery corrections: Miles—1 at 204, 206; Schumacher at 233–234, 237–238.
- "This being my first book": Morgan & Peters at 43–44 (letter of Allen Ginsberg to Lawrence Ferlinghetti, 3 July 1956).
- "Everything worked out fine": Ginsberg—1 at 158 (letter of Allen Ginsberg to Lawrence Ferlinghetti, 9 August 1956).
- Complimentary copies: Schumacher at 238; Silesky at 69.
- Ezra Pound: Miles—1 at 202; Schumacher at 239.
- Richard Eberhart's piece: Richard Eberhart, "West Coast Rhythms," *New York Times Book Review*, 2 September 1956, p. 4.
- *Life* and *Mademoiselle*: Schumacher at 240.
- "Beginning to get long admiring letters": Ginsberg—1 at 159 (letter of Allen Ginsberg to Jack Kerouac, Fall 1956).
- Cowley & Jennison acceptance report: Theado—1 at 169–170 (reproduction of the manuscript acceptance report). See also Amburn at 260; Howard Cunnell, "Fast This Time: Jack Kerouac and the Writing of *On the Road*," in Kerouac—16 at 46.
- "Sterl, I'm real worried": Kerouac—5 at 53–54 (letter of Jack Kerouac to Sterling Lord, 26 June 1957).
- A dozen more books: Leland at 17; see also Maher—3 at 491.
- "I wouldn't be surprised if Viking Press got chickenshit": Kerouac—5 at 52 (letter of Jack Kerouac to Gary Snyder, 24 June 1957).
- "[H]ow absurd of that man": Morgan & Peters at 59 (letter of Gregory Corso to Allen Ginsberg, 6 May 1957).
- "Morning Report": Abe Melinkoff, "Morning Report: Iron Curtain on the Embarcadero," *San Francisco Chronicle*, 28 March 1957.
- Villiers & *Miscellaneous Man*: Lawrence Ferlinghetti, "Horn on 'HOWL'," *Evergreen Review*, vol. 2 (1957), p. 145.
- "I think MacPhee": Lawrence Ferlinghetti Interview with Authors, San Francisco: City Lights Bookstore, 27 July 2001.
- ACLU: Lawrence Ferlinghetti, "Horn on 'HOWL'," *Evergreen Review*, vol. 2 (1957), at 146; Miles—1 at 224–225; Schumacher—1 at 252.
- Photo-offset edition: Lawrence Ferlinghetti, "Horn on 'HOWL'," *Evergreen Review*, vol. 2 (1957), p. 146; Miles—1 at 224–225; Morgan & Peters at 58–59 (letter of Allen Ginsberg to Don Allen, 18 April 1957); Schumacher—1 at 252.
- "I guess this puts you up shits creek": Ginsberg—17 at 149–150, Morgan & Peters at 56–58 (letter of Allen Ginsberg to Lawrence Ferlinghetti, 3 April 1957).
- Ferlinghetti's statement in William Hogan's column: William Hogan, "Between the Lines," *San Francisco Chronicle*, 19 May 1957, p. 34.
- U.S. Attorney & Customs release: Cherkovski at 102; Lawrence Ferlinghetti, "Horn on 'HOWL'," *Evergreen Review*, vol. 2 (1957), p. 147; Miles—1 at 224–225.

- "Sting" operation: Cherkovski at 102; Morgan & Peters at 61; Schumacher at 254; Silesky at 70.
- "looked like a Japanese sage": Morgan—3 at 50.
- June 3 arrest & charges: Cherkovski at 103; Miles—1 at 224; Schumacher at 254; Silesky at 70–71.
- "it is all in the line of duty, ma'am" & "terribly nice": Silesky at 70 (quoting Kirby Ferlinghetti's recollections of officers).
- "Shigeyoshi Murao, a Japanese-American": Shigeyoshi Murao, "Footnotes to My Arrest for Selling *Howl*," in Ginsberg—1 at 170.
- Fingerprinting, mug shots: Shigeyoshi Murao, "Footnotes to My Arrest for Selling *Howl*," in Ginsberg—1 at 170; Miles—1 at 224; Schumacher at 254.
- "piss-stained mattress" & "cocksuckers": Shigeyoshi Murao, "Footnotes to My Arrest for Selling *Howl*," in Ginsberg—1 at 170.
- "elbows of rock": Kerouac—14 at 14–15.
- ACLU bail: Shigeyoshi Murao, "Footnotes to My Arrest for Selling *Howl*," in Ginsberg—1 at 171; Miles—1 at 224; Schumacher at 254.
- Ferlinghetti turns himself in: "Bookshop Owner Surrenders," *San Francisco Chronicle*, 7 June 1957, p. 2.
- "picturesque return": Lawrence Ferlinghetti, "Horn on 'HOWL'," *Evergreen Review*, vol. 2 (1957), p. 147.
- Ferlinghetti receives word of bust while in Big Sur: Ginsberg—17 at 154–158, Morgan & Peters at 62 (letter of Allen Ginsberg to Lawrence Ferlinghetti, 10 June 1957). We base this assertion on the following line in Ginsberg's letter: "Received your June 4 letter today, with clipping."
- "local dumb Irish cops": Kerouac—5 at 46 (letter of Jack Kerouac to Allen Ginsberg, 7 June 1957).
- "I guess this is more serious": Morgan & Peters at 62, 63–64 (letter of Allen Ginsberg to Lawrence Ferlinghetti, 10 June 1957).
- *Chronicle* pieces: "Making a Clown of San Francisco," *San Francisco Chronicle*, 6 June 1957, reprinted in Morgan & Peters at 111–112; William Hogan, "Bookman's Notebook: Orwell's 'Big Brother' Is Watching over Us," *San Francisco Chronicle*, 6 June 1957, reprinted in Morgan & Peters at 113–114; "Hanrahan's Law," *San Francisco Chronicle* 1957, reprinted in Morgan & Peters at 110.
- "We have purchased" & "They are not fit for children": "Making a Clown of San Francisco," *San Francisco Chronicle*, 6 June 1957, reprinted in Morgan & Peters at 111 (quoting Captain William Hanrahan).
- "Here is a new and startling doctrine": "Making a Clown of San Francisco," *San Francisco Chronicle*, 6 June 1957, reprinted in Morgan & Peters at 111.
- "How many children will read HOWL?": Morgan & Peters at 59 (letter of Gregory Corso to Allen Ginsberg, 6 May 1957). Although Corso opined on censorship efforts of Customs Collector MacPhee, his commentary was equally applicable to those of Captain Hanrahan.
- "I think that you are perhaps the only great publisher": Morgan & Peters at 66 (letter of Gregory Corso to Lawrence Ferlinghetti, late July 1957).

CHAPTER 6

- Ferlinghetti's reactions to his arrest: Ginsberg—1 at 71 (letter of Allen Ginsberg to Lawrence Ferlinghetti, 23 September 1957), 78 (letter of Allen Ginsberg to Law-

rence Ferlinghetti, 10 October 1957), 107 (quoting Ferlinghetti's *San Francisco Chronicle* article of 19 May 1957); Morgan & Peters at xiii.
- Murao's reactions to his arrest: Ginsberg—1 at 170; Morgan & Peters at xiii.
- Hanrahan's declaration: David Perlman, "How Captain Hanrahan Made 'Howl' a Best-Seller," *The Reporter*, 12 December 1957, p. 37.
- "America": Ginsberg—9 at 39.
- Legal cases: *Speiser v. Randall*, 48 Cal. 2d 903, 311 P.2d 546 (Cal. 1958); *Speiser v. Randall*, 357 U.S. 513 (1958); *Roth v. United States*, 354 U.S. 476 (1957); *Alberts v. California*, 354 U.S. 476 (1957).
- Footnote on Emerson: Emerson at 195.
- Supreme Court setting for *Roth-Alberts*: Eisler at 142.
- Oral exchanges with Justices Frankfurter and Brennan: Friedman at 15, 54.
- Opinion excerpts: *Roth v. United States*, 354 U.S. 476, 484–485, 487–489 (1957)
- Original schedule for trial: Morgan & Peters at 3.

CHAPTER 7

- *Ten Commandments* sentence: "Court Rules on Biblical Essays—1 Wins, 1 Loses," *San Francisco Chronicle*, 7 August 1957, p. 1.
- Press reactions to *Ten Commandments* sentence: Editorial, "Creative Writing in Horn's Court," *San Francisco Chronicle*, 8 August 1957, p. 20.
- Albert Bendich: Al Bendich Interview; Morgan & Peters at 213–220.
- Jake Ehrlich: Silesky at 71; "Jake Ehrlich, Criminal Lawyer Who Won Murder Cases, Dies," *New York Times*, 25 December 1971, p. 20; "Jake Ehrlich Sr. Quotes" at www.neverpleadguilty.com.
- Ralph McIntosh: de Grazia at 335; Morgan & Peters at 203, 215–216; Fiona Paton, "Banned Beats," at lib.newpaltz.edu/events/bannedbooks.html.
- "sustained shrieks of frantic defiance": M. L. Rosenthal, "Poet of the New Violence," *The Nation*, 23 February 1957, p. 162.

CHAPTER 8

- Headlines: Carolyn Anspacher, "Battle of the Books Is On: 'Howl' Trial Starts—Big Crowd," *San Francisco Chronicle*, 17 August 1957, p. 1.
- "nakedness of mind": John Clellon Holmes, "This Is the Beat Generation," *New York Times Magazine*, 16 November 1952, p. 10.
- censored works: Sova at 209–212 (*Scarlet Letter*), 166–167 (*Leaves of Grass*), 237–239 (*Well of Loneliness*); de Grazia at 7–13 (*Ulysses*).
- Petition: "Bookmen Ask Mayor to Ban Cop Censors," *San Francisco Chronicle*, 16 August 1957, p. 1.
- Description of Ferlinghetti, Murao, Ehrlich, and of the booklets on display at the trial hearing: Carolyn Anspacher, "Battle of the Books Is On: 'Howl' Trial Starts—Big Crowd," *San Francisco Chronicle*, 17 August 1957, p. 1; Ginsberg—1 at 171.
- Proceedings at the August 16th hearing: Ehrlich—1 at 3–5.
- Arguments at the August 22nd hearing: Ehrlich—1 at 6–23.

- Description of the August 22nd hearing: Carolyn Anspacher, "'Obscene' Book Trial: Dismissal for 'Howl' Clerk Indicated," *San Francisco Chronicle*, 23 August 1957, p. 4.
- Footnote on *Time* interview: Miles—1 at 227.
- Epigraph quote: Al Bendich, "Award to Lawrence Ferlinghetti," 12 December 1999, reprinted in Charters—2 at 17.
- Defense witnesses: "Clark, Walter van Tilberg," in *Encyclopedia Britannica*, at www .britannica.com/eb/article-9024214; "Lowenthal, Leo (1900–1993)," in "Glossary of People," *Encyclopedia of Marxism*, at www.marxists.org/glossary/people/l/o.htm# lowenthal-leo; "Rexroth, Kenneth," in *Encyclopedia Britannica*, at www.britannica .com/eb/article-9063377; "Schorer, Mark 1908–1977, in "Notable Wisconsin Authors," *Wisconsin Library Association*, at www.wla.lib.wi.us/lac/notable/index.htm; Ehrlich—1 at 23–69.
- Direct testimony of defense witnesses: Ehrlich—1 at 26–27 (Schorer), 39 (Nichols), 54 (Van Tilburg Clark),
- Cross-examination testimony of defense witnesses: Ehrlich—1 at 30–31 (Schorer), 49–52 (Nichols).
- Book reviews of *HOWL*: Richard Eberhart, "West Coast Rhythms," *New York Times Book Review*, 2 September 1956; M. L. Rosenthal, "Poet of the New Violence," *The Nation*, 23 February 1957, p. 162.
- Admissibility of book reviews: Ehrlich—1 at 72–75.
- David Kirk testimony: Ehrlich—1 at 76–91.
- Gail Potter testimony: Ehrlich—1 at 91–94; David Perlman, "How Captain Hanrahan Made 'Howl' a Best-Seller," *The Report*, 12 December 1957, pp. 37, 39.
- Summations: Ehrlich—1 at 94–113.
- Memorandum: *People v. Ferlinghetti* and *People v. Murao*, Memorandum of Points and Authorities, Municipal Court of the City and County of San Francisco, Nos. B-27585 & B-27083 (filed September 1957).

CHAPTER 9

- Epigraph quote: Norman Podhoretz, "A Howl of Protest in San Francisco," *New Republic*, 16 September 1957, p. 26.
- Negative reviews of *HOWL*: James Dickey, "From Babel to Byzantium," *Sewanee Review*, vol. 65, July-September 1957, p. 510; John Ciardi, "Writers As Readers of Poetry," *Saturday Review*, 23 November 1957, p. 33; John Hollander, "Poetry Chronicle," *Partisan Review*, vol. 24, Spring 1957, p. 298; McNally—1 at 241, 375.
- Footnote quotation: Allen Ginsberg, "Notes Written on Finally Recording 'Howl,'" reprinted in Parkinson at 30.
- *Life* magazine: "Big Day for Bards at Bay: San Francisco Muse Thrives in Face of Trial over Poems," *Life*, 9 September 1957, p. 105.
- *HOWL*'s commercial success: Morgan & Peters at 78 (letter of Allen Ginsberg to Lawrence Ferlinghetti, 10 October 1957).
- *On the Road*'s commercial success: Watson at 253–254.
- "Jack had been grumbling": Miles—2 at 36.

- Ginsberg letter to Kerouac (28 September 1957): Kerouac—5 at 73; Miles—2 at 36; Schumacher at 268.
- Kerouac letter to Ginsberg (1 October 1957): Kerouac—5 at 76–77.
- Ginsberg letter to Ferlinghetti (10 October 1957): Morgan & Peters at 78.
- Ferlinghetti letter to Ginsberg (17 September 1957): Morgan & Peters at 70–71.
- "offered the most fantastic collection": David Perlman, "'Howl' Not Obscene, Judge Rules," *San Francisco Chronicle*, 4 October 1957, p. 1.
- Description of opinion: Ginsberg—1 at 173–174; Morgan & Peters at 197–199.
- Ferlinghetti after decision: Silesky at 78; David Perlman, "'Howl' Not Obscene, Judge Rules," *San Francisco Chronicle*, 4 October 1957, p.1
- *Chronicle* report and editorial: David Perlman, "'Howl' Not Obscene, Judge Rules," *San Francisco Chronicle*, 4 October 1957, p. 1; "'Howl' Decision Landmark of Law," *San Francisco Chronicle*, 7 October 1957, p. 18.
- "PR genius": Kerouac—6 at xvi (quoting Ann Douglas).
- Ginsberg reactions: Morgan & Peters at 78 (letter of Lawrence Ferlinghetti to Allen Ginsberg, 10 October 1957); Ginsberg—7 at 189 (letter of Allen Ginsberg to Neal Cassady, 3 December 1957).
- Epigraph quote: Hyde at 32 (quoting Rexroth from 1957 *Evergreen Review* piece titled "San Francisco Letter").
- "Godfather": "Rexroth, Kenneth," in *Encyclopedia Britannica*, at www.britannica.com/eb/article-9063377.
- Rexroth reflections: Kenneth Rexroth, "Disengagement: The Art of the Beat Generation," 1957, reprinted in Charter—2 at 507, 508.
- Kerouac in Goody's Bar: Jeremy Talmer, "Back to the Village," reprinted in Maher—2 at 44.

CHAPTER 10

- Lenny Bruce: Collins & Skover at 222–224.
- Footnote re letter to Kuh: Ginsberg—17 at 296 (letter of Allen Ginsberg to Richard Kuh, 16 June 1964).
- "We are here": Miles—1 at 410 (quoting Allen Ginsberg).
- Yippie press conference: Nicholas von Hoffman, "Yippies Unveil 'Politics of Ecstasy,'" *Washington Post*, 20 March 1968, sec. A, p. 3; Miles—1 at 410 (mistaking the date of the press conference); Schumacher at 503–504 (mistaking the date of the press conference as March 17, 1968).
- "16,000 Chicago police officers": Miles—1 at 444.
- Chicago demonstrations: Kurlansky at 272–283; Miles—1 at 412–413; Morgan—1 at 452–456; T. Morgan at 444–446; Sylvan Fox, "300 Police Use Tear Gas to Breach Young Militants Barricade in Chicago Park," *New York Times*, 27 August 1968, p. 29; D.J. Bruckner, "Chicago Police Use Tear Gas to Rout Thousands," *Los Angeles Times*, 28 August 1968, p. 1; J. Anthony Lukas, "Police Battle Demonstrators in Streets," *New York Times*, 29 August 1968, p. 1; "Ginsberg Enters Hall After Startling Police," *New York Times*, 29 August 1968, p. 23.
- Ginsberg statements: Quoted in J. Anthony Lukas, "Police Battle Demonstrators in Streets," *New York Times*, 29 August 1968, pp. 1, 23.

- "Statement on Censorship": Federal Communications Bar Association, "What's Indecent? Who Decides?" program materials, 18 April 1990 (on file with authors); Ginsberg—4 at 177–180.
- Reading "Howl" in front of U.S. Court of Appeals: Laura Lippman, "Ginsberg 'Howls' Again as Lawyers Battle FCC Rule," *Baltimore Sun*, 20 October 1994, sec. D, p. 1.
- Footnote re National Endowment of the Arts funding: Ginsberg—17 at 440–442 (letter of Allen Ginsberg to Randy "Duke" Cunningham, 4 April 1995); John M. Broder, "Lawmaker Quits after He Pleads Guilty to Bribes," *New York Times*, 29 November 2005.
- Sotheby catalogue & auction events: Sotheby's—Ginsberg (cover portrait & listing of lots); Michael Ellison, "The Beat Goes On at Ginsberg Auction," *The Guardian* (London), 8 October 1999, p. 19; "Ginsberg's Belongings Auctioned Off at Sotheby's," *The Globe and Mail* (Canada), 8 October 1999, sec. A, p. 19; Kathryn Shattuck, "Sotheby's to Auction Ginsbergiana," *New York Times*, 7 October 1999, sec. E, p. 3; "They'll 'Howl' over Ginsberg Sales," *New York Post*, 5 October 1999, p. 9; David Usborne, "Sotheby's Sells Off Allen Ginsberg Estate, *Hamilton Spectator* (Ontario, Canada), 8 October 1999, sec. F, p. 11.
- Ginsberg Obituary: Wilborn Hampton, "Allen Ginsberg, Master Poet of Beat Generation, Dies at 70," *New York Times*, 6 April 1997, sec. A, p. 1.
- Lennon Obituary: Les Lesbetter, "John Lennon of Beatles Is Killed; Suspect Held in Shooting at Dakota," *New York Times*, 9 December 1980, sec. A, p. 1.
- Presley Obituary: Molly Ivins, "Elvis Presley Dies; Rock Singer Was 42," *New York Times*, 17 August 1977, p. 1. Of course, the deaths of Lennon and Presley were unexpected, unlike Allen's. Moreover, the number of stories about Lennon and Presley in the immediate aftermath of their deaths and thereafter far exceeded those about Ginsberg. Still, it is noteworthy that the Ginsberg story received the coverage and placement that it did.
- Kerouac Obituary: Joseph Lelyveld, "Jack Kerouac, Novelist, Dead; Father of the Beat Generation," *New York Times*, 22 October 1969.
- Ginsberg's achievements & influences: Morgan—1 at 491–492; Molly Hall, "In the Spirit of Kerouac: School Is Born from the Beat Generation," *Chicago Tribune*, 4 August 1994, sec. C, p. 8.
- "The poet laureate": Wilborn Hampton, "Allen Ginsberg, Master Poet of Beat Generation, Dies at 70," *New York Times*, 6 April 1997, sec. A, p. 1.
- Cadets read *Howl* at the Virginia Military Institute: Holly George-Warren, ed., *The Rolling Stone Book of the Beats* (New York: Hyperion, 1999), pp. 60–61.
- Ginsberg canon: see Bibliography in this book.
- Ginsberg letter to Ferlinghetti: Morgan—7 at 264, 265 ("I have been amiss").
- Ginsberg dedication to Ferlinghetti: Ginsberg—1 at v.
- Ferlinghetti letter to Ginsberg: Morgan—7 at 266.
- Copies and translations of *Coney Island of the Mind*: see www.citylights.com.
- City Lights bookstore, City Lights Books, and honors: William Lawlor, "Ferlinghetti, Lawrence," in Hemmer at 98–101.
- Pocket Poet Series: Lawrence Ferlinghetti, ed., *City Lights Pocket Poets Anthology* (San Francisco: City Lights Books, 1995).
- Ferlinghetti's publications: see Bibliography in this book.

- Re PEN award: Christopher Young, "Beat This: Lawrence Ferlinghetti Refuses Hungarian Cash Award," *Daily News*, 12 October 2012.
- Footnote re Wiesel: Alexander Nazaryan, "Elie Wiesel to Hungary: Keep Your Award," *Daily News*, 19 June 2019.
- *Daily News*: *ibid.* ("was unsatisfied with the organization's efforts"). See also Carolyn Kellogg, "Lawrence Ferlinghetti Declines Hungarian Award over Human Rights," *Los Angeles Times*, 11 October 2012.
- *Poetry as Insurgent Art*: Ferlinghetti—6 at 8, 31.

CHAPTER 11

- Al Bendich epigraph quote: Morgan & Peters at 220.
- Ferlinghetti epigraph quote: Ferlinghetti—3.
- Dennis McDougal, "FCC Firm on Decency Code; 'Howl' Muffled," *Los Angeles Times*, 8 January 1988.
- "an FCC spokesman said": *Ibid.*
- *NYT* story: Patricia Cohen, "'Howl' in an Era That Fears Indecency," *New York Times*, 4 October 2007.
- "Steven Pinker Comes to the 'F' Word's Defense," *Talk of the Nation*, National Public Radio, 17 October 2017, www.npr.org/templates/transcript/transcript.php?storyId=15370150.
- "broadcast a poetry reading": Lisa Hollenbach, "Broadcasting *Howl*," *M/M*, 12 July 2018.
- "*Howl* was rebroadcast": *Ibid.*
- "KPFA declared October 30": *Ibid.*
- "As recently as 2014": *Ibid.*
- Copies and translations of *Coney Island of the Mind*: see www.citylights.com.
- City Lights bookstore, City Lights Books, and honors: William Lawlor, "Ferlinghetti, Lawrence," in Hemmer at 98–101.
- Pocket Poet Series: Lawrence Ferlinghetti, ed., *City Lights Pocket Poets Anthology* (San Francisco: City Lights Books, 1995).
- Ferlinghetti's publications: see Bibliography in this book.
- *Poetry as Insurgent Art*: Ferlinghetti—6 at 8, 31, 73.
- WBAI flap: Joe Garofoli, "'Howl' Too Hot to Hear," *San Francisco Chronicle*, 3 October 2007; Lydia Hailman King, "'Howl' Obscenity Prosecution Still Echoes 50 Years Later," First Amendment Center, 3 October 2007, at www.firstamendmentcenter.org; Patricia Cohen, "'Howl' in an Era That Fears Censorship," *New York Times*, 4 October 2007, sec. B, p. 3.
- Footnote re NYT editorial: "A Muse Unplugged," *New York Times*, 8 October 2007, sec. A, p. 22.
- Pacifica interview & Ferlinghetti reading: "Howl against Censorship," Pacifica.org, 3 October 2007.

EPILOGUE

- "Great Oracle": Lawrence Ferlinghetti, "To the Oracle at Delphi," *The Nation*, 20 September 2001.

- Dylan epigraph quote: V. A. Musetto, "'Ferlinghetti: A Rebirth Of Wonder' review," *New York Post*, 8 February 2013.
- John Milton, "corruptions of power" and "detested rigidity": Vincent Blasi, *Milton's Areopagitica and the Modern First Amendment*, Yale Law School Occasional Paper, second series, # 1, pp. 1–19.
- "pandemonium": Jonathan Rosen, "Return to Paradise," *The New Yorker*, 2 June 2008.
- "wrote the *Areopagitica* at the behest of the journeymen printers": Blasi at 6.
- celebrated the howls of the nonconformist: Steven H. Shiffrin, *The First Amendment, Democracy, and Romance* (Cambridge, MA: Harvard University Press, 1990), at 72–79.
- "Paths of the Untrodden": Whitman at xix.
- "Populist Manifesto #1": Ferlinghetti—6 at 69.
- "I greet you at the beginning": Whitman at xxi; Morgan—7 at 1.
- "voices speaking out": Ferlinghetti—6 at 73.

Acknowledgments

$\mathscr{T}$he prime mover, the man who made this book happen, is Jonathan Sisk. Jon is old school in this sense: he still believes in big ideas; he still values good writing; and he still holds to the conviction that books can change minds. Given that, we hope that this book does justice to his faith in us (and the faith of his colleagues at Rowman & Littlefield, too).

The pages of this book trace back decades in time to when we were first researched *The Trials of Lenny Bruce: The Fall & Rise of an American Icon* (2002) and thereafter returned to the scene with our *Mania: The Story of the Outraged and Outrageous Lives That Launched a Cultural Revolution* (2013). Both books made this one possible. The constant in those two works was Al Bendich (1929–2015), the ACLU lawyer who successfully represented both Lenny Bruce, the uninhibited comedian, and Lawrence Ferlinghetti, the dissident poet.[†] Al was a source of great information and inspiration. He embodied what is best in defending our First Amendment freedoms. He became a friend, a close one, to both of us, and we miss him dearly.

Much gratitude is owed to Alex Lubertozzi, who guided us through many chapters with his astute editorial insights and who oper-

---

[†] See Margalit Fox, "Al Bendich, Defender of 'Howl' and Lenny Bruce's Comedy, Is Dead at 85," *New York Times*, 13 January 2015; Abdi Soltan, "Remembering Al Bendich, ACLU Northern California," 12 January 2015, https://www.aclunc.org/blog/remembering-al-bendich; "Al Bendich Tribute," Berkeley FILM Foundation, *YouTube*, 19 November 2015, https://www.youtube.com/watch?v=fpn-1MG6lME.

ated as our copyright clearance agent. Our debt to Alex has continued over the years; so too does our appreciation.

Bill Morgan and Nancy Peters (the latter of City Lights fame) assisted us indirectly with their *Howl on Trial* book. There is also Lawrence Ferlinghetti's significant essay "Horn on 'Howl.'" And we are grateful to him, as well, for granting us an interview.

The folks at Seattle University School of Law were supportive in countless ways. We are immensely grateful for the generous research and travel budgets provided by Dean Annette Clark (S.U.) and former Dean Kellye Testy (U.W.). We owe thanks for the unstinting and excellent library assistance given by Susan Kezele, Kelly Kunsch, and Bob Menanteaux; and for the superb research work done by Jason Eric Bernstein and Stacey Scriven Bernstein, who helped us reinsert authoritative citations in the *People v. Ferlinghetti* opinion found in the Appendix. Thanks go out at well to Jackie Farmer of FIRE (Foundation for Individual Rights in Education) for transcribing the Pacifica interview and commentary.

Ron Collins: First and foremost, there is Susan A. Cohen, who has made my uncommon life journey possible, even when it seemed difficult to continue. Her patience and perseverance, coupled with an overarching love, continue to allow me to chase after my dreams, wild though they are. I take great solace in the fact that our son, Dylan, treasures the world of wide-eyed poets yearning to break out of the bounds that cabin that mysterious life-spirit within us.

I would be remiss if I did not enter a note of posthumous gratitude to my mother-in-law, the late Shirley V. Cohen (1928–2018) whose generosity of heart was a model to us all of how love comes to the rescue when fate does not.

To Linda Hopkins—who in the musical bard's words "knows too much to argue or to judge." Her counsel returns faithfully despite this or that turn of fate. And yet, she rolls the roulette wheel time and again towards an ever hopeful tomorrow.

And then there is David Skover, who knows where all my failures are hidden. Even so, he, too, spins that same roulette wheel for his own reasons. One of David's strengths is his open-mindedness, a rare willingness to judge ideas and people on their merits, which can be a dangerous trait in these conformist times. Our writing relationship traces back to 1988, when we offered up our ideas in the *Michigan Law Review*. They were unorthodox then and, happily, they continue to be so. To be sure, we are an odd couple given how very different our upbringings were and our styles are. Still, we managed to square the circle and then circle the square—ah, and what a splendid joy it has been.

David Skover: My sole personal acknowledgment is dedicated to Ron Collins—my stalwart coauthor and steadfast friend. Clearly, no one has been more influential in my evolution as a scholar and my development as a writer. When my reasoning became too convoluted, Ron encouraged me to clear out the conceptual brush and clarify my ideas. When my style became too turgid, he modeled the elegance and flair that my prose required. When my spirits sagged under performance pressures, he shouldered a good portion of the burden until my energy bounced back. It is Cicero who declared, "A friend is, as it were, a second self." Thank you, Ron, for being my second self, but also for improving my first.

Index

About the Authors

The authors David Skover (left) and Ron Collins (right) with
Peter Maravelis (center) at City Lights Bookstore, 2013.
R. Collins.

Ronald K. L. Collins is the Harold S. Shefelman Scholar at the University of Washington Law School. Before coming to the law school, Collins served as a law clerk to Justice Hans A. Linde on the Oregon Supreme Court, a Supreme Court Fellow under Chief Justice Warren Burger, and a scholar at the Washington, DC, office of the Newseum's First Amendment Center.

Collins has written constitutional briefs that were submitted to the Supreme Court and various other federal and state high courts. In addition to the books that he coauthored with David Skover, he is the editor of *The Fundamental Holmes: A Free Speech Chronicle and Reader* (2010)

and coauthor with Sam Chaltain of *We Must Not Be Afraid to Be Free*
(2011). His last solo book was *Nuanced Absolutism: Floyd Abrams and
the First Amendment* (2013). His next book is: *First Things First—A
Modern Coursebook on Free Speech Fundamentals* (coauthored with Will
Creeley and David Hudson, Jr., 2019). Collins is the book editor of
SCOTUSblog and writes a weekly blog (First Amendment News),
which appears on the FIRE website. In 2010, Collins was a fellow
in residence at the Norman Mailer Writers Colony in Provincetown,
Massachusetts. He is also the co-founder of the History Book Festival
(Lewes, Delaware).

* * *

David M. Skover is the Fredric C. Tausend Professor of Constitutional
Law at Seattle University School of Law. He teaches, writes, and lec-
tures in the fields of federal constitutional law, federal jurisdiction, and
mass communications theory and the First Amendment.

Skover graduated from the Woodrow Wilson School of International and Domestic Affairs at Princeton University. He received his
law degree from Yale Law School, where he was an editor of the *Yale
Law Journal*. Thereafter, he served as a law clerk for Judge Jon O. Newman at the Federal District Court for the District of Connecticut and
the U.S. Court of Appeals for the Second Circuit. In addition to the
books that he coauthored with Ronald Collins, he is the coauthor with
Pierre Schlag of *Tactics of Legal Reasoning* (1986).

* * *

Together, Collins and Skover have authored *The Death of Discourse*
(1996 and 2005), *The Trials of Lenny Bruce: The Fall & Rise of an Ameri-
can Icon* (2002 and 2012), *Mania: The Outraged & Outrageous Lives
That Launched a Cultural Revolution* (2013), *On Dissent: Its Meaning in
America* (2013), *When Money Speaks: The McCutcheon Decision, Cam-
paign Finance Laws, and the First Amendment* (2014), *The Judge: 26
Machiavelian Lessons* (2017), and *Robotica: Speech Rights & Artificial
Intelligence* (2018). They have also coauthored numerous scholarly arti-
cles in various journals including the *Harvard Law Review, Stanford
Law Review, Michigan Law Review, Texas Law Review*, and the
Supreme Court Review, among other publications. The *Trials of Lenny
Bruce* (revised and expanded) and *Mania* are available in e-book form.
They are also the co-directors (with Lee Levine) of the First Amend-
ment Salons (Washington, D.C, New York City, and New Haven).